Reagan as President

Reagan as President

*Contemporary Views of the Man,
His Politics, and His Policies*

EDITED WITH COMMENTARY BY
Paul Boyer

Ivan R. Dee, Publisher
CHICAGO

Grateful acknowledgment is made to authors, newspapers, periodicals,
and publishers noted herein for permission to reprint copyrighted materials.

Library of Congress Cataloging-in-Publication Data
Reagan as president: contemporary views of the man, his politics, and
   his policies / edited with commentary by Paul Boyer.
      p.   c.m.
   ISBN 0-929587-27-8 (cloth)
   ISBN 0-929587-28-6 (pbk.)
   1. Reagan, Ronald.   2. Presidents—United States.   3. United
States— Politics and government—1981–1989.   I. Boyer, Paul S.
E876.R3929   1990
973.927'092—dc20   89-78111
                                                         CIP

Contents

Reagan as President

INTRODUCTION
Reaganism: Reflections on an Era

In 1931, when the heady decade of the 1920s was still fresh in memory, the journalist Frederick Lewis Allen produced a book which captured his impressions of the decade just ended. Almost at once, Allen's *Only Yesterday* took its place as a minor classic of popular social history.

Although different in approach and more targeted in subject matter, *Reagan as President* attempts something similar for the 1980s, a decade dominated by the looming figure of Ronald Reagan. Rather than offering an anecdotal narrative history, however, this book presents a careful selection of almost one hundred articles, editorials, and essays, dating from 1980 to 1989, by journalists, columnists, and cultural observers, commenting on the unfolding Reagan presidency, its policies, its ideology, its style, and its leader.

Some Presidents—Jackson, FDR, and Eisenhower come immediately to mind—have so shaped or epitomized their times that we speak not just of their presidencies but of their *eras*. Prediction is a risky business (notwithstanding Nancy Reagan's faith in astrology), but it seems likely that by the same gradual process of historical and popular consensus, the 1980s will become "the Reagan Era." This book offers a potpourri of contemporary perspectives on that era—seemingly so recent, yet already receding into that penumbral region we call the past. It should be richly evocative for those who remember these events, and instructive for those who do not.

The boundaries of most historical "eras" are fuzzier than they appear at first glance, and certainly the sources of the Reagan Era long antedate Ronald Reagan's entry into the White House. For years before 1980, conservative organizations, think tanks, and periodicals—especially William F. Buckley's *National Review*—had been preaching the gospel of small government, militant anticommunism, laissez-faire economics, and a return to traditional moral values. Senator Barry Goldwater, the 1964 Republican presidential candidate, was Reaganism's John the Baptist. Indeed, it was a half-hour network television speech on behalf of Goldwater in 1964 which gave the

13

relatively obscure Ronald Reagan his first big boost as a political figure of national stature.

The turbulent 1960s laid the groundwork for the Reagan revolution in other ways as well, as New Left student activists denounced the tepid liberalism of their parents' generation. In one of the ironies of recent American political history, not the Left but the Right ultimately benefited most from the assault on liberalism by 1960s radicals.

Liberalism suffered from internal strains in these years also, as the federal welfare and regulatory bureaucracies—and high tax rates—that were the legacy of successive waves of Democratic reform seemed to many Americans increasingly bloated, sclerotic, and generally irksome. The proportion of Americans who told pollsters they believed Washington could be trusted to "do the right thing" plummeted from 76 percent in 1964 to 25 percent in 1980.

Affirmative-action programs, the women's movement, and a heavily publicized sexual revolution fed the conservative backlash as well, as many Americans, especially white heterosexual males, concluded that the pace of social change was out of hand, jeopardizing their status and threatening the familiar contours of their cultural world. The technological transformations of the post–World War II years, producing an increasingly electronic and automated social and economic order, also proved unsettling. By the end of the seventies, the sense of disorientation, and the longing for a return to a half-remembered, half-mythical era when life was simpler and values clearer, had become almost palpable.

A series of public events fed the underlying malaise. On the heels of the Vietnam debacle came the collapse of the Nixon presidency and then a series of economic shocks administered by OPEC, the Organization of Petroleum Exporting Countries. As gasoline prices and the inflation rate soared, America again seemed on the ropes, buffeted by forces it could barely understand, let alone control. The Iranian hostage crisis of 1979–1980, when more than fifty Americans languished as captives for 444 days in the U.S. embassy in Tehran, provided the bitter coda to two decades of trauma. These frustrations came to a head in November 1980 as a sullen electorate repudiated Jimmy Carter and chose in his place a sixty-nine-year-old former radio sports announcer, former movie actor, and former governor of California, Ronald Wilson Reagan.

Reagan offered America a seemingly clear-cut conservative agenda honed over years of political speechmaking. On the domestic front he advocated cutbacks in welfare programs and in the Washington bureaucracy. As he put it in his acceptance speech at the Republican convention, capitalizing on the national obsession with physical fitness: "... Our Federal Government is overgrown and overweight. Indeed, it is time Government should go on a diet."

Economically, Reagan and his conservative advisers such as Arthur Laffer of the University of Southern California preached what came to be called Reaganomics: big tax cuts and a sharp reduction in Washington's regulatory activities. Lower taxes and deregulation, so the hopeful theory went, would encourage capital investments and consumer spending, producing an economic boom which would generate higher tax revenues even at the lower rates.

Internationally, Reagan preached militant anticommunism. On the rhetorical plane, at any rate, he summoned America to an Armageddon struggle against atheistic communism and to decisive action against leftist and revolutionary movements wherever they cropped up, especially in Latin America. To back up the tough talk he called for—and got—massive increases in military spending.

Reaganism was a matter of mood and symbolism as much as of specific programs. On the campaign trail and as President, Reagan called for renewed patriotism and pride. America must again "stand tall," he insisted, after the humiliations of recent years. This oldest of U.S. presidents evoked the era of America's confident and expansive youth. The crowds at the 1984 Summer Olympics in Los Angeles, waving flags and endlessly chanting, "We're Number One," were the authentic voice of Reaganism.

Reagan also spoke to the concerns of those rattled by the social changes sweeping the nation and worried that America was drifting from its moral moorings. He praised the traditional values—religion, family, patriotism, hard work, individual effort. His sermonlike Detroit acceptance speech would have pleased his devout mother Nelle; it was laced with quasi-religious pieties ("We must teach our children the virtues handed down to us by our families") and it closed with "God bless America" and a silent prayer.

The social agenda of Protestant evangelicals, epitomized by TV evangelist Jerry Falwell's Moral Majority, won Reagan's support. He called for a war on pornography; a school prayer amendment to the Constitution; a reversal of the Supreme Court's 1973 ruling upholding women's constitutional right to an abortion; and a general restoration of "morality" to public life.

Exuding sincerity as he read his skillfully crafted speeches into the TV camera, Reagan brilliantly articulated and wove into a cohesive whole the amorphous fears and longings of millions of Americans. Just as FDR was the first President to master the trick of effective radio communication, so Reagan was the first to exploit television to the fullest.

The underside of the Reagan ideology of individualism and a diminished role for government was a muted social consciousness and a blatant flaunting of personal success and material gain. To be sure, Reagan's calls for reduced federal social spending were accompanied by rhetorical summonses to Americans to increase the private charity that, as he put it, "flows like a deep and mighty river through the history of our nation." But the deep and mighty river flowed sluggishly in the Reagan years. The "haves" generally turned a deaf ear to the claims of the underclass in the eighties—a decade when, as Sidney Blumenthal has observed, "Belief in a common good was seen by many conservatives as a pathology, a dangerous liberal attitude that needed to be searched out and destroyed."*

This dimension of Reaganism found expression not only in the politics but also in the popular culture of the decade, as capitalist tycoons such as automaker Lee Iacocca, real estate baron Donald Trump, and (until his conviction for fraud) stock market wizard Ivan Boesky were idolized as cultural heroes. Three of the decade's top TV serials, *Dallas, Dynasty,* and *Falcon Crest* (the latter starring Reagan's ex-wife Jane Wyman) revolved around the lives of the super rich. The stereotypical American of the period was the Yuppie, the "young urban professional" (it came in both male and female models) preoccupied with generating the kind of income necessary to sustain a way of life based on the latest in trendy consumer goods, from BMW automobiles and health club memberships to designer jeans, Reebok running shoes, and Japanese VCRs and CD players.

Reagan's first inaugural set the tone for the materialism, ostentation, ersatz traditionalism, and preoccupation with media celebrities that would characterize the decade to follow. The Mormon Tabernacle Choir, Johnny Carson, and Frank Sinatra entertained the Hollywood stars, fashion celebrities, and corporate executives who gathered to pay their homage to the new President and his wife, the latter resplendent in a $25,000 gown.

To some, the nation seemed in a kind of schizophrenic trance through much of the eighties. Americans swelled with patriotic pride, took comfort in soothing rhetoric and incantatory phrases, and reaffirmed the familiar public pieties—while at the same time pursuing private agendas and starring in one-person dramas entitled *Making It.*

Reagan's Washington, too, was a place of paradox and contradiction. The critics of big government presided over vast increases in federal spending. The champions of balanced budgets and fiscal responsibility launched policies that produced deficits of breathtaking magnitude. The President who lauded the values of an earlier, simpler, more virtuous age relied on Hollywood techniques and state-of-the-art communications technology to beam his message into every home. Most amazingly of all, the grand marshal of the Cold War's ideological battalions ended his presidency by flying to Moscow to embrace Mikhail Gorbachev, the Evil Empire's general secretary.

And, in true Hegelian fashion, Reaganism called forth its antithesis. The very stridency of the Reagan themes gave rise to a grassroots nuclear-weapons freeze movement, won recruits for the environmental cause, and aroused feminists and civil rights leaders to renewed efforts.

*Sidney Blumenthal, "Reaganism and the Neokitsch Aesthetic," in Sidney Blumenthal and Thomas Byrne Edsall, eds., *The Reagan Legacy* (New York, 1988), p. 289.

Reagan himself posed another set of enigmas. On TV he seemed larger than life, yet beneath the rehearsed speeches, the staged appearances, and the flickering electronic image, the real Reagan proved remarkably elusive. Reagan watchers endlessly marveled at the vast chasm between the carefully cultivated media figure—charismatic, eloquent, masterful, deeply thoughtful about politics and the human condition—and the elderly gentleman behind the image: detached, bored by details, and fairly inarticulate except when repeating hoary anecdotes which "proved" his stock of ideas and notions. Like the Wizard of Oz, this man who so dominated his era seemed, close up, diminished, inconsequential, even a bit pathetic. The surge of retrospective affection for Harry Truman in the eighties perhaps reflected Americans' awareness of the degree to which they knew their current President only as an electronic image on a screen, and their nostalgia for a down-to-earth, plain-spoken leader for whom, they sensed, the gap between the public persona and the man himself had been far narrower.

But this is hindsight speculation from the perspective of the minority that remained immune to the lure of Reaganism. During Reagan's years in the White House, his almost mesmeric hold over millions of Americans was remarkably strong. As the first President since Eisenhower to complete two full terms, Reagan brought a welcome stability and continuity to the office. His almost flippant bravado when a would-be assassin's bullet nearly killed him in March 1981 cemented his place in the public's affection.

But above all, it was Reagan's ability to articulate with such apparent conviction the simple verities that defined the meaning of America for many of his fellow citizens that assured his place in the pantheon of American political heroes. So powerful was his hold that his penchant for malapropisms, garbled statements, and *faux pas* hurt him not at all. Like Eisenhower, Reagan seemed immune to the controversies that swirled around his administration and its policies. In embracing Reagan, millions of citizens were also embracing a vision of America that seemed increasingly jeopardized by social change, economic transformation, and world upheaval. To give up on Reagan would have been to give up on the vision, and few were prepared to do that.

This book is centered at the intersection of two pillars of American political culture: journalism and the presidency. The relationship between the two is as troubled as it is ancient. From the earliest days of the republic, journalists have criticized Presidents, and Presidents have complained bitterly about journalists' unfairness and irresponsibility. In the Gilded Age, the patrician Adams brothers, Henry and Charles Francis Jr., raised investigative journalism to a high art with their scathing exposés of the scandals and knavery of the Grant Era. In the 1920s, H. L. Mencken of the *Baltimore Sun* produced satirical columns on the public figures of the Harding and Coolidge years which stand as masterpieces of political journalism. Of more recent memory, it was two journalists, Carl Bernstein and Robert Woodward of the *Washington Post*, who broke the Watergate scandal wide open.

This long tradition of journalistic scrutiny of the presidency continued at an unabated pitch in the Reagan years. Whatever else he accomplished or failed to accomplish, President Reagan stimulated a remarkable outpouring of vigorous, passionate, and often strikingly insightful journalistic comment. *Reagan as President* brings together a rich selection of this comment. While no attempt has been made to achieve a precise and mechanical ''balance'' of pro and con opinion on every issue, the essays, taken as a whole, reflect the broad spectrum of American views of Reagan and his presidency, from the enthusiastically favorable to the scathingly critical. (The President himself is liberally represented by speeches in which he articulated his vision and defended his policies.) Wherever they fall on the ideological spectrum, the selections have in common the tang of immediacy that retrospective assessments often lack. This is history's raw first draft, written against a deadline by men and women deeply involved with the matters they are discussing. Taken together, the articles not only examine the political issues of the Reagan Era but also evoke the texture and flavor of its political culture. Historians will eventually have their say about the Reagan years, as they have have had about other presidential ''eras,'' but when they do, they will draw upon contemporary documents like those assembled here.

Not every possible topic could be covered here, despite attempts to be comprehensive. For example, a section on Reagan and the courts could not be included for considerations of length. Still, this anthology includes a rich and varied selection of contemporary comment.

A note about editorial practice. All the documents are reproduced precisely as they first appeared, with the following exceptions. A few of the longer articles have been cut. These cuts do not alter the thrust of the authors' argument, and all excisions are indicated by ellipses (...). Footnotes have been dropped from a few of the articles, and in two or three others dealing with economic matters, graphs and charts have been omitted. The original place and date of publication of each selection are indicated at the beginning of the individual pieces; those who wish to read the full version of edited articles are urged to consult these original sources.

I wish to thank the editors and authors who graciously gave permission to reprint these articles, in many cases waiving or reducing reprint fees so that the book's price could be kept within the range of student budgets.

Finally, I wish to thank Ivan R. Dee, who originally suggested a book on the Reagan Era and who, in an age of corporate conglomerates, is carrying on an older tradition of book publishing. In the course of my work on this project, Ivan Dee has become my friend as well as my publisher, and we ourselves have vigorously debated many of the same issues discussed by the journalists represented in this book.

P.B.

Institute for Research in the Humanities
Madison, Wisconsin
October 1989

A Man and a Movement

1. THE 1980 CAMPAIGN AND ELECTION

Ronald Reagan's speech accepting the Republican presidential nomination, delivered on August 15, 1980, before a hall of ecstatic delegates at the party convention in Detroit—and a vast television audience beyond—set the central themes not only of his campaign but of his presidency. After ritualistic denunciations of President Jimmy Carter and the Democrats, Reagan set forth his own agenda: a renewed commitment to work and family, a revitalization of the free-enterprise system, lower taxes and a reduced federal regulatory role, a beefed-up national defense, vigorous anticommunism worldwide, and a deepening of patriotic pride in "this . . . beloved and blessed land."

The Reagan nomination set off the first wave of what would prove an eight-year torrent of journalistic reflection, prognostication, and speculation. Writing in the Nation *shortly before the election, the Texas journalist Ronnie Dugger combed Reagan's radio speeches of the 1970s to find a series of belligerent pronouncements that convinced him the Republican candidate was "the most dangerous person ever to come this close to the Presidency" ("Ronald Reagan and the Imperial Presidency,"* Nation, *November 1, 1980).*

With the election, what had been a possibility became a certainty: a Reagan presidency. In one of many post-election analyses, Morton Kondracke, executive editor of the New Republic, *found Reagan's "John Wayne" world view simplistic but thoroughly American, and expressed the hope that the Democrats would profit by their defeat to redefine their ideology and purpose ("A Doubtful New Order,"* New Republic, *November 15, 1980). *Time* columnist Hugh Sidey, meanwhile, summed up the national mood of*

21

uncertainty and watchful waiting: "We are off on a special adventure,"
Sidey intoned, "for which there is no travel guide and no reassuring pre-
cedent." In the eight years ahead, American journalists would endlessly
explore the dimensions of this "special adventure"—the presidency of
Ronald Reagan.

RONALD REAGAN
Acceptance Speech
[Republican National Convention, Detroit, August 15, 1980]

With a deep awareness of the responsibility conferred by your trust, I accept
your nomination for the Presidency of the United States. . . .

I'm very proud of our party tonight. This convention has shown to all
America a party united, with positive programs for solving the nation's
problems; a party ready to build a new consensus with all those across the
land who share a community of values embodied in these words: family,
work, neighborhood, peace and freedom.

Now I know we've had a quarrel or two but only as to the method of
attaining a goal. There was no argument here about the goal. As President, I
will establish a liaison with the 50 Governors to encourage them to eliminate,
wherever it exists, discrimination against women. I will monitor Federal laws
to insure their implementation and to add statutes if they are needed.

More than anything else, I want my candidacy to unify our country; to
renew the American spirit and sense of purpose. I want to carry our message
to every American, regardless of party affiliation, who is a member of. this
community of shared values.

Never before in our history have Americans been called upon to face three
grave threats to our very existence, any one of which could destroy us. We
face a disintegrating economy, a weakened defense and an energy policy
based on the sharing of scarcity.

The major issue of this campaign is the direct political, personal, and
moral responsibility of Democratic Party leadership—in the White House and
in the Congress—for this unprecedented calamity which has befallen us.
They tell us they've done the most that humanly could be done. They say that
the United States has had its day in the sun, that our nation has passed its
zenith. They expect you to tell your children that the American people no
longer have the will to cope with their problems; that the future will be one of
sacrifice and few opportunities.

My fellow citizens, I utterly reject that view. The American people, the
most generous on earth, who created the highest standard of living, are not
going to accept the notion that we can only make a better world for others by

moving backward ourselves. And those who believe we can have no business leading this nation. . . .

Isn't it once again time to renew our compact of freedom; to pledge to each other all that is best in our lives; all that gives meaning to them—for the sake of this, our beloved and blessed land?

Together, let us make this a new beginning. Let us make a commitment to care for the needy; to teach our children the virtues handed down to us by our families; to have the courage to defend those values and virtues and the willingness to sacrifice for them.

Let us pledge to restore, in our time, the American spirit of voluntary service, of cooperation, of private and community initiative; a spirit that flows like a deep and mighty river through the history of our nation.

As your nominee, I pledge to you to restore to the Federal Government the capacity to do the people's work without dominating their lives. I pledge to you a Government that will not only work well but wisely, its ability to act tempered by prudence, and its willingness to do good balanced by the knowledge that government is never more dangerous than when our desire to have it help us blinds us to its great power to harm us. . . .

First, we must overcome something the present Administration has cooked up: a new and altogether indigestible economic stew, one part inflation, one part high unemployment, one part recession, one part runaway taxes, one part deficit spending seasoned with an energy crisis. It's an economic stew that has turned the national stomach.

Ours are not problems of abstract economic theory. These are problems of flesh and blood; problems that cause pain and destroy the moral fiber of real people who should not suffer the further indignity of being told by the Government that it is all somehow their fault. We do not have inflation because—as Mr. Carter says—we've lived too well.

The head of a Government which has utterly refused to live within its means and which has, in the last few days, told us that this coming year's deficit will be $60 billion, dares to point the finger of blame at business and labor, both of which have been engaged in a losing struggle just trying to stay even.

High taxes, we are told, are somehow good for us, as if, when government spends our money it isn't inflationary, but when we spend it, it is.

Those who preside over the worst energy shortage in our history tell us to use less, so that we will run out of oil, gasoline and natural gas a little more slowly. Well, now, conservation is desirable, of course. We must not waste energy. But conservation is not the sole answer to our energy needs.

America must get to work producing more energy. The Republican program for solving economic problems is based on growth and productivity.

Large amounts of oil and natural gas lay beneath our land and off our shores, untouched because the present Administration seems to believe the

American people would rather see more regulation, more taxes and more controls than more energy.

Coal offers a great potential. So does nuclear energy produced under rigorous safety standards. It could supply electricity for thousands of industries and millions of jobs and homes. It must not be thwarted by a tiny minority opposed to economic growth which often finds friendly ears in regulatory agencies for its obstructionist campaigns.

Now make no mistake. We will not permit the safety of our people or our environmental heritage to be jeopardized, but we are going to reaffirm that the economic prosperity of our people is a fundamental part of our environment. . . .

It is essential that we maintain both the forward momentum of economic growth and the strength of the safety net between those in our society who need help. We also believe it is essential that the integrity of all aspects of Social Security be preserved.

Beyond these essentials, I believe it is clear our Federal Government is overgrown and overweight. Indeed, it is time our Government should go on a diet. Therefore, my first act as chief executive will be to impose an immediate and thorough freeze on Federal hiring. Then, we are going to enlist the very best minds from business, labor and whatever quarter to conduct a detailed review of every department, bureau and agency that lives by Federal appropriation.

And we are also going to enlist the help and ideas of many dedicated and hard-working Government employees at all levels who want a more efficient Government just as much as the rest of us do. I know that many of them are demoralized by the confusion and waste they confront in their work as a result of failed and failing policies.

Our instructions to the groups we enlist will be simple and direct. We will remind them that Government programs exist at the sufferance of the American taxpayer and are paid for with money earned by working men and women and programs that represent a waste of their money—a theft from their pocketbooks—must have that waste eliminated or that program must go. It must go by Executive Order where possible, by Congressional action where necessary.

Everything that can be run more effectively by state and local government we shall turn over to state and local government, along with the funding sources to pay for it. We are going to put an end to the money merry-go-round where our money becomes Washington's money, to be spent by states and cities exactly the way the Federal bureaucrats tell us it has to be spent.

I will not accept the excuse that the Federal Government has grown so big and powerful that it is beyond the control of any President, any administration or Congress. We are going to put an end to the notion that the American taxpayer exists to fund the Federal Government. The Federal Government exists to serve the American people and to be accountable to the American people. On January 20, we are going to reestablish that truth.

Also on that date we are going to initiate action to get substantial relief for our taxpaying citizens and action to put people back to work. None of this will be based on any new form of monetary tinkering or fiscal sleight-of-hand. We will simply apply to government the common sense that we all use in our daily lives.

Work and family are at the center of our lives, the foundation of our dignity as a free people. When we deprive people of what they have earned, or take away their jobs, we destroy their dignity and undermine their families. We can't support families unless there are jobs; and we can't have jobs unless the people have both money to invest and the faith to invest it.

These are concepts that stem from an economic system that for more than 200 years has helped us master a continent, create a previously undreamed-of-prosperity for our people and has fed millions of others around the globe, and that system will continue to serve us in the future if our Government will stop ignoring the basic values on which it was built and stop betraying the trust and good will of the American workers who keep it going.

The American people are carrying the heaviest peacetime tax burden in our nation's history—and it will grow even heavier, under present law, next January. We are taxing ourselves into economic exhaustion and stagnation, crushing our ability and incentive to save, invest and produce.

This must stop. We must halt this fiscal self-destruction and restore sanity to our economic system.

I've long advocated a 30 percent reduction in income tax rates over a period of three years. This phased tax reduction would begin with a 10 percent "down payment" tax cut in 1981, which the Republicans in Congress and I have already proposed.

A phased reduction of tax rates would go a long way toward easing the heavy burden on the American people. But we shouldn't stop there....

It's time to put America back to work, to make our cities and towns resound with the confident voices of men and women of all races, nationalities and faiths bringing home to their families a paycheck they can cash for honest money.

For those without skills, we'll find a way to help them get new skills.

For those without job opportunities we'll stimulate new opportunities, particularly in the inner cities where they live.

For those who've abandoned hope, we'll restore hope and we'll welcome them into a great national crusade to make America great again.

When we move from domestic affairs, and cast our eyes abroad, we see an equally sorry chapter in the record of the present Administration....

—A Soviet combat brigade trains in Cuba, just 90 miles from our shores.

—A Soviet army of invasion occupies Afghanistan, further threatening our vital interests in the Middle East.

—America's defense strength is at its lowest ebb in a generation, while the Soviet Union is vastly outspending us in both strategic and conventional arms.

—Our European allies, looking nervously at the growing menace from the East, turn to us for leadership and fail to find it.

—And incredibly, more than 50, as you've been told from this platform so eloquently already, more than 50 of our fellow Americans have been held captive for over eight years—eight months—by a dictatorial foreign power that holds us up to ridicule before the world.

Adversaries large and small test our will and seek to ccnfound our resolve, but we are given weakness when we need strength; vacillation when the times demand firmness.

The Carter Administration lives in the world of make-believe. Every day, drawing up a response to that day's problems, troubles, regardless of what happened yesterday and what'll happen tomorrow.

But you and I live in a real world, where disasters are overtaking our nation without any real response from Washington.

This is make-believe, self-deceit and, above all, transparent hypocrisy. . . .

Who does not feel a growing sense of unease as our allies, facing repeated instances of an amateurish and confused Administration, reluctantly conclude that America is unwilling or unable to fulfill its obligations as leader of the free world?

Who does not feel rising alarm when the question in any discussion of foreign policy is no longer, "Should we do something?" but "Do we have the capacity to do anything?"

The Administration which has brought us to this state is seeking your endorsement for four more years of weakness, indecision, mediocrity and incompetence. No. No. No American should vote until he or she has asked: Is the United States stronger and more respected now than it was three-and-a-half years ago? Is the world safer, a safer place in which to live?

It is the responsibility of the President of the United States, in working for peace, to insure that the safety of our people cannot successfully be threatened by a hostile foreign power. As President, fulfilling that responsibility will be my No. 1 priority.

We're not a warlike people. Quite the opposite. We always seek to live in peace. We resort to force infrequently and with great reluctance—and only after we've determined that it is absolutely necessary. We are awed—and rightly so—by the forces of destruction at loose in the world in this nuclear era.

But neither can we be naïve or foolish. Four times in my lifetime America has gone to war, bleeding the lives of its young men into the sands of island beachheads, the fields of Europe and the jungles and rice paddies of Asia. We know only too well that war comes not when the forces of freedom are strong, it is when they are weak that tyrants are tempted.

We simply cannot learn these lessons the hard way again without risking our destruction.

Of all the objectives we seek, first and foremost is the establishment of lasting world peace. We must always stand ready to negotiate in good faith, ready to pursue any reasonable avenue that holds forth the promise of lessening tensions and furthering the prospects of peace. But let our friends and those who may wish us ill take note: the United States has an obligation to its citizens and to the people of the world never to let those who would destroy freedom dictate our future course of life on this planet. I would regard my election as proof that we have renewed our resolve to preserve world peace and freedom. That this nation will once again be strong enough to do that.

Now this evening marks the last step, save one, of a campaign that has taken Nancy and me from one end of this great nation to the other, over many months and thousands and thousands of miles. There are those who question the way we choose a President, who say that our process imposes difficult and exhausting burdens on those who seek the office. I have not found it so.

It is impossible to capture in words the splendor of this vast continent which God has granted as our portion of His creation. There are no words to express the extraordinary strength and character of this breed of people we call Americans.

Everywhere we've met thousands of Democrats, Independents and Republicans from all economic conditions, walks of life bound together in that community of shared values of family, work, neighborhood, peace and freedom. They are concerned, yes, they're not frightened. They're disturbed, but not dismayed. They are the kind of men and women Tom Paine had in mind when he wrote, during the darkest days of the American Revolution, "We have it in our power to begin the world over again."

Nearly 150 years after Tom Paine wrote those words, an American President told the generation of the Great Depression that it had a "rendezvous with destiny." I believe this generation of Americans today also has a rendezvous with destiny.

Tonight, let us dedicate ourselves to renewing the American compact. I ask you not simply to "trust me," but to trust your values—our values—and to hold me responsible for living up to them. I ask you to trust that American spirit which knows no ethnic, religious, social, political, regional or economic boundaries; the spirit that burned with zeal in the hearts of millions of immigrants from every corner of the earth who came here in search of freedom.

Some say that spirit no longer exists. But I've seen it—I've felt it—all across the land, in the big cities, the small towns and in rural America. It's still there, ready to blaze into life if you and I are willing to do what has to be done; we have to do the practical things, the down-to-earth things, such as creating policies that will stimulate our economy, increase productivity and put America back to work. . . .

The time is now to redeem promises once made to the American people by another candidate, in another time and another place. He said:

"For three long years I have been going up and down this country preaching that government—Federal, state and local—costs too much. I shall not stop that preaching. As an immediate program of action, we must abolish useless offices. We must eliminate unnecessary functions of government.

"We must consolidate subdivisions of government and, like the private citizen, give up luxuries which we can no longer afford." And then he said:

"I propose to you my friends, and through you, that government of all kinds, big and little, be made solvent and that the example be set by the President of the United States and his Cabinet."

That was Franklin Delano Roosevelt's words as he accepted the Democratic nomination for President in 1932.

The time is now, my fellow Americans, to recapture our destiny, to take it into our own hands. And to do this it will take many of us, working together. I ask you tonight, all over this land, to volunteer your help in this cause so that we can carry our message throughout the land.

Isn't it time that we, the people, carry out these unkept promises? That we pledge to each other and to all America on this July day 48 years later, that now we intend to do just that.

I have thought of something that's not a part of my speech and worried over whether I should do it. Can we doubt that only a Divine Providence placed this land, this island of freedom, here as a refuge for all those people in the world who yearn to breathe free? Jews and Christians enduring persecution behind the Iron Curtain; the boat people of Southeast Asia, Cuba and of Haiti; the victims of drought and famine in Africa, the freedom fighters in Afghanistan, and our own countrymen held in savage captivity.

I'll confess that I've been a little afraid to suggest what I'm going to suggest. I'm more afraid not to. Can we begin our crusade joined together in a moment of silent prayer?

God bless America.

Thank you.

HUGH SIDEY
We Are Off on a Special Adventure

[*Time*, November 17, 1980]

A few days before the election, Cartoonist Garry Trudeau extracted from his vivid imagination a huge cross section of Ronald Reagan's brain, in which he placed the intrepid television reporter Roland Hedley Jr. With microphone and camera, Hedley Jr. searched for behavioral patterns in the cortex and the cerebellum with its maze of neurons and their dendritic spines.

Some editors detected a certain prejudice against Reagan, and they threw the cartoon out or put it on the editorial page. Trudeau was guilty as charged, a practitioner of marvelous bias and political deviltry. But any serious student of why Presidents say what they say and do what they do knows that Trudeau, who comes from a family of physicians, had his observer in the right place pondering the ingredients of leadership.

same w/ reporters

Our system, of course, is designed with its web of checks and balances, and open scrutiny that can halt a good deal of presidential caprice and anger, and prevent excess and foolishness. Yet, in our time, the need for quick, authoritative action is so important that we have piled up more power in the Oval Office than those who designed the system ever imagined. That power is unleashed by the sequence of events inside the very individualistic mind of the President—any President. So it will be with Ronald Reagan.

Many wonder if we poke and prod too much at Presidents, speculating on their moods, their IQs, grasp of history, courage and honor. That may be so, but the search is not likely to cease. Too much rides on the man's conclusions for it to be otherwise. Yet at the same time we must recognize the discomforting fact that the analysis of presidential intelligence and wisdom remains a difficult and error-ridden public sport.

Franklin Roosevelt was hardly envisioned as the midwife to social revolution nor was Harry Truman suspected of being the resolute student of history he turned out to be. Lyndon Johnson, the most brilliant legislator we have ever had in the White House, flopped when he tried to apply the techniques of compromise to a war. Jimmy Carter, who collected more facts than his predecessors about the problems that came to him, could not put them together in a way that gave direction to his presidency.

What all this proves is that we can make a pretty good judgment about the individual qualities of a man before he gets to the White House, but we cannot confidently predict how these characteristics will finally interact within the presidential context. . . .

The journey that Ronald Reagan has taken from his prairie hamlet of Dixon, Ill., to the White House, via Hollywood and the Governor's mansion in Sacramento, is an astonishing American pilgrimage. Reagan is not brilliant in any sense, but his mind had to be practical and persistent in a special way to bring him this distance. Those instincts nurtured in simpler times and places seem to have served him well so far. Football, swimming, campus politics, sportscasting and acting are the strata in his evolution. He mimicked real life until he became Governor of California, and then he amazed many people by performing credibly.

But no test of his skills has been like the one he now faces. Not even Reagan fully understands how far his new world is from those old haunts where every talent a healthy person had could be developed and opportunity was as wide as the horizon. There is no way now to fix Reagan up with new genius or to rearrange his convictions. The interaction of the events of this world with the mind of this genial progeny of the heartland will affect us all. As with other Presidents, we are off on a special adventure for which there is no travel guide and no reassuring precedent.

2. THE REAGAN ERA IS LAUNCHED

Reagan's inaugural address displayed both his deepest ideological commitments and the rhetorical skills that won him the nickname the Great Communicator. Even as he extolled the evocative symbols of federal power that surrounded him, Reagan engaged in a long philippic against Washington. "Government is not the solution to our problem," he declared, "government is the problem."

While some post-inaugural editorials adopted a conciliatory stance toward Reaganism, Lewis H. Lapham, editor of Harper's *magazine, offered a deeply mordant view of its cultural meaning. The 1960s were over at last, reflected Lapham; Sinatra had replaced Dylan. Reagan was the new Adam in a materialistic Eden where young people aspired not to service in the Peace Corps but to public relations jobs with big corporations. Reagan's America, Lapham concluded, quoting historian Richard Hofstadter, was a "democracy in cupidity."*

Meanwhile, wildly divergent assessments of the new administration, reflecting deep ideological differences, quickly emerged. Introducing a symposium in the Nation *in November 1981, Mark Green cited chapter and verse to show that the Reagan White House was fatally "out of step with modern America" for its "blatantly pro-business bias" and its hostility to consumer and environmental concerns. But in the January 1983 issue of* Nation's Business, *the magazine of the U.S. Chamber of Commerce, conservative columnist James J. Kilpatrick looked at the same reality Green found so dismaying and pronounced it generally good. Harebrained liberal reform schemes had ceased bubbling up in the Congress, the gushing Niagara of social-welfare spending had been at least slowed, and in the federal regulatory agencies "the zeal of social reformers" had been replaced by a narrower "commonsense" approach. All in all, Kilpatrick concluded, the Reagan years were proving very good for American business—and for America.*

RONALD REAGAN
Inaugural Address
[January 20, 1981]

To a few of us here today this is a solemn and most momentous occasion. And, yet, in the history of our nation it is a commonplace occurrence.

The orderly transfer of authority as called for in the Constitution routinely takes place as it has for almost two centuries and few of us stop to think how unique we really are.

In the eyes of many in the world, this every-four-year ceremony we accept as normal is nothing less than a miracle. . . .

The business of our nation goes forward.

These United States are confronted with an economic affliction of great proportions.

We suffer from the longest and one of the worst sustained inflations in our national history. It distorts our economic decisions, penalizes thrift and crushes the struggling young and the fixed-income elderly alike. It threatens to shatter the lives of millions of our people.

Idle industries have cast workers into unemployment, human misery and personal indignity.

Those who do work are denied a fair return for their labor by a tax system which penalizes successful achievement and keeps us from maintaining full productivity.

But great as our tax burden is, it has not kept pace with public spending. For decades we have piled deficit upon deficit, mortgaging our future and our children's future for the temporary convenience of the present.

To continue this long trend is to guarantee tremendous social, cultural, political and economic upheavals.

You and I, as individuals, can, by borrowing, live beyond our means, but for only a limited period of time. Why then should we think that collectively, as a nation, we are not bound by that same limitation?

We must act today in order to preserve tomorrow. And let there be no misunderstanding—we're going to begin to act beginning today.

The economic ills we suffer have come upon us over several decades.

They will not go away in days, weeks or months, but they will go away. They will go away because we as Americans have the capacity now, as we have had in the past, to do whatever needs to be done to preserve this last and greatest bastion of freedom.

In this present crisis, government is not the solution to our problem; government is the problem. . . .

Our Government has no power except that granted it by the people. It is time to check and reverse the growth of government which shows signs of having grown beyond the consent of the governed.

It is my intention to curb the size and influence of the Federal establishment and to demand recognition of the distinction between the powers granted to the Federal Government and those reserved to the states or to the people.

All of us—all of us need to be reminded that the Federal Government did not create the states; the states created the Federal Government.

Now, so there will be no misunderstanding, it's not my intention to do away with government.

It is rather to make it work—work with us, not over us; to stand by our side, not ride on our back. Government can and must provide opportunity, not smother it; foster productivity, not stifle it.

If we look to the answer as to why for so many years we achieved so much, prospered as no other people on earth, it was because here in this land we unleashed the energy and individual genius of man to a greater extent than has ever been done before.

Freedom and the dignity of the individual have been more available and assured here than in any other place on earth. The price for this freedom at times has been high, but we have never been unwilling to pay that price.

It is no coincidence that our present troubles parallel and are proportionate to the intervention and intrusion in our lives that result from unnecessary and excessive growth of Government.

It is time for us to realize that we are too great a nation to limit ourselves to small dreams. We're not, as some would have us believe, doomed to an inevitable decline. I do not believe in a fate that will fall on us no matter what we do. I do believe in a fate that will fall on us if we do nothing.

So, with all the creative energy at our command let us begin an era of national renewal. Let us renew our determination, our courage and our strength. And let us renew our faith and our hope. We have every right to dream heroic dreams. . . .

Can we solve the problems confronting us? Well, the answer is a unequivocal and emphatic yes.

To paraphrase Winston Churchill, I did not take the oath I've just taken with the intention of presiding over the dissolution of the world's strongest economy.

In the days ahead I will propose removing the roadblocks that have slowed our economy and reduced productivity.

Steps will be taken aimed at restoring the balance between the various levels of government. Progress may be slow—measured in inches and feet, not miles—but we will progress.

It is time to reawaken this industrial giant, to get government back within its means and to lighten our punitive tax burden.

And these will be our first priorities, and on these principles there will be no compromise. . . .

And as we renew ourselves here in our own land we will be seen as having greater strength throughout the world. We will again be the exemplar of freedom and a beacon of hope for those who do not now have freedom.

To those neighbors and allies who share our freedom, we will strengthen our historic ties and assure them of our support and firm commitment.

We will match loyalty with loyalty. We will strive for mutually beneficial relations. We will not use our friendship to impose on their sovereignty, for our own sovereignty is not for sale.

As for the enemies of freedom, those who are potential adversaries, they will be reminded that peace is the highest aspiration of the American people. We will negotiate for it, sacrifice for it; we will not surrender for it—now or ever.

Our forbearance should never be misunderstood. Our reluctance for conflict should not be misjudged as a failure of will.

When action is required to preserve our national security, we will act. We will maintain sufficient strength to prevail if need be, knowing that if we do we have the best chance of never having to use that strength.

Above all we must realize that no arsenal or no weapon in the arsenals of the world is so formidable as the will and moral courage of free men and women.

It is a weapon our adversaries in today's world do not have.

It is a weapon that we as Americas do have.

Let that be understood by those who practice terrorism and prey upon their neighbors.

I am told that tens of thousands of prayer meetings are being held on this day; for that I am deeply grateful. We are a nation under God, and I believe God intended for us to be free. It would be fitting and good, I think, if on each inaugural day in future years it should be declared a day of prayer.

This is the first time in our history that this ceremony has been held, as you've been told, on this West Front of the Capitol.

Standing here, one faces a magnificent vista, opening up on this city's special beauty and history.

At the end of this open mall are those shrines to the giants on whose shoulders we stand.

Directly in front of me, the monument to a monumental man. George Washington, father of our country. A man of humility who came to greatness reluctantly. He led America out of revolutionary victory into infant nationhood.

Off to one side, the stately memorial to Thomas Jefferson. The Declaration of Independence flames with his eloquence.

And then beyond the Reflecting Pool, the dignified columns of the Lincoln Memorial. Whoever would understand in his heart the meaning of America will find it in the life of Abraham Lincoln.

Beyond those monuments, monuments to heroism, is the Potomac River, and on the far shore the sloping hills of Arlington National Cemetery with its row upon row of simple white markers bearing crosses or Stars of David. They add up to only a tiny fraction of the price that has been paid for our freedom.

Each one of those markers is a monument to the kind of hero I spoke of earlier.

Their lives ended in places called Belleau Wood, the Argonne, Omaha Beach, Salerno and halfway around the world on Guadalcanal, Tarawa, Pork Chop Hill, the Chosin Reservoir, and in a hundred rice paddies and jungles of a place called Vietnam.

Under such a marker lies a young man, Martin Treptow, who left his job in a small town barber shop in 1917 to go to France with the famed Rainbow Division.

There, on the Western front, he was killed trying to carry a message between battalions under heavy artillery fire.

We are told that on his body was found a diary.

On the flyleaf under the heading, "My Pledge," he had written these words:

"America must win this war. Therefore I will work, I will save, I will sacrifice, I will endure, I will fight cheerfully and do my utmost, as if the issue of the whole struggle depended on me alone."

The crisis we are facing today does not require of us the kind of sacrifice that Martin Treptow and so many thousands of others were called upon to make.

It does require, however, our best effort, and our willingness to believe in ourselves and to believe in our capacity to perform great deeds; to believe that together with God's help we can and will resolve the problems which now confront us.

And after all, why shouldn't we believe that? We are Americans.

God bless you and thank you. Thank you very much.

LEWIS H. LAPHAM
The Precarious Eden
[*Harper's*, March 1981]

Writing in the January issue of *Commentary*, Norman Podhoretz, the editor of that journal, described President Ronald Reagan "as a political figure . . . unmistakably offering himself as the legitimate heir to Richard Nixon's usurped throne." For the last four or five years *Commentary* has strenuously supported a number of conservative and neo-conservative causes, and, as one of the leading apologists for what he construes to be Mr. Reagan's foreign and economic policies, Mr. Podhoretz enjoys access to the highest levels of corporate opinion. I can well understand his wish to establish the principle of a Republican monarchy; even so, I think he does Mr. Reagan an injustice. President Nixon, like President Jimmy Carter, was a crouching and suspicious man, obsessed with politics, perpetually warding off the swarm of his enemies—both real and imagined—in whom he hoped to instill a respectful mood of fear. Mr. Reagan appears to be a genial man, worldly and accommodating, a politician more in the line of succession from Presidents Eisenhower and Kennedy. He gives the impression of being at his ease in Zion, and he has about him the air of comfortable opulence of a man familiar with the pleasures of the successful middle class, accustomed to the safer suburbs, expensive cars, the scent of jasmine on a golf course, Bob Hope's geopolitics, and the smiling camaraderie of Frank Sinatra.

Despite all his years in what some of his supporters undoubtedly regard as the Sodom of Hollywood, Mr. Reagan gives no sign of having been troubled by the local standards of morality. Harlots come and harlots go, and so do transvestite movie producers and dealers in cocaine; every year somebody one knows commits suicide, and the criminal syndicates take their customary percentage of distribution deals. But such is the way of the world, and what's a fellow to do about it? It is also true that every year the Rose Bowl Parade renews the miracle of flower arrangement, and Jerry Lewis raises another $10 million for children afflicted with muscular dystrophy. Mr. Reagan remains content with the benign deism of an American business oligarchy long since divorced from the existential questions of religion. He subscribes to the American belief in property, self-help, and individualism (as who among his compatriots would not), and he leaves to miserable naysayers and ingrates the thankless task of crying in the wilderness. Self-righteousness has gone out of fashion, and I don't expect that a devout Baptist would find himself any more welcome in the councils of the Reagan administration than would a renegade atheist. Obviously it will be necessary to maintain the proprieties of a belief in the god of one's choice. Jerry Falwell and the Moral Majority, Inc. proclaimed January 20 a day of fasting and prayer, and it would be unkind, as well as foolish, to mock their festivals.

President Reagan campaigned in the cultural rather than the political theaters of opinion, and his audiences understood that he proposed to substitute a crass realism for the crass moralism that had made a mess of things ever since Bob Dylan started singing those revolutionary songs. Mr. Reagan's political theories, which were as chaotic as those of Mr. Carter, didn't matter as much as his instincts, his sentiments, and his prejudices. He was on the side of property, the family, and the flag—against the officiousness of federal bureaucrats, against pornography, drugs, the ghost of Jane Fonda, and the stale, metropolitan sensibility of public television. In 1976 Mr. Carter had appealed to much the same constituency, promising to lead the faithful out of this desert of modernism. But Mr. Carter proved himself a parody of the dynamic leader in the despised liberal tradition. He brought to Washington the agents of the Trilateral Commission and in four years had reduced the illusions of the 1960s to a record of sophism, sleaze, and sanctimony.

If Mr. Reagan had been elected in 1970 instead of 1980, his triumph might have been said to represent the hope of a new beginning, but it takes at least a decade for a political idea to seep into the groundwater of a society as diverse as that of the United States, and by the time Mr. Reagan was able to command a majority of his 225 million fellow citizens his agenda had been accepted as self-evident.

The extent to which Mr. Reagan represented attitudes already in place was made clear to me two years ago in Dallas, during a conversation with the dean of the School of Journalism at Southern Methodist University. The dean asked me to guess how many of the sixty-five students in the graduating class intended to follow careers in the newspaper business. She scoffed at my naïveté when I suggested that only twenty students might be willing to go to fires and elections. "Two," she said, "the rest of them want to become vice presidents in charge of public affairs." They had it in mind to follow in the steps of Herbert Schmertz of the Mobil Oil Corporation, to ride around the country in corporate aircraft, earning $250,000 a year formulating policy and dispensing patronage to symphony orchestras. On an examination dealing with events of the 1960s, nobody in the class recognized Bob Dylan's name.

For the time being, maybe for as long as two or three years, or at least until an unforeseen event announces a reality as yet undiscussed at a White House conference, Mr. Reagan's election and administration will stand as confirmation of the news that the revels of the 1960s have ended at last. I suspect that this will prove the entire sum of his accomplishment, but it is substantial enough to revise the pieties of the age. What it was once mandatory to say in public (about foreigners, for example, or women, or blacks) will now become a matter of whispered confidence; what was once the stuff of private confession will become the subject of Sunday sermons. The conventions changed some years ago (witness the prescient defections of Tom Hayden and Gary Hart from the beleaguered garrisons of the left), but Mr. Reagan's election gives people leave to admit publicly what in 1968 they were willing to say only to their attorneys and press agents.

Given the bias of the Reagan administration, I doubt whether it will still be possible to confuse art with politics, or politics with art. The official culture put together by the liberal coalition of the last twenty years amalgamated the temporal with the spiritual order of expression. The critics writing in the *New York Review of Books* discussed the war in Vietnam as if it were a literary text. President Carter asserted his concern for humanity with the proclamation of metaphors. When John Lennon was killed last December in New York, his devotees perceived his death as a state execution. They gathered in Central Park to mourn the passing of an era in which individuals had claimed the powers of governments. Like the academic ideologues, Mr.

Lennon had become an instrument through which cultural constituencies could make political statements. Even those of his admirers who couldn't remember the lyrics or hum the tunes could see in the person of John Lennon (as with Dylan and Joan Baez) a heroic figure, allegedly in the process of becoming, conquering time past, and transforming himself into the symbol of a world order balanced on a rose petal.

Mr. Reagan's friends look for their heroes among the likes of General Alexander M. Haig. They tend to think of artists as accordion players, and I don't expect that they will have much patience with anything that fails to flatter their vanity. They will find a use for court painters and court intellectuals (i.e., for the photographs of business magnates in *Fortune* and for the metaphysics supplied, at bargain rates, by the contributors to *Commentary*), but the cry of rage once accepted as a conventional art form no longer will find favor with the patrons in the box seats. Maybe this is why so many people mourned the death of John Lennon; henceforth it would not be so easy to make common cause with the cultural opposition.

Maybe this also is why the Reagan administration has found it so difficult to recruit an elite corps of government functionaries. The administration had hoped to appoint at least 200 deputies, assistant deputies, secretaries, and undersecretaries before Christmas: the people necessary to the governing of a bureaucracy. On January 9 the *Wall Street Journal* reported that only one of the available positions had been filled. That same day I spoke to three acquaintances, all blessed with impeccable Republican connections, each of whom had had some experience of politics in the 1960s and 1970s, and all of whom might have proved useful to the new regime. None of them had any intention of going to Washington. Disillusioned with the possibilities of government, impressed not by its properties of redemption but by its stupidity and inefficiency, they had chosen to devote themselves to the amassing of wealth.

Twenty years ago it would have been thought insensitive to admit so middle-class an interest in money. Only philistines went willingly to Wall Street, and the guests at the imperial masquerades staged by the Kennedy administration prided themselves on their aristocratic distance from people who had spent thirty years making automobile tires. But the new administration speaks for the makers of automobile tires, and it has restored the sanctity of property, interpreting the American enterprise, in Richard Hofstadter's phrase, as "a democracy in cupidity rather than a democracy of fraternity." Once again, it has become possible to talk about money without a feeling of guilt or embarrassment. Yes, it is true that the Cambodians continue to starve, but that is no reason for a young man with a Harvard education (bought at a cost of $10,000 per annum) to go mooning about in some dull and fever-ridden rice field. . . .

It isn't that Mr. Reagan and his friends cherish a wish for vengeance. Unlike Mr. Nixon and Mr. Carter, both of whom arrived in office with the lists of their enemies firmly in hand, Mr. Reagan prefers to think that he doesn't have enemies. Given the chance, I'm sure Mr. Reagan would try to make friends with Jane Fonda, Idi Amin, or the editor of the *Nation*. At least in the beginning the Reagan administration will probably look on its opponents not as villains but merely as carping misanthropes, either silly or misinformed and making gratuitous complaints. Of course Mr. Reagan means nobody any harm, and of course he wouldn't dream of wrecking the environment or forcing the Mexican population of Los Angeles into armed rebellion. What nonsense. He would be delighted to invite Sammy Davis, Jr., to dinner, and the foreman of Rancho Mirage undoubtedly takes exquisite care of the swallows and the ferns. But over the last twenty years the legal guarantees extended to the innocent have been so grossly exaggerated as to afford equal protection to the guilty. Surely somebody has got to draw a line somewhere. The law is not a department of social philosophy, and it's about time somebody said a good word on behalf of the FBI and the CIA.

This tone has also been dominant in the public conversation for the last four or five years, expressing itself in the recent Justice Department ruling vis-à-vis busing, and in the repeated jibes (presented as witticisms in the *National Review*) at the futility of the environmentalists and the absurdity of affirmative action.

The other day in New York, a distinguished publisher informed me that the world had become "fragile." These were dangerous times, he said; the Russians were moving around in the mountains and God knows what kind of trouble lay hidden under the floor of the domestic economy. A depression was not out of the question; neither was a devaluation of the currency or a revolution in Central America. The bottom could fall out; things could go from bad to worse. Why then cast unnecessary aspersions on the chieftains of the political and intellectual establishments? Clearly nobody was perfect, but they were trying their best, and maybe it would be a good thing for once to go easy on the criticism.

The national press has already endorsed such a delicate view of events. For at least a year hardly anybody has mentioned an outrage against the First Amendment. During the whole of last summer's campaign, the press, which had been expected to hold Mr. Reagan up to public scorn and ridicule, behaved itself in a manner remarkably soft-spoken and polite. Even Anthony Lewis and Tom Wicker found pleasant things to say about Mr. Reagan's charming smile. Elsewhere in its pages, *The New York Times,* for the last several months, has been publishing a series of articles in praise of wealth. Every few days the paper celebrates the magnificence of yet another rich man (William Paley and Oscar de la Renta come to mind as the most recent subjects of flattering portraits), and the reporters choose their adjectives with the tact of a couturier fitting a client for a dress. The food and fashion columnists elaborate the theme of the precarious American Eden, reminding their readers of the cornucopia of material rewards available to the shoppers in the department stores of the free world. Given the fondness of the media for the moral beauty of the status quo, I don't expect them to find much fault with the Reagan administration, certainly not in its initial phases and probably not for as long as it can continue to keep its more prominent members out of jail or foreign wars.

The Reagan administration in its cultural aspects presents itself as the manifestation of an idea whose moment has already passed. Occasionally I have the odd feeling that the Reagan people meant to reenact the pageant of the 1960s, but this time with full knowledge of what they're about (cf. the supposed "realism" of Alexander Haig) and with a Republican repertory company. Maybe that is what accounts for this curious atmosphere of comic opera. Mr. Reagan proclaims a utopia for people already rich. In somewhat the same way that the Second Empire of Louis Napoleon aped the empire of Napoleon I, the Reagan administration mimics the vigor of President Kennedy's New Frontier. But Mr. Reagan is a little old for the leading role, and the supporting players give the awkward impression of actors and actresses dressed up in costumes of state. In the Paris of Napoleon III, the court accompanied its masquerade with the tunes of Offenbach. The Reagan administration seems to prefer the nostalgia of a Frank Sinatra song.

MARK GREEN
Rating Reagan: Trendlines, Faultlines
[*Nation*, November 7, 1981]

Why does Ronald Reagan confuse us so? For years he was routinely underestimated by the press and his opponents; now he is just as regularly overestimated. He's "King of the Hill." The "chairman of the board." A Republican F.D.R.

To be sure, a year after his election, President Reagan appears to be doing as well as his devotees had hoped and better than his critics had expected—and for reasons not terribly mysterious. Compared with Lyndon Johnson, Richard Nixon, Gerald Ford and Jimmy Carter, Ronald Reagan is stable, decisive, charming and damn nice.

The press has a way of magnifying both the victories and the defeats of a President—of apotheosizing the momentary. And it has a habit of focusing more on who's up and who's down than on the content and impact of the prevailing side's programs. But as the President is lionized for his winsome personality and domestic legislative wins, several less publicized trends and fault lines are discernible.

already an intention

In this symposium* seven writers attempt to trace some of these trends and faults. In doing so, they remind us that Reagan was elected largely because the voters thought he would do a better job than Carter; he was not given an ideological mandate for reactionary restructuring. For example, exit polls taken last November 4 found that while only 10 percent of those who had voted for Reagan said they supported him because he was "a conservative," nearly 40 percent simply cited that it was "time for a change."

To do Reagan's injustices justice would, of course, require several book-length analyses. This present collection represents an early contribution to what will no doubt be a growing body of opposition literature....

The connecting theme of these pieces is that Reaganism will fail, and perhaps Reagan as well. That is, the doctrinaire conservatism that guides this government will objectively and measurably fail as public policy, and the public will eventually associate that failure with a President who now enjoys substantial personal popularity. Let me suggest two political fault lines that, with enough sustained pressure, might grow into gaping fissures.

First, on a long list of important issues—abortion, nuclear energy, health and safety regulation, civil rights, social security, environmental protection, national health insurance—Ronald Reagan is a doctrinaire conservative, out of step with moderate America. Over four years, this disharmony can only lead to tension and unpopularity. Already, for example, a July Harris poll found that by 57 percent to 34 percent, most of the public thought that Reagan's economic policies would be "unfair to the poor and cause hardship on them."

Second, the blatantly pro-business bias of this Administration—and its ostentatious displays of affluence as poverty programs are cut back—is increasingly offensive to the large number of Americans who are concerned about overweening corporate power and privilege. There is no doubt that Reagan sincerely believes that getting government off the back of business will make the United States more prosperous. There is also no doubt that the business elite that has helped him succeed in politics sees him as their champion. They know that he owes them a lot. Without the visibility he enjoyed as the spokesman for General Electric in the late 1950s and early 1960s, and without the financial backing of his "kitchen cabinet" of millionaire businessmen, he never would have been elected governor of California or President. Verne Orr, Governor Reagan's Director of Finance and President Reagan's Secretary of the Air Force, once described the role of these corporate supporters: "It is natural that the type of special-interest group that puts you there [in office] is the one that you're going to listen to more closely. In our case it was the conservative groups, the business groups, that put this administration in. They are our constituency."

---

*This essay by Mark Green introduced a special issue of the *Nation* offering assessment of different aspects of the Reagan administration by various writers.

Fóurteen years later, banker and longtime Reagan friend Charles Z. Wick said, "We won the election. We don't intend to lose the government." Alfred Bloomingdale, department store magnate and Reagan intimate, added, "We're surrounding Ronnie with the best people—the ones we'd hire for our own businesses."   *education guy?*
Wick can stop worrying about "losing the government." Almost all of the people the President has named to business-sensitive posts either previously represented the regulated industry or are philosophically opposed to the regulatory mission entrusted to them, or both. A pro-development cattleman runs the Bureau of Land Management; a former Exxon lawyer is the general counsel of the Environmental Protection Agency; an Occupational Safety and Health Act violator now runs the agency that enforces this law. Allowing business to police itself makes no sense—unless one wants to repeal legislation without bothering to go back to the legislature.

If Reagan's appointments have pleased his business constituency, the same is true of his policies.

§ The Administration has tried to hasten the decontrol of oil and permit more oil and gas exploration on more Federal land. It also reduced the Department of Energy's enforcement unit by 67 percent.

§ The Administration abandoned the automatic seat belt and airbag requirement for new cars despite overwhelming evidence that many lives would be saved. G.M., Ford and Chrysler lauded the decisions.

§ The new chairman of the Federal Trade Commission, James Miller 3d, said his agency should stop protecting consumers against false advertising and defective products.

§ In 1980, after more than two years of deliberations, OSHA enacted its landmark Access Rule, which allows workers and their union representatives to inspect company medical records. Secretary of Labor Raymond Donovan has recently announced that the department plans to review the standard with an eye toward rewriting it.

§ American companies that sell infant formula abroad complained to the White House about a proposed voluntary code against deceptive marketing practices. Companies like Nestlé, Bristol-Myers, Abbott Labs and American Home Products, along with the Grocery Manufacturers of America, told Reagan aides that their infant formula sales totaled $2 billion annually and that the market was growing. The Reagan White House then overruled the Reagan State Department to cast the only vote in the World Health Organization against the code.

§ William Baxter, head of the Justice Department's Antitrust Division, announced that "vertical" mergers between suppliers and dealers and acquisitions by large conglomerates did not trouble him, which helps explain the recent paroxysm of mergers. Many antitrust division lawyers are demoralized by what they regard as Baxter's "pro-trust" policy.

never heard a complaint about that

§ The Administration spearheaded a drive that led to $142 billion in tax cuts for corporations over the next five years.

The President periodically demonstrates that he understands the peril of being too closely identified with the big-business community, which is as unpopular in America as big government. "The new Republican Party I envision," he told biographer Frank Van Der Linden, "will not, and cannot, be limited to the country-club-Big-Business image that it is burdened with. . . . It is going to have to make room for the men and women in the factories." Yet when faced with a decision, he almost invariably comes down on the side of corporate interests.

The point is not that the corporate position on an issue is always or even usually wrong, but rather that it is not *always* right, as Reagan's decisions in office would imply. Nor do his speeches show any openness to opposing views. He has rarely expressed sympathy for the victims of business discrimination, pollution, oligopoly, payoffs, corruption or fraud. In his world there is only government bungling; flammable Pintos, exploding Firestone 500s and cancer-breeding toxic-waste dumps simply do not exist.

The costs to the American people of the President's policies are becoming evident. They will be even more visible in his second year in office. And *Fortune* magazine recently reported that 51 percent of Americans making more than $25,000 a year believe that "big business is becoming a threat to the American way of life." This growing skepticism could produce a backlash against an Administration that is an apologist for big business. Out of this discontent will emerge a new generation of "economic democrats" to develop alternatives to the old generation of "economic royalists" now running a government they don't believe in.

JAMES J. KILPATRICK

The Reagan Presidency: A Pattern of Significant Change

[*Nation's Business*, January 1983]

We come now to the end of the first two years of Ronald Reagan's presidency. The 97th Congress has limped off the field; the 98th is trotting out of the locker room. It is an appropriate time for the business community to have a look at whither we have been and whither we are going. The second half, unless I am vastly mistaken, will be tougher than the first.

These have been two good years, politically speaking, for American business. (Economically speaking, the two years have been lousy, but let us table a motion to talk of corporate profits.) Think back, if you will, to the elections of 1980. It is a rare event in our political history that sees anything approaching a "mandate" from the voters, but we saw one then.

This mandate was not to be discerned in Reagan's victory over Jimmy Carter. Such was the popularity of the unfortunate gentleman from Georgia that almost any Republican candidate could have toppled him. . . . The presidential outcome, important as it was, carried no clear ideological message.

There could be no mistaking the message left by returns from the Senate contests, however. With the sole exception of Connecticut's seat, every Senate seat that changed hands changed in a more conservative direction. Some of the Senate's most liberal members fell—Birch Bayh in Indiana, Gaylord Nelson in Wisconsin, Frank Church in Idaho, George McGovern in South Dakota, John Culver in Iowa.

If this was not a revolution, it was something very close to it. The Republicans took control of the Senate; they took over the committee chairmanships: they named their committee staffs. There is no rational way to pooh-pooh this phenomenal upheaval. Taken in conjunction with the Reagan victory, the Senate returns spoke volumes. It was the clearest mandate for change since Franklin Roosevelt licked Herbert Hoover in 1932.

And we have indeed seen change in these past two years.

Reagan defined his program of economic recovery in several ways. He wanted to reduce the total burden of federal taxation. He wanted to attain a stable monetary policy. He wanted to eliminate some of the regulatory red tape in which business has been strangled. His hope was that this combination would revitalize the economy and generate new revenues that would more than offset the loss of revenues resulting from the lower tax rates.

The operation was a success, but the patient hasn't recovered. Congress gave the President most of what he asked for. As a percentage of national income, the federal tax burden has been reduced. Tight monetary policies have indeed favorably affected the rate of inflation. Many excessive regulations have been eased. Through the Budget Reconciliation Act, entitlement programs have been curbed. Interest rates have been forced down. However, the doldrums persist, and the prospect of a balanced budget grows steadily more remote. Anticipated deficits for 1983 and 1984 will dominate the capital market; the private sector will be scrambling for what is left.

Still, the pattern of significant change is now fixed, and these past two years have witnessed other changes. Among them is a palpable shift in attitude at executive agencies.

This can be seen clearly at the Occupational Safety and Health Administration, under Thorne Auchter; at the Environmental Protection Agency, under Anne Gorsuch; at the Interior Departments under James Watt; at the Federal Trade Commission, under James C. Miller. We see new attitudes at the Federal Communications Commission and the Consumer Product Safety

Commission. The Justice Department has replaced the zeal of social reformers with a commonsense policy of law enforcement.

In one of the Sherlock Holmes stories, the key element was that the dog didn't bark. Nothing had happened. We find a similar situation in considering the 97th Congress—political things that were not done and in many cases were not even attempted. . . .

In the 96th Congress, Democratic leaders pushed hard for national health insurance; such proposals were not even discussed in the 97th. Organized labor formerly was seeking reorganization of the National Labor Relations Board, effective repeal of the Hatch Act and a nationwide scheme of postcard registration for voting. Gone, all gone. Liberal pressure groups wanted a new consumer protection agency. It was a lost cause in Reagan's first Congress.

This is not to suggest that liberal forces on the Hill were entirely impotent over these past two years. Of course not. Reagan got nowhere in his efforts to abolish the Departments of Energy and Education. . . . The President couldn't win his first-year tax cut of 10 percent; he had to settle for 5 percent instead.

Yet even the President's defeats, more often than not, were partial defeats. Reagan wanted to abolish the Consumer Product Safety Commission; Congress voted instead to reauthorize the CPSC for a few more years, but to keep it on a tight leash.

Looking back at the first half of the Reagan term, we see the pattern of change most clearly in the things that were in fact achieved. For a prime example, consider the Economic Recovery Tax Act of 1981 (Public Law 97-34). This was the act that gave the business community its accelerated cost recovery system, fixing new depreciation schedules. The act created new benefits for small business; it provided for carryover of unused tax credits; it set up incentives for additional research and development; and of course it reduced actual tax rates on corporate income. Taken as a package, the act will reduce taxes on business by annual increments reaching $54 billion in 1986.

Yes, it is quite true that the tax act of 1982 took back a substantial part of the benefits that had been granted in 1981. . . . Yet on balance, or so it seems to me, the 1982 changes have to be regarded as bearable changes. The tax increases were legislatively married to spending decreases. This was a compromise package, and not a gravely damaging package at that.

The important trend of these past two years appears plainly in such aspects as speed and direction. The Reagan program never envisioned a net cut in outlays; no informed person would have expected any such thing. What has happened is that Reagan's leadership has produced a startling change in the rate of increase.

We still will be pouring billions of dollars a year into such programs as food stamps, Medicaid, student loans, child nutrition, subsidized housing and aid to the arts, but in every instance the rate of increase has been significantly slowed. The course of legislative direction has changed; it no longer is seriously proposed to expand the bureaucracy or to create new areas of federal pre-emption of state responsibilities. The direction goes in the other way—toward a reduction in the regulatory burden, toward block grants instead of categorical grants.

Little of the Reagan record could have been set without the cooperation of conservative Democrats—the Boll Weevils—in the House. Notably in 1981, less so in 1982, the Republicans' own ranks held steady; but the Boll Weevils made the difference. Matters will be quite different in the incoming 98th Congress. The Boll Weevils will be back, but 26 Republicans won't be back, and assuming even a modicum of party solidarity under Speaker Thomas O'Neill, we can anticipate two years of impasse and stalemate.

The question has been kicked around for the past two months: Were the elections of 1982 a referendum on, and a repudiation of, Reagan's program of economic recovery? In my own view the answer is, plainly, no. . . .

The conservative mandate of 1980, in my own view, has been weakened, but it has not been rejected. The prolonged recession, with rising unemployment and diminishing corporate profits, plainly has taken its toll.

We are an impatient people, spoiled by a society wedded to instant gratification, and we are forever asking of our leadership: What have you done for us *lately*? Both interest rates and inflation rates have been halved, but these immense benefits are quickly forgotten.

The business community cannot expect much from the incoming 98th Congress, but there will be no major defeats, either. If business leaders have the good sense and quick wit they are widely presumed to have, they will look past the prospects for 1983 and begin focusing at once on the political situation in 1984, when the Presidency and 19 Republican seats in the Senate will be up for grabs. At the moment, 1983 promises little more than a tepid tale of three-up, three-down; in 1984, my brothers and sisters, it is the whole blessed ball game.

[Adapted by permission from *Nation's Business*. Copyright © 1983 U.S. Chamber of Commerce]

3. THE MANY REAGANS

Thinker and World Leader

Like Franklin Roosevelt and John Kennedy before him, Reagan the man proved endlessly fascinating to political journalists. Much of this attention focused on the quality of the President's mind. In March 1982, Morton Kondracke of the New Republic publicly broached what had theretofore been largely a matter of gossip: that Reagan was out of touch, perhaps even senile. Kondracke approached the subject cautiously: Reagan's brain, he suggested, was perhaps less important than his administration's policies. This view was challenged in the same periodical two weeks later, when Jack Beatty argued that any President's mental processes, or lack thereof, were a matter of vital concern. Reagan's tendency to reduce complex issues to simplistic—and often false—anecdotes, suggested Beatty, demonstrated a triumph of ideology over pragmatism rare in American politics.

The same topic was implicitly addressed in September 1983 by conservative columnist John McLaughlin. Commenting on Reagan's handling of the Russians' shooting down of a Korean airliner that strayed into Soviet airspace, McLaughlin concluded that the President had adopted just the right response to win a maximum of support at home and abroad—hardly the actions of a doddering incompetent.

But the debate went on. In a lengthy article devoted to "The President's Mind" (New York Times Magazine, October 6, 1985), Leslie Gelb concluded that Reagan often did, indeed, resort to simplistic, anecdotal modes of expressing rigid ideological positions formed during his years as spokesman for the General Electric Corporation. While Reagan's intellectual style made it hard for him to grasp complicated policy issues, Gelb went on, it equipped him ideally for the "simpler, negative tasks of hammering away at 'big government' and rhetorically bashing the Soviet Union." When the Iran-Contra scandal broke (see p. 221), concern about Reagan's day-to-day mental grasp surfaced with fresh urgency.

MORTON KONDRACKE
Reagan's I.Q.
[*New Republic,* March 24, 1982]

In each of America's recent failed Presidencies, the press has managed to discover, disclose, and then inculcate into public consciousness a nasty little secret that finally came to dominate the President's image. Lyndon Johnson was a boor, Richard Nixon a crook, Gerald Ford a clown, and Jimmy Carter a mean-spirited incompetent. Right now, with a good bit of help from other politicians and from the President himself, the press is working itself up to declare aloud that our latest emperor also has no clothes. All that remains in doubt is exactly how Ronald Reagan's nakedness will be characterized for posterity.

A pattern is developing. Last September, after two Libyan jets were shot down by U.S. planes, and aides did not awaken the President, *Newsweek* described Reagan as "disengaged," and quoted an unnamed White House aide as saying "he probably spends two or three hours a day on real work. . . . All he wants to do is tell stories about his movie days." Twice in January, Lou Cannon of the *Washington Post* was painfully direct. "More disquieting than Reagan's performance or prospects on any specific issue is a growing suspicion that the President has only a passing acquaintance with some of the most important decisions of his Administration." Cannon cited a long list of Presidential press conference misstatements, and concluded that "as [Reagan] begins his second year he has raised anew one of the principal issues of his Presidential candidacy. Simply put, the question is: is Reagan up to the job?" Cannon's second article, a probing review of Reagan's press conference *faux pas,* said there was concern in the White House that "further verbal fumbling by Reagan may contribute to the impression of a President whose grasp is slipping." . . .

On February 22 the *Wall Street Journal* carried a front-page story headlined: REAGAN'S MANAGEMENT BY DELEGATION BEGINS TO CONCERN SUPPORTERS. THEY FEAR THAT A FEELING HE ISN'T ON TOP OF THINGS MAY HURT HIS AUTHORITY, and *New York Times* columnist Anthony Lewis accused the press of going easy on Reagan, in view of his economic and foreign policy shortcomings. Lewis said the most important reason might be that reporters and editors who watch Reagan "are frightened by what they see . . . a man who acts without real information . . . a man with an anecdotal view of the world, who may apply in El Salvador lessons of imagined history in Vietnam. They see a man who gives simplistic answers to complicated questions." These press people "care about their country, and they find it too upsetting to acknowledge . . . that the enormous power of its leadership is in such hands."

Then, on March 2, the *New York Times*'s new "Washington Talk" page carried a story by White House correspondent Howell Raines, headlined: REAGAN JOKES STIR AIDES' CONCERN, which observed that editorial cartoons and comedians' wisecracks were portraying the President as an "amiable muddler," as Robin Hood in reverse, or as a man not in control of his White House. The same day, the Associated Press carried the most damaging piece of all—damaging because it came not from the press itself or from the Democratic opposition (which has, in fact, been relatively tame about attacking Reagan personally), but from Senator Robert Packwood of Oregon, chairman of the Senate Republican Campaign Committee. Packwood said that Reagan responds to the concerns of Republican senators "on a totally different track." If senators tell him they are worried about the projected $120-billion deficit, Packwood said, Reagan responds with an anecdote. "The President says, 'You know a person yesterday, a young man, went into a grocery store and he had an orange in one hand and a bottle in the other and he paid for the orange with food stamps and he took the change and paid for the vodka. That's what's wrong.' "

Reports subsequently emerged from other members of Congress and from the public that Reagan deals in anecdotal non sequiturs all the time. One Northeastern group of shoe industry representatives sought to express concern about foreign competition, for example, and was treated to a Presidential lecture on the difficulty nowadays of buying a pair of cowboy boots as good as the ones available in days of yore.

So far the criticism has been reasonably gentle and euphemistic. Reagan is "detached," and there is "concern" about his being "in charge" or "out of touch." Cartoonists still portray him as captain of a storm-tossed ship or as a cowboy riding a ferocious economic horse. But the pressure is on to be more frank. Sometimes it's editors who are putting pressure on reporters, but in most cases, it's reporters who are convinced that the President is lazy, passive, stupid, or even senile, and are pushing their editors to let them say so. According to one White House correspondent, "For almost everybody in Washington, Reagan was a new beat, and you don't write that kind of stuff until you're pretty sure of yourself. Reporters are just beginning now to feel that what they feared is true, that he is detached. They've got a notebook full of stuff, and they are beginning to try to sell stories to their editors. The editors are very reluctant to use it. They've seen it with many other Presidents, Gerald Ford in particular, and you hate to reinforce that kind of thing. It's a devastating thing, but it's going to happen, and once he gets tagged with the image, it's going to be hard to get rid of, mostly because he's so old."

There is some faint reason to hope that the patterns of the past will not repeat themselves. For one thing, editors are reluctant to plaster labels on the

President that the facts may not sustain. . . . A *Washington Post* editor said, "My experience in such matters is that history will show that what we all believe to be true will be true—plus about 30 percent or even 50 percent. But at this point it's very difficult to nail it down with specifics in a way that you could write a story saying that the President is not in charge. The White House people regard it as unsayable. We try to be as specific and hard as possible, and we are. If we had real evidence of his being in the Bozo zone, we'd write it. We have not restrained ourselves."

White House aides are aware that the question of Reagan's competence is becoming an issue, but they deny its premise, which may be a valid thing to do. They also tend to discount its importance, which I think is neither valid nor wise. One aide's response was: "Is the President on top of his job? I find that a stunning question after the year in which he won seven straight Congressional victories. It may be that the press demands a big victory every so often to prove that he's still there. He does not fit the press's pattern of the Presidency, but he's got control. I don't think the Presidency requires that someone be deeply immersed in the detail of government or be deeply read in the great works of political literature. It requires someone with a strong sense of where he wants to go and a good sense of leadership, and I think he's got those in abundance." . . .

According to an Administration official who has observed Reagan for a long time, "The worst you can say about him is that he has a passive personality, and he does relate to things through anecdotes. He's nowhere near stupid. If you're talking about intellectually academician-bright, half those people are stupid because they lack common sense. No man is stupid with that kind of a sense of timing, that kind of sense of people. That's not just actor's training; no other actor's done what he's done. He's passive not in the sense of not being able to make a hard decision, but in the way he gets information. He doesn't go out to seek it, reach out for it, and pursue it, but lets it come to him conveniently. 'Intellectually lazy' is probably fair. He's without a constant curiosity."

To Reagan aides, the proof that the President is in charge of his Administration came in January, when he rejected all of their advice that he cut defense and raise taxes to bring his budget closer to balance. "He made the decision. He makes the decisions here, all the major ones. In foreign policy, he makes all the decisions that come to him, and quite a few do. He made the decision on the Rumanian debt against the desires of State and Defense. He sat through many meetings and made the decision on the Soviet pipeline and East-West technology transfers and what to do about Libya. He makes all those decisions. He's not as involved as Jimmy Carter in the day-to-day operations of the Presidency, but I don't think he has to be. He is very well read and up to speed on anything that's given to him—perhaps to a fault. We can't send him too much stuff or he'll stay up till two or three in the morning reading it. The suggestion that he's only going through just the ceremonial motions is just not true."

Reagan's top aides deny that his tendency to indulge in anecdotes shows he is out of touch with reality. According to them, the Republican leadership meeting that Packwood referred to consisted of a senatorial rehash of the same antideficit arguments that Reagan had heard repeatedly during his budget deliberations. "Was he supposed to argue with them all over again, or was it better to change the subject in his own way?" That would plausibly explain the President's desire to deflect the conversation with an anecdote (though it doesn't excuse the unbecoming undertone of prejudice in the anecdote itself). And in the shoe manufacturers' meeting, "they were coming in to talk about protectionist measures to a free trader. There is no doubt where Ronald Reagan was coming down on that issue, and rather than sit there and be disingenuous—telling them he might do something for them when he wouldn't—he related an anecdote that had some relation to the subject." Other aides note that Franklin Roosevelt also put off unpleasant subjects by telling stories, that Americans took Chairman Mao's unintelligible aphorisms for wisdom, and that, until the economy turned bad, Reagan's anecdotes were considered charming.

"I agree with George Will," said one White House assistant, citing Will's remark on an ABC-TV "Nightline" program on the subject of Reagan's competence. "There's nothing here that a 6 percent prime interest rate wouldn't cure." Unfortunately for Reagan, the prime rate is far from 6 percent, and Reaganomics is perceived to be one of the reasons. As a result, Reagan's overall approval ratings are down, and his "leadership" ratings are beginning to dip. The latest Harris results show that more Americans disapprove of Reagan's performance now than approve. When asked whether Reagan inspires confidence in the White House, 56 percent said yes at the end of January, and 39 percent said no. In mid-February, the figures were 48 to 48. Political analyst Kevin Phillips sees other signs of decay. "Watch the chimpanzee cartoons—the number of editorial cartoons each month that conjure up *Bedtime for Bonzo*. You get some measure of what the cartoonists think is fair game. It wasn't fair game last fall, but it's beginning to be now."

What's Reagan to do? His White House aides now have him hold one press conference a month to get him in practice, although so far the results have been more damaging than helpful. Additional press sessions simply increase the opportunity for misstatements. But the President is being more intensively primed for press conferences than he was previously, and each Monday he has an "issues lunch" with ten White House aides who brief him on important pending activities. What matters in the end, though, is not how well Reagan performs in front of reporters, but how well his Administration performs on the major issues of domestic and foreign policy. The results will show whether Ronald Reagan is a political wizard or just the Wizard of Oz. An intellectual genius whose policies fail is a failure, and an imbecile is a success in the unlikely event that his policies succeed. The country will be better off if the press keeps its eye on the prime interest rate, not on Ronald Reagan's I.Q.

JACK BEATTY
The President's Mind
[New Republic, April 7, 1982]

In his typically fair and tough-minded discussion of "Reagan's I.Q.," . . . Morton Kondracke tries to lay to rest the issue of what might be called the President's Oakland problem—is there any there there?—saying that the press should forget about Ronald Reagan's intelligence quotient and attend to the numbers that really matter, like the prime rate and the unemployment rolls. These are indeed important numbers, but reporters and the public generally, I think, should pay the closest attention to the President's intelligence—and, more important, to his mind.

Mind refers to the quality and kind of a person's thoughts, feelings, and volitions, and to the fusion of these things in the complex whole we call the self. Intelligence is to a mind as a limb is to a body. When we apply this wider idea of mind to Mr. Reagan, we have reason to tremble that the country is in his hands, because the mark of his mind is its lack of seriousness.

By seriousness of mind, I mean three relatively modest qualities: first, the ability to recognize logical contradiction; second, the ability to change or modify one's ideas when confronted with facts that contradict them; and third, the ability to monitor the consequences of one's actions and to adopt a different course if those consequences are not as one's ideas represented them. The first two qualities are sheerly cognitive; the third, both cognitive and moral. Mr. Reagan shows no sign of possessing any of them. Dumb he may or may not be, but he clearly is not serious.

The President's economic policy—to cut taxes, increase expenditures, and balance the budget simultaneously—shows that he is a stranger to the law of logical contradiction. But his relation to facts is even more tenuous. He finds it next to impossible to say anything that is not in some crucial way untrue. He has a disposition to distort and to caricature. It's not a credibility gap, for there is no evidence of cynical or even conscious duplicity. The President is so far out of touch that it amounts to a reality gap.

His mind does not proceed according to logical or empirical principles. It works in an essentially imagistic way. Its most characteristic device is the figure of speech known as synecdoche: the use of a part to stand for a whole.

Again and again Mr. Reagan uses this device, in the form of anecdotes. And again and again the parts he uses to stand for the whole—from the celebrated Chicago "welfare queen" who did not exist to the recent slander of the disabled Virginia welder whom the President accused of taking welfare while working—are shown to be false. Even if they were true, that would be small comfort, for complex social realities still would have been reduced to simple, and by no means typical, examples. But the President's anecdotes are not true. Which means that he represents social reality to himself with false images, and then, guided by a light that is darkness, acts into that reality. All is illusory—except the real pain caused by these false metaphors.

The President styles himself a quintessential American, yet as the most ideological of our Presidents, he rarely evinces the native bent of mind called pragmatism. Pragmatism, as an explicit philosophy, was a complex intellectual development, but in its main emphases it was an attempt to apply the scientific method to the perennial questions of philosophy. The pragmatist does not merely believe his ideas are right in the manner of the ideologue, he tests them by their consequences. If the consequences are other than those predicted by his ideas, he changes his ideas accordingly. He is saved not by belief but by works. His motto is: by their fruits ye shall know them.

This intellectual procedure is the genius of American civilization. By all the evidence of his Presidency, it is unknown to Mr. Reagan. His economic policies were to have produced a surge of confidence among business people; instead, the massive budget deficits created by the logical and empirical flaws of his economic program have created dismay in those very circles. Has the President changed his policy in line with these consequences? He has not. He remains fixed in *a priori* belief.

Blind to the cognitive side of pragmatism, the President also fails to display its moral side. For if he really believes that his cuts in social programs are not inflicting pain on thousands of our most vulnerable citizens, then he is not attending to the consequences of his actions, and is a careless man in the literal sense of that word: he does not care.

All of our recent Presidents have been victims of the Xanadu effect. Prisoners of their office, they see no one outside the ring of the sycophants and lickspittles who surround them. Most of them have been rich, with the accompanying incurable ignorance of what life is like for most people. And all of them, from Kennedy to Reagan, have repeatedly politicized the facts of our condition. But in Reagan these structural flaws of the office in the media age are compounded by an intellectual slovenliness which, in a job where power could not disguise incapacity, would brand a man a fool. At a dangerous moment in our history, we are being led by such a man. That, whatever the prime rate, is reason to worry.

[Reprinted by permission of *The New Republic*, copyright © 1982 The New Republic, Inc.]

JOHN MC LAUGHLIN
A Leader for the West

[*National Review,* September 30, 1983]

In August of 1968, about three days before the Soviets invaded Czechoslovakia, Alexander Dubcek, the First Secretary of the Czechoslovakian Communist Party, met with Janos Kadar, the First Secretary of the Hungarian Communist Party, whom the Soviets had placed in power in 1956. The meeting took place at a town on the Czechoslovakian-Hungarian border. Before Dubcek departed, Kadar asked him, "Do you know what kind of people you are dealing with?" When Dubcek did not answer, Kadar said, "They are animals."

This is how the free world felt about the Soviets when it learned that a Korean 747 jetliner had been hit by a Russian rocket, killing 269 defenseless civilians. Demands for reprisals were insistent and sweeping. Certain conservatives in the United States urged the President to end all commerce with the Soviets, break off arms talks at Geneva and Vienna, cancel the Shultz-Gromyko meeting in Madrid, rescind wheat and technology deals, nationalize U.S. loans to Soviet satellite states, expel Russian diplomats and KGB agents (together totaling about 150) from their walled fortress in Washington. The pressure on Mr. Reagan was immense. The fury peaked over the Labor Day weekend.

Before giving his TV address to the nation on September 5, the President reached a decision. He would not impose piecemeal, ad hoc strictures against the Soviets, however warranted and cathartic. The President reasoned that such tactics would be temporary at best, requiring early or late reversal, and that they would entail hopeless policy, hurt us more than the Soviets, run athwart our charter principles (nationalizing private-sector loans), breed division among our allies and squabbles in Congress, and, most important, defeat the larger purpose of building international public opprobrium toward the Soviets.

So Mr. Reagan decided to position the Soviets against the world, not against us. The President's role would be to marshal the world's rage toward a long-term, wide-arc goal: the overriding realization by nations outside the Soviet bloc that strong military defenses must exist to counter continued Soviet aggression.... Short-term band-aid "punishments" were really no punishments at all, and would undercut the larger defense design. A climate of worldwide anti-Soviet opinion, on the other hand, would make it possible for governments to increase their military preparedness. Internal resistance to those defense budgets would ebb in the face of mounting anti-Soviet world feeling occasioned by the Korean airline slaughter. "A bipolar U.S.-USSR confrontation would only let lagging countries off the hook," notes a White House counselor. "We wanted them to carry their water, too. Reagan is building a cathedral, not the pews."

If the President had opted for Carteresque sanctions, the impact on European-American relations might well have been disastrous. Instead of isolating the Soviet Union, the sanctions could have isolated us. Western Europeans, who cannot even agree among themselves to deny Aeroflot landing rights for sixty days, would hardly have endorsed more stringent measures, and so we would have been left sitting on the end of a limb as we were with the Siberian pipeline embargo.

Their reluctance to act against the Soviets is understandable, if not wholly admirable. Europeans are worried sick about whether their territories will be targeted by Soviet SS-20s when Pershing and cruise missiles are emplaced in December. If the President had canceled the START and INF talks, which deal with the fate of 600 million people, our allies would then have had to choose between a paranoiac Russian bear on the one hand and a U.S. President perceived as a bomb-throwing jingo on the other. But by seeking long-term public-opinion mileage rather than short-term quick-fix reprisals, Mr. Reagan has focused the anger of the world.

At home, Mr. Reagan's tactics will be similarly efficacious. He can reasonably expect Congress to condemn the Soviet Union for its wickedness in the most searing language, and not become fragmented by partisan, dove/hawk wrangling over discrete retaliatory acts.

During the Carter years, this nation cried out for a leader. Now, it appears, we may have one. Mr. Reagan has a leader's ability to conceptualize broadly, to persuade, and to stick to his principles calmly and tenaciously. The most impressive aspect of his TV address was the way in which he presented himself as a principled person representing a principled government that, despite the gravest of international provocations, sedulously refused to compromise those principles or to yield to counterproductive reprisals.

Is Mr. Reagan emerging as a statesman able to fill the power vacuum in Western leadership? Helmut Schmidt of West Germany is through. Helmut Kohl is decent and courageous, but perforce absorbed in domestic German problems. Valéry Giscard d'Estaing is gone, and his successor, the grey, dull socialist intellectual, François Mitterrand, has all he can do to hold his bankrupt economy and government together (although that doesn't keep him from meddling mischievously in Central America). Margaret Thatcher has leadership qualities, as the Falklands episode abundantly showed, but aspires to no mission beyond her borders. In Japan, Mr. Nakasone shows vision and courage, but he is consumed by parochial responsibilities, to say nothing of European resistance to a Japanese as leader of the West.

Archimedes once said that if he had a lever big enough and knew where to stand, he could move the earth. The Russians have given Mr. Reagan his lever—world opinion—and he knows where to stand—center stage, where circumstances and timing have thrust him. He will try to use his new fulcrum to lever the planet into a stronger defense against Soviet aggression and, in so doing, make the world safe for freedom.

Chief Executive

Many conservative observers warmly seconded Reagan's denunciation of government. After all, he was simply amplifying the grumblings of ordinary Americans frustrated by their encounters with an unwieldy, often officious government bureaucracy. But in a thoughtful 1982 essay in the democratic socialist journal New Leader, *Steven Kelman of Harvard's Kennedy School of Government suggested that Reagan's endless badmouthing of "government" was not only unfair to many dedicated and idealistic public employees but could cause an insidious demoralization—contributing to the very inefficiency and callousness that most people had in mind when they complained about the government.*

As for Reagan's own management style, assessments varied as well. Writing in the business magazine Fortune *in 1986, Ann Reilly Dowd presented Reagan as a model manager whose techniques corporate executives could well emulate. A rather different picture emerged from the 1988 memoir of Donald T. Regan, White House chief of staff from 1985 until he was forced out during the Iran-Contra affair. Although Regan had many positive things to say about his former boss, the overall picture that emerged was just about as damning as one could imagine. Regan not only revealed that First Lady Nancy Reagan consulted an astrologer in planning her husband's schedule, but he described a passive President surrounded by advisers obsessed with "image." Reagan, wrote his former top aide, cared only about "the outer presidency" and had little interest in the substance of power or the nitty-gritty of decision-making: "He listened, acquiesced, played his role, and waited for the next act to be written." The President's schedule for one typical day, revealed by ABC newsman Sam Donaldson and published in* Harper's *magazine in May 1988, revealed that almost every moment of the Reagan presidency was quite literally scripted, down to the most trivial offhand comment to Oval Office visitors.*

STEVEN KELMAN
Reaganism and Managing the Government
[*New Leader,* April 5, 1982]

Two images of the Federal bureaucracy have fueled the popular resentment against "big government" that the Reagan Administration has so richly exploited. One pictures bureaucrats as slothful and ineffectual—wasting tax dollars through a propensity to dole out money for research on the sex lives of butterflies. The other sees bureaucrats as all too zealous about what they do—diligently seeking new ways to oppress citizens with onerous requirements for the design of workplace ladders and the installation of wheelchair ramps in every public building.

There is, of course, an implicit contradiction between these two views. The blast against bureaucratic laziness is part of the "waste, fraud and abuse" charge leveled at Washington that includes such other complaints as cheating by welfare recipients. On the whole it is the less radical critique: It does not necessarily question Federal purposes, only their misuse by some citizens and the competence of government workers. The alternative lament, dubbed the "getting government off our backs" approach, is more an ideological assault against the very notion that government has an active role to play in society. This reflects the President's expressed philosophy, but the Reagan camp has not hesitated to take advantage of both sentiments in pursuit of its desire to reduce the Federal presence.

Perhaps it suspects, as I do, that the incompetence of public servants gets most Americans angrier than the fact of their existence. Analyzing survey data about attitudes toward taxes and government (in connection with the passage of Proposition 13 in California), Seymour Martin Lipset has pointed out that the bulk of the voters favored both lower taxes and the continuation of most important domestic programs. They saw no inconsistency because they believed that high levels of bureaucratic waste made it possible to significantly cut budgets while retaining services. Between 1964-80 the percentage of Americans who said they believe the Washington bureaucracy wastes "a lot" of tax dollars jumped from under half to an overwhelming 78 per cent. During the same period, the percentage agreeing that "government is run by people who don't know what they're doing" rose dramatically from just over one-fifth to 63 per cent....

"Getting government off our backs" appeals most to traditionally Republican constituencies. Although the abstract slogan undoubtedly sounds attractive to many Americans, no majority support existed for its specific content until very recently. As late as 1979, opinion surveys found Americans were about evenly divided on the essence of the issue, with 48 per cent favoring the same or more Federal regulation of business and 47 per cent favoring less. In 1980 the figures did swing to a 54-38 per cent majority for reducing regulation. Yet this is new, and there is still evidence of strong public approval for strictly regulating the environment and workplace safety, two of the biggest sources of Republican "off our backs" hostility.

In any event, since he assumed the Presidency, Reagan's policies have been aimed more at meeting the concern of those who consider the government overbearing than at coping with the inefficiency that seems to trouble most Americans. Much of the budget cutting, whatever else one might say about it, is not directed at what the average citizen has in mind when he thinks of waste or fraud or abuse. The promised "regulatory relief" is an unambiguous ideological bow. Even the Reagan tax program, as communicated by the Great Communicator himself, took on a distinctly "off our backs" ring with his talk of letting people decide how to spend their money instead of having Washington make the decision for them.

But the dilemma facing Reaganism in terms of the management of the Executive Branch is that efforts to minimize the importance of the Federal bureaucracy are likely to increase laziness and incompetence where the government must continue to function. The reasons for this are simple. First, in a hostile atmosphere most domestic policy agencies lose many of their best people, while much of the dead weight is left in place. Second, bad-mouthing the bureaucracy severely damages attempts to instill Federal employees with a sense of mission, a vital element in promoting dedicated performance. And these problems are exacerbated by the reductions in force many agencies are experiencing, by pay hikes being held to less than half the inflation rate, as well as by retaining ceilings on salaries for top career managers (at about $50,000 a year) so that many of them have received no raises for several years.

Why, after all, do people go to work for the government? To begin with, many idiosyncratic factors that would apply anywhere are involved, ranging from the chance recommendation of a friend to commuting convenience. Blacks and women have been said to seek government jobs because they believe there is less discrimination in the public than in the private sector. Others are thought to be attracted by the power inherent in the ability to make or influence decisions that take on the force of law. Still others, preferring to avoid the vicissitudes of the private job market, have been drawn by the relatively superior job security of government. Then there is the age-old bane of the Civil Service: To the extent that the pay and/or chances for advancement are not on a level with private business, government tends to be the refuge, everything else being equal, of the less able.

Be that as it may, things have not been equal since the establishment of the Great Society in the mid-'60s, and of the environmental, consumer protection and safety/health regulatory programs in the early '70s. In fact, I think that just as the potential for making America a better place inspired bright, idealistic people to take up mid-level career positions in Washington during the New Deal, a significant number of the past decade's bureaucrats have chosen their jobs out of a commitment to the substantive goals of their departments. Especially over the last few years as economic stress has limited the possibilities for contributing to the shaping of our society, Washington has become attractive to younger managers loath to join the corporate world, an appealing alternative to working for a poverty law center in a migrant labor camp or as a freelance writer. . . . That many domestic policy agencies today have devoted employees has not escaped notice. Some neoconservative writers, particularly Irving Kristol, have emphasized the increasing affinity of educated people of liberal persuasion— the so-called "new class"—for public work. Kristol sees something sinister in this: Such individuals become the main constituency for government activism out of self-interest. But it is obscure to me why those pursuing government jobs compatible with their inclination to do good are subject to question, while those entering the private sector to satisfy their inclination to make money raise no comment. Indeed, I would suggest that the availability of jobs that allow individuals to work without doing violence to their convictions, liberal or conservative, is a healthy social underpinning for political pluralism. Certainly managers in any organization, public or private, will welcome the availability of people who work hard and care about what they do.

Reaganism's ideological assault on government, in contrast, deals a direct blow to bureaucrats who believe in the programs they are a part of. Those still holding office are likely to either languish in inner exile or leave as quickly as the job market allows. Nor is it probable that they will be replaced by enthusiastic junior level personnel. Instead, the dead weights and the indifferent will listlessly carry on, and the Civil Service will thus gradually become more freighted down with time-servers. . . .

It is difficult to sound the alarm about the effects of Reaganism on managing the government. Most Americans seem to have such a low opinion of civil servants that they would be skeptical whether performance could be any worse than it already is. I think those who have had intimate experience with the bureaucracy, though, would agree that the popular view is highly exaggerated. In a number of interviews after arriving in Washington, for example, Secretary of the Treasury Donald T. Regan noted that one of his greatest surprises was the dedication and intelligence of the top career people at Treasury.

In addition to the public's skepticism, the results of declining competence and demoralization are likely to be perceived only indirectly—as the environment gets even dirtier than the Administration would want to allow, consumers are less protected, the poor become more desperate. Conceivably, corruption scandals among Federal regulatory officials or inspectors could occur and be noticed, yet the public might not appreciate just how uncommon scandals of that kind among Federal civil servants have been in the past.

Further, my own entire line of criticism may be dismissed with the charge that it appears to be saying liberal domestic policies must be followed for government to have any chance of being well managed. To be sure, the Reagan conception of government at its most extreme does not embrace the concerns I have presented. In January 1976 the New York *Times* quoted Ronald Reagan as declaring, "I've always thought that the best thing government can do is nothing." In the light of that opinion, how the government performs its functions hardly matters, since the government shouldn't have any functions to perform. An agency with zero appropriations can't get on the backs of the people, much less wallow in waste, fraud and abuse.

But the reality is that the President has not yet proposed the total elimination of the social welfare or regulatory functions of government. Apparently there is a consensus among most of his political associates that *some* level of regulatory effort in pollution control, safety and health regulation and social welfare is desirable. On top of that, the Administration needs efficient people to provide facts and figures and arguments to meet the judicial and political challenges to its deregulatory and anti-redistributive initiatives.

Granted, liberals have a far broader agenda for government and consequently a greater interest in seeing it managed effectively. And the damage that Reaganism can do to the Civil Service by driving out the good people and leaving the system in the hands of the time-servers is long term. But even Reaganites should be concerned about the competent performance of the domestic policy functions of government that they agree need to be carried out. It is therefore not only liberals who have to worry that the present ideological assault on the bureaucracy will make government worse. It is a problem for the Reagan Administration as well.

ANN REILLY DOWD

What Managers Can Learn from Manager Reagan

[*Fortune*, September 15, 1986]

A fire burned cheerfully in the fireplace in the Oval Office. Still, presidential pollster Richard Wirthlin felt a bit chilled on that cold December day in 1982

when the economy looked as bleak as the weather. "Mr. President," he said,
"I have some bad news for you. For the first time in your presidency, our
surveys show that more people disapprove of your performance than support
it." The President flinched slightly. Then he relaxed, reached out his arm,
touched his pollster's sleeve, and said with a grin: "Well, I could always get
shot again..."

Classic Reagan: funny, reassuring, confident. The President went on,
"With taxes and inflation down, I really believe this economy will soon start
growing again. And when people get back to work, those ratings will start
coming up again." Many of his advisers were skeptical. But Reagan was
persistent, optimistic, and right.

You don't have to support Reagan to concede that he has had remarkable
success in achieving most of the goals he brought to Washington. Principal
exception: reducing the deficit, which has mushroomed into his most significant failure. But Reagan has, as he promised, rebuilt the military, cut taxes,
slowed the growth of domestic spending, reduced regulation, and put a
conservative stamp on the nation's judicial system. The economy is in its
45th month of expansion, however modest, and inflation is low. Radical tax
reform—of which Reagan is not the sole author but for which he can, and
will, take much of the credit—is on the verge of enactment. The jury is still
out on the eventual effects of these changes, but for better or worse the
Reagan Revolution has largely succeeded, and the world will feel its effects
for years.

Many pundits continue to regard Reagan's successes as the dumb luck of a
good old Irish actor who stumbled onto the right set. Even members of his
Administration denigrate his intellect and lambaste his hands-off management
style. It's true that Reagan is lucky. He took over the presidency near the
bottom of a business cycle, so by some arguments he had nowhere to go but
up. As with most lucky people, though, he makes much of his own luck, and
managers can learn a lot from him about how to do the same.

Reagan's management principles are few and clear. "Surround yourself
with the best people you can find, delegate authority, and don't interfere as
long as the policy you've decided upon is being carried out," he told
Fortune. He brings a strong vision to his job but constantly, skillfully
compromises. His message to his team and the public is consistent and
upbeat. He is painstaking in choosing subordinates but otherwise avoids
details. He encourages staff members to speak their minds and defuses
tension with an endless repertoire of jokes. Perhaps most important, his
decisions, at least on major matters, are fast and firm.

His leadership style strikes a constantly recalculated balance between
idealism and realism. Reagan demonstrates a realization that his kinds of
goals are achieved not overnight, but slowly, day by day, year by year. "I've
never understood people who want me to hang in there for 100% or
nothing," he told a senior adviser. "Why not take 70% or 80%, and then

come back another day for the other 20% or 30%?'' So he does, again and again, on defense, taxes, budget cuts, all his major initiatives. Says Warren Bennis, who teaches at the University of Southern California's graduate business school: "Reagan is a master of compromise. Like Abraham Lincoln, he will temporize, but he will never lose sight of his vision.''

More than other recent Presidents and many corporate leaders, Reagan has also succeeded in translating his vision into a simple agenda, with clear priorities that legislators, bureaucrats, and constituents can readily understand. . . . Independent pollster Gerald Goldhaber says that nearly 70% of the American people can name at least one of Reagan's top four priorities. By contrast, such ratings for the Johnson, Nixon, Ford, and Carter Administrations ranged from 15% to 45%.

The President makes communicating seem easy partly because he works hard at it. He understands, as too few chief executives do, that communication is a two-way street. Like all shrewd politicians, he keeps in touch with his constituents by studying polls, reading newspapers, watching TV, meeting with different groups, and getting out on the hustings whenever possible. But Reagan is better than most at reading, and shaping, the public mood. When he gives speeches, he speaks in language his audiences can readily understand— simple, stark phrases brought to life by tales from the real world. His message is generally encouraging. The President's speechwriters prepare drafts for him, but they say that he reworks all his major addresses, sometimes scribbling in the margins, other times rewriting whole sections in longhand on a yellow legal pad. Invariably, Wirthlin maintains, the lines that move people most are the President's own. . . .

The President's plan to make his vision reality started with a thorough search for the right people to help him. In November 1979, nearly nine months before he won the GOP nomination, he asked executive recruiter E. Pendleton James to begin thinking about staffing his Administration. Working with candidate Reagan, James quickly developed a set of criteria for hiring. Topping the list was loyalty—not just to the Republican Party, but to Reagan and his program. "Reagan has been criticized for picking people who shared his philosophy," says Defense Secretary Caspar Weinberger. "But doing otherwise would have been perfectly absurd. Reagan came here to change the direction of the country.''

During the first two years of his Administration, Reagan spent two hours a week working with James on presidential appointments down to the lowest levels. Longtime White House observers say such presidential attention to personnel is unprecedented. Today Reaganites can be found throughout the top ranks of the bureaucracy and judiciary, ensuring that the President's influence will be felt long after he is gone.

Reagan's emphasis on loyalty, sometimes to the exclusion of other qualifications, has obvious drawbacks. The so-called sleaze factor in his Administration has been unusually high: Labor Secretary Raymond Donovan was indicted for fraud, former White House deputy chief of staff Michael Deaver is under investigation for influence-peddling and perjury, and many lesser officials have left office after charges of unseemly behavior, usually some kind of cupidity. But in most top posts Reagan has been able to attract and keep loyalists with enough integrity and talent to be independent.

Picking competent people who are on his wavelength has also enabled Reagan to delegate more effectively than most Presidents. Former Transportation Secretary Drew Lewis recounts an incident during the 1981 air traffic controllers' strike that set the tone for labor-management relations throughout the Reagan era. Lewis worried that Reagan's friends, whose private planes were grounded, might urge him to back down on his decision to fire the controllers, which Lewis had recommended. So the transportation chief called Reagan to test his resolve. Recalls Lewis: "The President said: 'Drew, don't worry about me. When I support someone—and you're right on this strike—I'll continue to support you, and you never have to ask that question again.' From that day on, it was clear to me—whether in increasing the federal gasoline tax in 1983 or selling Conrail—that once he said, 'Fine,' I never had to get back to him. I had the authority."

Some longtime Reagan associates speculate that his capacity to delegate stems from his Hollywood experience. Says John Sears, his former campaign manager: "A lot of people in political and corporate life feel that delegating is an admission that there's something they can't do. But actors are surrounded by people with real authority—directors, producers, scriptwriters, cameramen, lighting engineers, and so on. Yet their authority doesn't detract from the actor's role. The star is the star. And if the show's a hit, he gets the credit."

Reagan sees his role as that of a leader who establishes the direction for the organization, not that of a hands-on manager or idea man. He delegates day-to-day management to Chief of Staff Donald Regan, the former chairman of Merrill Lynch, who has streamlined White House operations and reduced much internal bickering. Reagan looks to his Cabinet and White House staff to put the flesh on major initiatives and to serve up new ideas, such as Treasury Secretary James Baker's plan for coordinating interest rate policies among several nations. Meanwhile, Reagan focuses on big issues like tax reform or on opinion-shaping events like the summit with Soviet leader Mikhail Gorbachev. . . .

Critics fault Reagan for not wading deeply into the substance of decision-making. Insiders confirm that he is not a detail person, but they insist he receives enough information to make the right decisions on the most important issues. On each one, he gets a two- or three-page memo prepared by Cabinet Secretary Alfred Kingon's office outlining options and their pluses and minuses, and detailing which Cabinet members and top White House aides are pushing what. The agencies involved also prepare longer papers, which, aides say, the President reads and remembers. Then he calls a meeting of principals to debate the issue. Says Porter: "Reagan has a high tolerance for hearing competing views argued very intensely."

Most modern Presidents—and corporate chiefs—have demanded more detail in preparing for important decisions. Carter, for example, read reams of Treasury documents on tax reform and plunged into the drafting of a final proposal, which got nowhere. Reagan relies on staff analysis plus his own principles and instincts. In his tax reform drive he established his objectives—among them lower rates, fairness, simplicity, revenue neutrality, and stimuli for growth. Then he delegated the details to Treasury and weighed in at key moments with appeals to Congress and the voters, plus strategic advice to Baker on pushing the program. His formula worked fine, but management experts caution corporate leaders against disdaining detail to the extent Reagan does.

Past Presidents, among them Richard Nixon and Franklin Roosevelt, built conflicting views into their staffs to ensure a diversity of opinion. Reagan did not do this consciously. But his choice of strong lieutenants and his willingness to let them knock heads over key issues has had much the same effect. In Reagan's first term, the clash between the tax hikers, led by Budget Director David Stockman and Baker, then White House staff chief, and the antitax team, led by then Treasury Secretary Regan, yielded a wide range of opinion on budget policy. Persistent fights between Weinberger and Secretary of State George Shultz have ensured that Reagan hears different sides on arms control and other foreign policy issues. . . .

For all the jokes about his "burning the midday oil," aides argue that the President is a hard worker. He rises between 7 and 7:30 and typically looks at the *Washington Post, Washington Times, New York Times, USA Today,* and *Los Angeles Times* before his first meeting at 9. He almost always has working lunches. He does not, aides insist, take afternoon naps. He rarely leaves the office before 5:30. (Like many a good businessman, he lives above the store.) Usually he takes two to four hours of reading home, principally briefing papers on the next day's events and upcoming issues. But does he do his homework? "Religiously," says Edward Rollins, his 1984 campaign director. "The President has a clean-desk attitude. If you give him four hours of reading, he'll do it all. He won't talk about it. But you'll see his notes on page 40."

Reagan uses humor as a management tool. It helps that he likes jokes, many of them unprintable. A Cabinet member says Reagan can match anyone dirty joke for dirty joke, golf joke for golf joke, dialect joke for dialect joke. Critics cite Reagan's tendency to joke as a sign that he lacks seriousness; insiders say it serves a useful purpose. As [Robert] Waterman [Jr.] points out, "Humor facilitates change by taking the tension out of situations." Reagan says the President ends even the most serious meetings with a funny story, "so staffers go away smiling." . . .

Early in his Administration Reagan set up the so-called Cabinet Council system in which committees of Cabinet members regularly thrash out policy issues for the President. Fashioned after a similar system Reagan used in California, the council structure provides a convenient forum for balancing the interests of various agencies. When Cabinet members agree—as they did recently on a proposal to reform product liability law, for example—the President typically signs off. In a deadlock—as there was over whether to subsidize grain sales to the Soviets—he chooses a winner. In that case he sided with [Commerce Secretary Malcolm] Baldrige and Agriculture Secretary Richard E. Lyng, who supported the sale as a way to help troubled U.S. farmers. The losers were Weinberger and Shultz, who opposed it as too generous to the Soviets.

More than in any other way, Reagan has established his authority by sticking with his decisions. Says Donald Regan: "The President has a unique talent: He is serene internally. When he has made a decision, he lives with it. He doesn't fret over it. And most of all, he doesn't change his mind. Therefore he doesn't confuse Congress or the public as to what he stands for."

From where does this serenity spring? Reagan associates cite a combination of principle, instinct, self-confidence, and faith. Says Rollins: "Reagan is a great believer in destiny. That gives him an inner peace and an ability to do what he thinks is right, regardless of public opinion." . . .

Reagan also relies on a combination of principle and instinct in deciding when to hold and when to fold in negotiations. Says corporate raider T. Boone Pickens, chairman of Mesa Petroleum: "Reagan's timing is excellent. In certain transactions there may only be a few minutes in which a deal can be cut. A real negotiator is able to pick the right time and not let it get away." One example: Reagan's decision last December to go up to Capitol Hill and persuade Republicans to vote for the House tax reform bill, even though it was anti-investment. Reagan vowed to veto the bill if the Senate did not improve it. That timely promise kept the bill moving toward changes Reagan wanted, including lower rates, a higher personal exemption, and more generous depreciation allowances than the House version proposed. The result was a bill he could enthusiastically endorse. Eugene Jennings, a professor at Michigan State's graduate business school, sees a lesson for executives: "The ability to adapt and adjust tactics while sticking to principles is extremely important. One of the biggest problems with C.E.O.s is that they are flexible on principle and inflexible on plans."

Reagan's management of crises carries another lesson most executives know but sometimes forget: Don't dissemble. Through the several disasters on his watch, from the terrorist bombing of the Marine barracks in Beirut to the *Challenger* explosion, Reagan has escaped much of the blame by going quickly to the people with a relatively full account. Says James Kouzes, director of Santa Clara University's Executive Development Center: "Credibility is very fragile. It's built day by day, and a President or a corporate leader can lose it in an instant by covering up." Some of the best executives handle disasters much as Reagan does. In the Tylenol poisonings, Johnson & Johnson Chairman James Burke limited the corporate damage by going right on TV to explain the situation simply and honestly. Jennings of Michigan State adds that the most effective C.E.O.s are "maze smart," like Reagan. "They have a sixth sense of how to get out of the brier patch without all those briers on their pants."

After many years in acting and politics, the President also seems to understand that everyone has his share of flops; the key is moving on to a hit next season. Says GOP presidential hopeful Donald Rumsfeld, the former chairman of G.D. Searle and White House chief of staff under President Ford: "Success tends to go not to the person who is error-free, because he also tends to be risk-averse. Rather it goes to the person who recognizes that life is pretty much a percentage business. It isn't not making mistakes that's critical; it's correcting them and getting on with the principal task."

Just about every President and C.E.O. gives at least a little thought to his legacy. Reagan's will hinge partly on how many goals he achieves, but probably more on how well the goals he chose serve the nation. With just over two years left in his presidency, it is too early to make those determinations. Still, one extraordinarily important if little-noted element of the Reagan legacy is already established: He has proved once again that the presidency is manageable.

DONALD T. REGAN

Inside the Reagan White House

[Excerpt from *For the Record: From Wall Street to Washington* (1988)]

Ronald Reagan seemed to be regarded by certain members of his inner circle not as the powerful and utterly original leader that he was, but as a sort of supreme anchorman whose public persona was the most important element of the Presidency. According to the rules of this school of political management, controversy was to be avoided at nearly any cost: every Presidential action must produce a positive public effect. In practice, this meant stimulating a positive effect in the media, with the result that the press, not the people, became the President's primary constituency.

As Secretary of the Treasury I had, of course, been aware of the power of the press in Washington. But I did not fully understand how closely the interests of the media and those of the Administration were intertwined until I became Chief of Staff. To say that I was surprised by this state of affairs would be an understatement. I was shocked by the extent to which the press determined the everyday activities, and even the philosophical tenor, of the Presidency. This is not to say that I did not know that the press plays an important role in the life of a democracy beyond its function as a watchdog of official morality. Publicity is a modern form of pomp, and if it were possible to govern without display, there would be no ruins in Rome or jewels in the Tower of London. But unless I have misread the histories of the great empires of the past, a preoccupation with outward style at the expense of inner conviction is not a favorable sign in the life of a superpower. . . .

It was [Michael] Deaver's job to advise the President on image, and image was what he talked about nearly all the time. It was Deaver who identified the story of the day at the eight o'clock staff meeting and coordinated the plans for dealing with it, Deaver who created and approved photo opportunities, Deaver who alerted the President to the snares being laid by the press that day. Deaver was a master of his craft. He saw—designed—each Presidential action as a one-minute or two-minute spot on the evening network news, or a picture on page one of the *Washington Post* or the *New York Times*, and conceived every Presidential appearance in terms of camera angles.

If the President was scheduled to make a ceremonial appearance in the Rose Garden, he could be sure that he and the recipients of whatever greeting or award was involved would be looking into the sun so that the cameras would have the light behind them. In the morning, when the sun was over the Treasury, this meant that the President stood on the steps right outside the Oval Office; in the afternoon he would stand on the long side of the colonnade. His position was always chosen with the idea of keeping him as far away as possible from the reporters who hovered at the edge of these events with the intention of shouting questions. Every moment of every public appearance was scheduled, every word was scripted, every place where Reagan was expected to stand was chalked with toe marks. The President was always being prepared for a performance, and this had the inevitable effect of preserving him from confrontation and the genuine interplay of opinion, question, and argument that form the basis of decision.

The President accepted these arrangements with what seemed to me to be practically superhuman good nature. *Second nature* might be the better term: he had been doing this kind of thing—learning his lines, composing his facial expression, hitting his toe marks—for half a century. They constituted no inconvenience to him. As Deaver (later Bill Henkel or Jim Kuhn, Reagan's personal assistant) rehearsed him for an appearance he would say: "You'll go out the door and down the steps. The podium is ten steps to the right and the audience will be in a semicircle with the cameras at the right-hand end of the half-moon; when you finish speaking take two steps back but don't leave the podium, because they're going to present you with a patchwork quilt. . . ." Larry Speakes would caution him that the press would be there and he should watch out for questions on X or Y. Reagan would smile and nod: Yup, yup, that's fine, all right; thanks fellows. . . .

The President is possessed of a philosophical agenda based on a lifetime of experience and thought. He is a formidable reader and a talented conversationalist with a gift for listening. It was precisely this gift that led to many of his gaffes and misstatements in encounters with the press: Ronald Reagan remembered nearly everything that was said to him. If someone told him (to use a wholly fictitious example) that there had been 35,987 hairs in Stalin's mustache, this fact would go into the Presidential memory bank, possibly to emerge weeks or months later in the middle of a press conference. It never seemed to occur to him that anyone would give him incorrect information. His mind was a trove of facts and anecdotes, something like the morgue of one of his favorite magazines, *Reader's Digest*, and it was impossible to guess when or why he might access any one of these millions of bytes of data.

Reagan started nearly every meeting with a story, no matter whether the participants were people he saw every day or the hereditary ruler of a remote kingdom who had never before laid eyes on an American President; he thought that laughter brought people closer together and dispelled the anxiety that they feel in the presence of the mighty, and of course he was right. The President knew more funny stories, ranging from jokes innocent enough for a Sunday-school class to the raunchiest locker-room humor, than anyone I had ever met. If you told Reagan an Irish joke, he'd come back with a better Irish joke, and could do the same in every category. Deaver had a new joke or bit of amusing gossip for him every morning as the first order of business—a practice I carried on with support from the Vice President (one of whose sons acted as a scout for new stories), after Deaver departed.

Reagan shunned the abstract, the theoretical, the cold and impersonal approach to problems. His love of stories was connected to this same tendency to see everything in human terms. Although even some of his intimates scoffed (ever so discreetly) at his bottomless fund of anecdotes about it, Reagan's experience as governor of California constituted a unique body of executive and political experience. He had a formidable gift for debate when he was allowed to debate in a spontaneous way. His problems in these matters, as in the first debate with Walter Mondale in 1984, nearly always resulted from his being overprogrammed. His briefers, forgetting that a President has a cast of thousands to remember facts for him, had crammed his mind with so many bits of information that he tried to rely on data instead of explaining the issue and defending his policy. I had seen him defend his ideas and critique the proposals of other heads of state with the best of them at six international economic summits, and it was not uncommon for him to render courageous decisions on domestic economic questions in the face of nearly unanimous advice and pressure to do the opposite. . . .

[Donald Regan goes on to describe his preparation for the President's consideration in August 1985 of a major working document laying out the White House's broad goals and strategies through the end of 1986 on a wide range of foreign and domestic issues.]

To borrow from the vocabulary of corporate practice, I was presenting a plan of action to the chief executive officer of the firm. According to the methods under which I had always operated, objectives were hammered out through discussion by the people who would have to carry them out, this consensus was reduced to writing, and the result was submitted to the man in charge. He then told you what he liked about the plan and what he did not like. You revised on the basis of his criticisms until you had a paper that he was willing to approve. Once he had signed off, debate ceased and you went to work to carry out the final plan.

This paper represented the first stage of this process. It was not a plan of action but an outline of goals. I expected that the President would read it, decide on his priorities, and call for more detailed suggestions. After that he could be expected to call in his department heads and give them their marching orders: cut the budget or increase it, fight for this policy on taxes and spending, concentrate on these bills before Congress, meet these objectives in research and development, develop a program to increase exports by X percent, make the following points to the Russians and offer the following reassurances to our allies, and explain it all to the public on the basis of these considerations.

Instead, Ronald Reagan read the paper while he was at the ranch and handed it back to me on his return without spoken or written comment.

"What did you think of it?" I asked.

It's good, the President replied, nodding in approval. It's really good, Don.

I waited for him to say more. He did not. He had no questions to ask, no objections to raise, no instructions to issue. I realized that the policy that would determine the course of the world's most powerful nation for the next two years and deeply influence the fate of the Republican party in the 1986 midterm elections had been adopted without amendment. It seemed, also, that I had been authorized as Chief of Staff to make the necessary arrangements to carry out the policy. It was taken for granted that the President would do whatever was asked of him to make the effort a success. We went on to the next item on the agenda.

I confess that I was surprised that this weighty matter was decided so quickly and with so little ceremony. In a way, of course, it was flattering: it is always gratifying to anticipate the boss's wishes with acceptable accuracy. Still, I was uneasy. Did the President really want us to do all these things with no more discussion than this? I decided that this must be the case, since always in the past, if he did not say no, the answer was yes. By now I understood that the President did not share my love of detail and my enthusiasm for planning. I knew that he was not an aggressive manager.

Perhaps I should have quizzed him on tax policy or Central America or our approach to trade negotiations; certainly my instincts and the practice of a lifetime nudged me in that direction. But I held my tongue. It is one thing brashly to speak your mind to an ordinary mortal and another to say "Wait a minute!" to the President of the United States. The mystery of the office is a potent inhibitor. The President, you feel, has his reasons.

Another President would almost certainly have had his own ideas on the mechanics of policy, but Reagan did not trouble himself with such minutiae. His preoccupation was with what might be called "the outer Presidency." He was content to let others cope with the inner details of running the Administration. In this he was the antithesis of most recent Presidents. Kennedy might call up a minor bureaucrat to check on a detail; Johnson might twist a senator's arm; Nixon might discuss the tiniest details of China policy with his staff; Carter might micromanage a commando raid in the Iranian desert from his desk in the Oval Office. But Reagan chose his aides and then followed their advice almost without question. . . .

Never—absolutely never in my experience—did President Reagan really lose his temper or utter a rude or unkind word. Never did he issue a direct order, although I, at least, sometimes devoutly wished that he would. He listened, acquiesced, played his role, and waited for the next act to be written. From the point of view of my own experience and nature, this was an altogether baffling way of doing things. But my own style was not the case in point. Reagan's method had worked well enough to make him President of the United States, and well enough for the nation under his leadership to transform its mood from pessimism to optimism, its economy from stagnation to steady growth, and its position in the world from weakness to strength. Common sense suggested that the President knew something that the rest of us did not know. It was my clear duty to do things his way.

[Excerpts from pp. 247–251 and 265–268 of Donald T. Regan, *For the Record: From Wall Street to Washington* (1988), copyright © 1988 by Donald T. Regan, reprinted by permission of Harcourt Brace Jovanovich, Inc.]

The President's Script

[*Harper's*, May 1988]

From President Reagan's private schedule for February 25, 1988. Attached to the schedule are "talking points" written by the White House staff to help the President prepare for meetings; Reagan sometimes copies the talking points onto index cards that he carries with him. The contents of this document were disclosed recently by ABC News Correspondent Sam Donaldson.

DROP BY MEETING WITH CEO'S

Time: 11:30 a.m. (20 minutes)

Location: Cabinet Room

Purpose: To brief CEOs of major corporations on the administration's budget initiatives and ask for their support. Also to discuss the INF Treaty and ask for their support.

Background: Support from the business community is important for success on the administration's budget initiatives and the INF Treaty...

Sequence of Events

11:30 a.m. You enter Cabinet Room, are introduced by Senator Howard Baker, and deliver remarks. At the conclusion of your remarks you open the meeting to discussion.

11:47 a.m. Rebecca Range will signal the end of the official portion of the meeting.

You move to the end of the Cabinet Room (under President Coolidge's picture) for handshake photos with the participants.

11:50 a.m. You depart.

Talking Points

—Let me start by saying thanks to all of you for coming today. This is certainly a much friendlier group than I faced at the press conference last night.

—I know you've already heard from Colin Powell on the INF Treaty and from Jim Miller on the budget package, but I would like to make a few remarks on both of these.

—First, on the INF Treaty, I'd like to repeat how important I believe this treaty is.

—It really represents a turning point in history. To actually reduce—not simply limit—the buildup of nuclear weapons.

—And to do that with the most stringent verification procedures in the history of arms control. Procedures that I believe will help pave the way to continued reductions in nuclear arms.

—It is a historic treaty, and I do hope I can count on your support to see that it is accepted by the Senate.

—Secondly, the budget. I'm sure Jim has given you the details, but I would like to make one thing clear.

—–As you know, I did agree with congressional leaders on a Bipartisan Budget Agreement last November.

—It isn't a perfect agreement, but it is a good first step. The two-year agreement will reduce the deficit by a total of $76 billion. . . .

—Under the agreement we will balance the budget by 1994—but only if Congress shows some discipline, avoids unnecessary pork and program expansions, and fixes the budget process.

—They are now promising to deliver all thirteen appropriation bills on a timely basis instead of wrapping them all into one and dropping them on my desk at the last minute.

—That's great if they really do it. But we also need some fundamental process changes.

—A balanced-budget amendment and a line-item veto would be a good place to start, but there are other options as well.

—I hope you agree on the critical need to fix the budget process and we can count on your support to make some changes this year.

—Now, let me stop there and ask for your thoughts on how we can keep Congress focused on the deficit and the budget process.

PHOTO WITH WAYNE NEWTON

Time: 1:45 p.m.

Purpose: To thank Wayne Newton for his tireless efforts on behalf of America's military men and women.

Background: In November 1987, Wayne Newton graciously volunteered two weeks of his time to give a Thanksgiving USO Tour aboard ships of our fleets in the Mediterranean, the Arabian Sea, and the Persian Gulf. With this recent trip, Mr. Newton is the only entertainer to have traveled and performed in Vietnam, Beirut, and now the Persian Gulf.

Sequence of Events
1:45 p.m. Participants enter the Oval Office.

Brief greetings are exchanged and photographs taken.

1:50 p.m. Participants depart the Oval Office.

MEETING WITH BIPARTISAN GROUP OF SENATORS

Location: Oval Office

Time: 2:00 p.m. (30 minutes)

Purpose: To receive a briefing from these senators on their recent trip to Europe and their meetings with our NATO allies concerning the INF Treaty.

Background: During the Presidents' Day recess (February 7–14) Senate Majority Leader Robert Byrd (Democrat, West Virginia) took a delegation of senators to several European capitals to discuss the pending INF Treaty with our NATO allies. . . .

Senator Byrd has requested this opportunity for the delegation to brief you on their meetings in Europe.

Talking Points

—Bob (Byrd), I appreciate you and your colleagues' coming down today.

—I know there has been a good deal of discussion in your hearings about the Treaty's implications for NATO.

—On that point, I'm pleased you were able to make this trip together, and Bob, I want to thank you especially for undertaking this and for handling your discussions over there so effectively. And I'm really glad that you made it to Turkey. I want to hear about that part of your trip in particular.

(Senator Byrd and other senators report on their trip.)

—I want to thank all of you for your input.

—The next several weeks will be critical in terms of your ratification activities on the INF Treaty, and I will continue to work closely with you.

PRESENTATION OF EASTER SEALS

Location: Oval Office

Time: 4:30 p.m.

Purpose: To meet and be photographed with the National Easter Seal Child and the Easter Seal Adult Representative and to receive the first sheet of 1988 Easter Seals.

Sequence of Events: Guests enter the Oval Office; Rebecca Range introduces each guest to you as individual photos are taken. Photos of each family are taken, then a group photo is taken. You make brief remarks. The 1988 Easter Seal Child, Shawn Dennsteadt, will present you with a plaque of the first sheet of 1988 Easter Seals and with a card and T-shirt signed by his fellow third-grade classmates at Hillside Elementary School. Then Shawn, who was born without hands and is missing bones in his feet and legs, will perform a headstand on his skateboard for you. Guests depart.

Talking Points

—Welcome to the White House as you continue your long tradition of service to this country's disabled citizens.

—Shawn, congratulations on being selected as the 1988 Easter Seal Child, and Colonel Cisneros (sis-ner-os), congratulations on being selected as the 1988 Easter Seal Adult Representative.

—You're both going to have a busy schedule over the next year, traveling all over the country representing the hundreds of thousands of disabled children and adults who receive rehabilitation services through Easter Seal facilities.

—Pat [Boone], I want to take this opportunity to thank you for all you've done on behalf of the Easter Seal Society. Your efforts have raised thousands of dollars that serve thousands of people who wouldn't otherwise receive care.

—God bless you all.

RECEIVE REPORT
OF THE PRESIDENT'S CANCER PANEL

Location: Oval Office

Time: 4:45 p.m. (10 minutes)

Purpose: To receive the report of your Cancer Panel from its chairman, Dr. Armand Hammer, and to hear from Dr. Hammer about his plans to raise private funds for cancer research.

Background: Armand Hammer has served as chairman of your Cancer Panel since October 1981.

The President's Cancer Panel was established by law as part of President Nixon's war against cancer. The panel provides advice on how our nation's efforts to curb cancer should be conducted . . . Dr. Hammer will also present a valuable first edition of *The Leonardo Codex,* a reproduction of the notebook in which Leonardo da Vinci recorded his scientific observations, to the Reagan Library Foundation. Fred Ryan will be there to accept the gift on behalf of the library.

Participants: Dr. Hammer; Secretary of Health and Human Services Otis Bowen; Director of the National Cancer Institute Vincent DeVita; Senator Baker; Nancy Risque; and Fred Ryan.

—Thank you, Armand, for coming here to present the report of the President's Cancer Panel. I'm sure you'd agree that within the federal government there is no one more important in our fight against cancer than these gentlemen, Dr. Otis Bowen and Dr. Vincent DeVita, with whom you've worked so closely.

—As someone who has had personal experience with cancer, I know the importance of our research effort.

—Our budget will provide $124 million more for cancer research next year than we have this year. Can you tell me more about your efforts to raise $500 million in the private sector?

(Armand Hammer)

—Otis, what are your thoughts?

(Secretary Bowen)

—Armand, good luck in your efforts to raise private funds for cancer research. If we had more citizens as energetic as you are in the fight against disease, we'd have a healthier country.

—Thank you for this handsome edition of *The Leonardo Codex*. It will be a great addition to the presidential library and we appreciate your generosity.

[Reprinted from *Harper's Magazine*.]

Cultural Icon

Beyond issues of ideology and managerial style, observers of the Reagan years endlessly puzzled over the President's almost mesmeric hold on the American people. Through most of his term, Reagan's personal approval ratings remained phenomenally high. Many commentators wrote of his skill as an actor, and this was certainly important, but the full story of Reagan's grip on the American consciousness clearly went deeper. In a speculative 1982 essay in the New Republic, *cultural critic Mark Crispin Miller turned to a nearly five-hundred-year-old handbook of political calculation and manipulation, Machiavelli's* The Prince, *to illuminate the deeper sources of Reagan's popularity. Reagan's mannerisms, his TV persona, and his entourage, Miller argued, all contributed to an image which the public found irresistible—Machiavelli's prince updated for the evening news. To understand his appeal, Miller contended, one had to steep oneself in the old movies, television shows, and other mass-culture detritus that had sunk deeply into the popular mind, and that Reagan brilliantly dredged up and exploited. Miller's characterization may have been overdrawn, but it was deliciously readable with its devastating portraits of Alexander Haig's "hints of madness"; James Watt's "incoherent jeering and his fits of hostile piety"; and Nancy Reagan, "who, glassy-eyed and overdressed, always looks as though she has just been struck by lightning. . . ."*

Garry Wills took a slightly different tack in his brilliant Reagan's America: Innocents at Home *(1987), whose introduction is reprinted here. For Wills, Reagan was "the great American synecdoche"—the prototypical embodiment of key components of the American dream: perennial optimism, eternal youth, infinite renewal. A walking montage of the bits and pieces of our national myth,* wrote Wills, *"Reagan runs continually in everyone's home movies of the mind."*

MARK CRISPIN MILLER

Virtù, Inc.

[*New Republic*, April 7, 1982]

"Everyone sees what you seem to be, few perceive what you are; and those few don't dare oppose the general opinion, which has the majesty of the government backing it up." Thus Machiavelli, in *The Prince*, suggests that most people put their trust in what they see, and that the would-be ruler must exploit this mass credulity by wielding his image with subtle skill. What everyone wants, above all, is a good show: "The masses are always impressed by appearances and by the outcome of an event—and in the world there are only masses. The few have no place there when the many crowd together." If he wants to stay in charge (and in health), a ruler has to please those staring and complacent multitudes with a public pose of sanctity, which will let him carry on the gruesome work of politics without losing his footing. The man who can thus remain on top, seeming good while doing necessary evil, is a figure of *virtù,* a term implying "power," "courage," "talent," "will," "strength of character," and other qualities of a heroic individualism.

Machiavelli showed considerable prescience when he wrote his bitter treatise in 1513: "The whole world is watching," *The Prince* points out, and now the networks and the satellites have translated that metaphor into literal truth. If politics has become less dangerous since the Renaissance, it has also, because of television, become a lot more superficial. In order to prevail today, the plucky office-seeker may not have to arrange clandestine stranglings, but he had better cultivate an understated manner and a level gaze, keep his statements short, and wear a light blue shirt at all times. This bland facility is now the main requirement for political success, even among those few who run for President.

And so, if Machiavelli were alive today, he would probably update his book with some reflections on how our Presidents use television, and vice versa. He was, for his era, an unusually scientific sort of theorist, basing his principles on actual cases. He based *The Prince* primarily on the example of that efficient monster, Cesare Borgia; and he would certainly base his new chapters on the career of Ronald Reagan, the smoothest surface this side of the Iron Curtain.

Reagan would seem to be the latest model in *virtù* itself. On the one hand, he approaches all the ugly tasks of his regime with the exalted ruthlessness of Frederick Barbarossa, "stout Cortez," or, to adopt a more appropriate model, Dirty Harry: Reagan, "shoots straight" and "gets tough," he goes by "horse sense," he's got plenty of "guts" and "balls" and other meaty attributes. And yet, even as he earns such right-wing plaudits, Reagan still manages to come across as an easygoing, *decent* fella. It is an impressive contradiction. Here is a President who takes from the poor to give to the rich, has supported infanticide abroad, ravages his own countryside, and props up brutal dictatorships; and yet, whenever he appears, he has you thinking, somehow, that he's "a nice guy."

Of course, if we judge Ronald Reagan by his actions, or by his inclinations, or even by the company he keeps, we have to conclude that he is not nice at all, if "nice" is taken to mean "kind" or "good." On the contrary, Reagan is "nice" as Iago is "honest"—that is, he is extraordinarily adept at affecting tones and postures which people trust without thinking. In other words, Reagan is considered "nice," not because he is nice, but in part because his image answers (temporarily) the emotional needs of quite a few Americans, who, tired of feeling cynical about their leaders, will swallow anything. And, like a good TV commercial, Reagan's image goes down easy, calming his audience with sweet inversions of the truth.

First of all, the image is meant to make the viewers think that Reagan is someone "just like you and me." Although this Administration has made a public point of dragging pomp and ostentation back into the White House, Reagan himself seems like a humble janitor at heart. Even at the dressiest affairs, and on the grandest state occasions, he has us thinking that he wears white socks and carries a pen-knife. Aside from partly obscuring the vulgar opulence of the Reagans and their tribe, this seeming averageness has the effect of distancing the President from his cruel strokes of policy—you wouldn't think such a *nice guy* could *do* such things, as shocked neighbors often put it on the evening news.

So far, this seems like basic statecraft, of the sort that Machiavelli would have grasped at once. However, he would have had a little trouble understanding how anyone could believe in Reagan's pose of commonness, which bears no clear relation to the world we commonly inhabit. In order to comprehend how Reagan can seem "just like you and me" without resembling anyone on earth, Machiavelli would have to sit through hours of bad old movies, pore over hundreds of dime novels and Horatio Alger stories, and otherwise school himself in the recurrent images of American myth. Only then would he perceive that Ronald Reagan is merely an anthology of the worst of American popular culture, edited for television. He comforts us, not by epitomizing what we are, but by reminding us of what we used to think we were or, perhaps, of what we think we used to be. In either case, his image is an eloquent symbol of reaction, forever promising the return of an illusory past.

Reagan seems to face us from within that past; he seems never to have fallen into modern times, or even into adulthood. Despite his advanced age, he comes across as a giant child who would be father to us frightened men and women. While we struggle in the world from day to day, making less and fearing more and more, homeless and uncertain, Ronald Reagan calls his wife "Mommy," and sports the same haircut that he wore when Hitler took over the Sudetenland. Although withered, he seems permanently boyish—not like an actual boy, of course, but something like a boy in an old movie: the lop-sided grin, the wavy thatch, the eyebrows impishly tilted, etc., remind us of all those scrubbed and hearty little guys in *Boys Town* and a hundred other movies of the Great Depression. Such a man, we sense, must be as sincere and innocent as anyone ever played by Mickey Rooney; and his policies, we hope, might let us live those happy days once brought to us by MGM.

Of course, the Reagan image also has its commanding aspect, but it too seems anachronistic, and faintly puerile: the big old sheriff, protector of the weak, loping toward Air Force One with his little lady at his side. Although this pose demands the obligatory Western gear, it comes through more in Reagan's oratorical style than in his boots and shirts. He speaks quietly, a little hesitantly, with his eyes to the ground, as if not used to public speaking, and he often punctuates his statements with a folksy little waggle of the head and shoulders, so that we won't take his specifying too seriously. All in all, the style suggests another complex pose of innocence—this President is a pure-hearted cowpoke, respectful to the ladies, wry and self-effacing with the boys.

Although these personae are derived from the movies, Reagan's Hollywood apprenticeship has, perhaps, been overemphasized by the casual students of his rise. His film career was undistinguished, because his celluloid image was basically too dim and vacuous to withstand the competition of more vivid presences. But this very emptiness has made him perfect for TV, which thrives on mundane types, demanding a pseudo-homely style which Reagan puts on easily. While he couldn't fill the grand patterns of the silver screen, then, he has managed, with immense success, to adapt those patterns to the smaller scale of television. Moreover, he has learned to liven up his every televised appearance with frequent shifts in expression, constant movements of the head, lots of warm chuckles and ironic shrugs and sudden frowns of manly purpose. Such perpetual motion is a must on television, and a must for Ronald Reagan, who tends to lose his charm when he comes to rest. At such terrifying moments of repose, all the boyishness drains out of him, and he suddenly starts looking like an anaconda, with his beady eyes and flat lipless head.

As long as he's running smoothly, however, Reagan is unfailingly attractive, not at all like a predator, nor, in fact, like anything other than what he seems—"a nice guy," pure and simple. However hard we try to glimpse the man concealed within that jovial disguise, Reagan remains impenetrable, a pleasing surface through and through. Machiavelli would have to marvel at such a thoroughgoing façade, and we too should appreciate the spectacle, after all the bad performances we've suffered through for years: LBJ, abusing his dogs and exposing his belly; Richard Nixon, hunched and glistening like a cornered toad; Gerald Ford, forever tipping over; Jimmy Carter, with his maudlin twang and interminable kin. While each of these men, appallingly, kept lunging at us from behind the mask of power, Reagan's mask and face are as one. It's been a long time since we've seen such integrity in government. Indeed, not since John Kennedy have we had such a united front for a chief executive.

How does Reagan do it? Or rather, how is it done? Machiavelli too would wonder about this, and would try, in his new afterword on modern politics, to work out an explication of Reagan's strange success. And he would find that this success is based not only on the original tenets of *The Prince,* but on those tenets modernized for the demands of television.

First of all, Machiavelli would try to account for the fact that Reagan, despite his daily atrocities, continues to seem "nice." Although this persistent air of sweetness owes much to Reagan's earnest yokelism, it also results from the clever use of prominent patsies, a strategy which Machiavelli recommends specifically in his treatise: "Princes should delegate the ugly jobs to other people, and reserve the attractive functions for themselves." Reagan is kept seemingly innocent by this device: David Stockman, a mere instrument, used to take the heat for Reagan's cuts and slashes, Al Haig often seems like the one who *really* wants to crush the Cubans, and so on. Thus people have been able to persist in the belief that their President is just and well intentioned, and that any ill consequences of his rule are only the capricious doings of his subordinates.

Although this tactic, in itself, does not depend on visual effects (it worked long before the invention of TV), it implies a corollary which has proven indispensable to this Administration, whose shrinking appeal is based entirely on appearances. In this age of television, it matters less what people do than what they look like. Therefore, the function of the President's men is not just to make his policies seem like their mistakes, but also to make the President himself look better by contrast with themselves. If Machiavelli were to update his directive in accordance with the current practice, he would say: "A president should surround himself with ugly people doing ugly jobs, in order to seem that much more attractive himself by doing no job at all."

Guided by the spirit of this precept, some unknown genius, or ingenious committee, assembled Ronald Reagan's Administration, employing that same skill and subtlety with which the President himself had been assembled. Few chief executives have gained so much from their associates; besides his aides, Reagan seems to take on warmth, authenticity, even vitality, and other alien qualities.

Everyone in this Administration has a real job, providing some of the essential contrast that makes Reagan seem credibly human. Even the qualities of the colorless serve this purpose. For instance, there are those unremarkable men, like Caspar Weinberger and Donald Regan, who simply look like Republicans, i.e., as if their one desire in life is to repossess your house. These sober corporate types serve to offset those maverick qualities that once made Reagan seem like something fresh. And then there are those solid staffers—Ed Meese, James Baker, Larry Speakes, etc.—who look something like an assortment of boiled eggs. Compared to them, Reagan seems like someone with a lot of character in his face, or at least like someone with a face.

Then there are the more important and misleading contrasts, involving Reagan and the superstars of this production. As the youth in charge of deprivations, for instance, David Stockman was, before his lapse, a perfect foil for Reagan. His was the zeal and excessive cleanness of the untried moralist, which allowed the craggy Reagan to seem (for a while) restrained and wise. General Alexander Haig has something of the same effect on Reagan's image. He is an openly belligerent cold warrior, and otherwise behaves like someone who should be watched at all times. He first made this impression during Nixon's twilight period, when he wrested sinister control over the household, like Mrs. Danvers in *Rebecca;* and then, after last year's shooting, he blurted, "'I am in control!'" which clearly suggested that he wasn't. Despite these hints of madness, or rather because of them, Haig stays firmly in his place, making Reagan seem moderate, and perhaps even necessary.

But the most perverse and daring stroke of contrast in this spectacle is, of course, the appointment of James Watt as Secretary of the Interior. Watt would be unbearable in any visible capacity, but placing him as guardian of our virgin spaces and small furry animals was a particularly sadistic move. Looking like something hewn from the very bedrock which he longs to disrupt, Watt has made a special talent of his loathesomeness, with his incoherent jeering and his fits of hostile piety. Reagan has suggested that forests cause lung cancer, but next to Watt he starts to look like Johnny Appleseed.

And, finally, there is Nancy, Reagan's own Mommie Dearest, whose frozen presence at her husband's side suggests, paradoxically, that Reagan is a man of passion. The President can also seem mellow and outdoorsy by appearing alongside this rigid wife. Making their way in and out of distant conveyances, the two of them act out a little pageant that celebrates the contradictory values of the right, he dressed as a lumberjack or wrangler, she in some lurid swatch of *haute couture.* Reagan does not ordinarily come across as very physical, but he seems as warm and earthy as a farm animal when accompanied by Nancy who, glassy-eyed and overdressed, always looks as if she has just been struck by lightning in a limousine.

Stockman, Watt, Haig, and Mommy have served their purpose beautifully, humanizing the President in the eyes of most Americans, and, at the same time, gladdening Reagan's true believers by appearing cold and hateful, which is, among the ultraright, not a shortcoming but a sign of grace. As useful as Reagan's satellites have been, however, neither they nor Reagan's charms would have accomplished anything without the full support of our journalists, particularly those who use a camera. "While it always helps to surround the President with freaks," Machiavelli would go on to say, "it is even more important that he learn to snow the press."

Why is it that we think of Ronald Reagan as "a nice guy"? And is it "we" who think it? In fact, it is not the growing numbers of the unemployed, the desperate single mothers, the students and teachers forced to leave school, or the farmers, or the union members, or the old, or the young, or the poor, or the middle class, who keep babbling about how "nice" the President is. Those who find him "nice" are in a dwindling group, comprised of some defense contractors, a few lunatics in Orange County, and most of our TV newsmen, who persist as Reagan's biggest boosters. . . .

The press, and TV in particular, elected Ronald Reagan by playing to his strengths, by letting him evince himself in all his "niceness," by politely avoiding any shots or revelations that might have compromised the seeming wholeness of his image. He came across as a man disinterested, natural, and pure, the innocent object of Carter's "mean campaign," which appeared, by comparison, to stink of politics.

Thus Reagan won because his image was a perfect television spectacle. Now that he's in power, however, it would seem that he might be in danger of extinction by the very medium that created him. His chummy style has created certain problems. For instance, it is still true, as Machiavelli once wrote, that "a prince must see to it that his actions bespeak greatness, courage, dignity, and strength"; and yet, evidently, a President now has to seem "nice" and approachable, everybody's pal. How can a leader seem both great and small? How does he get "closer" to television without succumbing to its equalizing tendencies? For television is, indeed, subversive, more dangerous to a President's well-being than any number of imaginary Libyans. It is an antiheroic medium, straining out charisma and amplifying little flaws; and it tends to exhaust the appeal of its stars very quickly.

It is therefore necessary for the would-be leader to cultivate a new kind of reserve. "Having encircled the President with truly odious people," Machiavelli would advise, "and having gotten him in good with the reporters, you must always take care to *keep him at a distance.*" This rule is not a simple one, as the example of Reagan's image demonstrates. First of all, a President should not be allowed to get too close to the cameras. Like Reagan, he should always appear far away and in transit, waving merrily at everyone, as if going to the beach. Such brief and cheerful appearances will keep the President looking young, and will lessen the risk of his saying something that someone else will only have to rephrase later.

However, keeping the President far away involves more than simply putting space between him and the minicams. One reason for this distancing is to obscure the fact that the President is mortal and this objective sometimes demands measures other than simply physically removing him. As in Reagan's case, it can demand plastic surgery, the liberal use of Grecian Formula 16 and an occasional outlandish fiction, such as last year's story that the President, after getting shot, came tap dancing into the emergency room and then did schtick during surgery. As one whose actions should "bespeak greatness," furthermore, the President must never be seen to do anything patently silly, a kind of distancing which sometimes calls for a little prudent suppression. Last May, for instance, the Dick Clark Company, for a show called "TV Censored Bloopers" tried to get hold of some old movie outtakes that (according to *Variety*) "included muffed lines by Reagan and others as well as failed props." The footage was refused. Even Richard Nixon once tried to cut loose on television grumbling "sock it to me!" on "Laugh-In"; but this President, seemingly so genial and relaxed, never appears televised without seeming carefully closed. . . .

Thus television has reduced our political culture to a succession of gestures, postures, automatic faces. Machiavelli, taking note of all this feeble imagery, would lay his pen down with a tired sigh. "So much for *virtù*," he would say to himself, wondering what became of those creative few whose fierce talents he had once sought to define. And, while thinking of that vanished strength, he would probably contemplate this new absurdity: that *virtù*, which once enabled the startling individual to control the impressions of his image, has itself declined into an image; and this image of the mighty individual is a corporate fiction, the careful work of committees and think tanks, repeatedly reprocessed by the television industry for daily distribution to a mass audience.

The modern prince, in other words, is entirely a creature of TV, which sets him up and breaks him down according to its own implicit schedule—he thrives only as a novelty, then turns at once into a joke or a nostalgia item. This precariousness is nothing new in the world of politics. "Let me observe," writes Machiavelli toward the conclusion of *The Prince*, "that we can see a prince flourishing today and ruined tomorrow, and yet no change has taken place in his nature or in any of his qualities." Machiavelli ascribed such reverses to the influence of the goddess Fortune, the fickle arbiter of all men's ups and downs. "The prince who relies entirely on Fortune comes to destruction the moment she changes," while the prince who counts on his own *virtù* might be able to endure.

But whereas a prince could presumably master Fortune if he made a hero's effort, no President can ever beat TV, no matter how slick and likable his image. Even the well-made Ronald Reagan is finally, and with great subtlety, being dismantled by the anchormen, who now begin to make him seem, although still "nice," a quaint and slightly ludicrous old figurehead. And if

Reagan's sturdy image can be thus subverted, any politician's can as every President's is. As with Reagan, so it was with Carter, with Ted Kennedy, with Gerald Ford, etc., and so it will surely be with all the rest. Our candidates will continue to flash by between commercials, seeming to inhabit no real space, offering nothing but a short performance; and so we'll watch as we watch everything, not bothering to participate, because participation won't be needed. The show, we'll figure numbly, must go on.

GARRY WILLS
An American Dream

[Introduction to *Reagan's America: Innocents at Home* (1987)]

The geriatric "juvenile lead" even as President, Ronald Reagan is old and young—an actor, but with only one role. Because he acts himself, we know he is authentic. A professional, he is always the amateur. He is the great American synecdoche, not only a part of our past but a large part of our multiple pasts. That is what makes many of the questions asked about him so pointless. Is he bright, shallow, complex, simple, instinctively shrewd, plain dumb? He is all these things and more. Synecdoche is just the Greek word for a "sampling," and we all take different samples from the rich store of associations that have accumulated around the Reagan career and persona. He is just as simple, and just as mysterious, as our collective dreams and memories.

He is capacious, surrounding contradictions. Different worlds cohabit the man—"Death Valley Days" and Silicon Valley, Des Moines and the District of Columbia, Sacramento and Eureka. Nor has he simply passed through these places as points of travel—he is still there, at each point. Return him to Eureka College, and he looks instantly at home. He is perfectly suited to the most varying scenes of his life, yet his manner never changes. He is the opposite of a chameleon: environments adapt themselves to him.

He spans our lives, culturally and chronologically. Born in the year the first studio opened in Hollywood, he reached that town just two years after Technicolor did. His second term as President runs through 1988, the two-hundredth anniversary of the ratification of the United States Constitution, and his life spans over a third of that history of constitutional government. His career as a public figure was already a fourth as long as the national government's in the year he went to the White House. Born eleven years into the twentieth, he is scheduled to leave the White House eleven years from the twenty-first century.

He began his regular radio career the year Franklin Roosevelt delivered his first fireside address. An adult during the Depression and World War II, he has known union crusades and corporate worries, spoken for civil liberties and for red hunting. He has been a Hollywood success and a Las Vegas flop. After two victories by wide margins in California, he went down to two defeats as a presidential candidate. He died for victory as the Gipper and won personal glory in the defeat of Barry Goldwater. We have been through it all with him. The GE "House of the Future" he lived in, and Star Wars for the outfitting of space. War movies, and real war (well, almost) in Grenada. Death from prop six-guns, and John Hinckley's real bullets. Reagan runs continuously in everyone's home movies of the mind. He wrests from us something warmer than mere popularity, a kind of complicity. He is, in the strictest sense, what Hollywood promoters used to call "fabulous." We fable him to ourselves, and he to us. We are jointly responsible for him.

He is aware of his own prototypical status, yet that awareness neither galls us nor discommodes him. It is simply "All-American" in his eyes for him to be all America; so, in his eyes, he is. His vast claims are made in ways that convey modesty, not megalomania. One psychobiographer has tried to trace Reagan's political views and actions to a deep insecurity derived from his father. But what must strike the candid observer is the President's almost preternatural security, the lack of inner division that he maintains despite so much contained diversity.

Self-assurance reassures others, and that has not been the least of Reagan's gifts to us, at a time when the nation needed some reassuring. President Carter had discovered such disorientation in the country, or in himself, that he scolded his countrymen for the crime of "malaise." More voters understood him to be the cause of this complaint than its cure; but there can be no doubt that it was a serious charge to bring against any American. Carter spoke of limits, of lowered goals as well as thermostats, of accommodation with the Russians and other unpleasant realities. That is not only demoralizing in a country that defines itself in terms of growth; it stirs a subtle panic, a claustrophobia, that has haunted the American consciousness all through this century. When the Census Bureau declared the frontier closed in 1890, it seemed to be announcing a doom upon the nation. What would we be without the frontier? It had shaped, conditioned, defined us, said Frederick Jackson Turner in 1892. A frontierless America would be non-America. So, once the physical line had been removed from our maps of the continent, we had to engage in metaphorical cartography, tracing "new frontiers" of various sorts, inner or outer, microfrontiers in the laboratory, macrofrontiers in space.

Beneath the spacial anxiety expressed in modern America, there is an even deeper *temporal* fear, that of aging. What if the New World should turn out no different from the Old? Progress may be our most important product, but youth is our oldest boast. As we passed through the various "birthdays" of the 1970s and 1980s, a litany of bicentennials, it should have been harder to maintain our political infancy. Yet, if we did *not* maintain it, what were we to make of claims that this alone preserved us from the gentle decrepitude or active corruption of our European forebears? We are now ruled by the oldest written constitution governing in any nation. Our plight resembles that of Mr. Crummles with his Infant Phenomenon, or Mary Pickford doing Pollyanna— we need an indulgent audience to make the act work.

Yet the rebound from malaise was accomplished in what seems, at first, a perverse way. We regained our youth by electing the oldest President in our history. Four years after the electorate had declared that it was worse off than it was in 1976, one could hardly distinguish Ronald Reagan's stunning re-election victory from the flags and gold medals of the 1984 Olympics. The young athletes seemed to draw strength from their aging leaders, not the other way around. In the famous exchange after John Kennedy's death, journalist Mary McGrory said, "We will never laugh again," and Patrick Moynihan answered, "No, we will laugh again; but we will never be young again." Reagan's success of 1984 was "big magic" by any measure: he made us young again.

How did he pull it off? It is not enough, I think, to say that he resummons our youth because he remembers it, as if anyone sufficiently old would do. Nor is Reagan like the other old men we have used, paradoxically, to symbolize America's youthful spirit—the wise old birds with white hair who seemed to defy the calendar: Mark Twain, or Thomas Edison, or Henry Ford. Those were progeny of Benjamin Franklin, men remembered for a youthful exploit they enacted or described so as to make it timeless—Franklin walking the streets of Philadelphia with his bulky inadequate bread rolls, Twain's eternal haunting of the youth gangs in Hannibal, Edison with his chemicals in the boxcar, or Ford in his workshop. They spoke for and out of a boyhood legend of themselves, authenticated by the fame and wealth such boyhoods led them to. Each, besides, was a genius (or was held to be one) who did not speak the language of the specialist, confirming our picture of America as natively shrewd yet naive. They offered us brilliance as an everyday matter, pairing wisdom with innocence.

Reagan has no archetypal boyhood achievement like Franklin's labor at the press or Ford's at the combustion engine. He has neither an author's nor an inventor's originality. He does not even have the warrior's glow that quickened Dwight Eisenhower's foxy-grandpa popularity. The key point is, precisely, that we do not think of Reagan as grandfatherly (no matter how many grandchildren he may have). Though he was only briefly a leading man on the screen, he has since acquired romantic luster in what passes for real life. He did not age gracefully into character roles, like Jimmy Stewart finally playing Lassie's owner's grandfather. Failure at the box office spared Reagan that honorable second and third life of the fading star who still finds work. But the alternative to such lessened grandeur is normally even worse—to become a fading nonstar, a Sunset Boulevard relic, the frail lacquered icon of an earlier self, as "ageless" and as unconvincing as Mae West. How did Reagan avoid all these traps? He did not age gracefully; he managed somehow not to age at all, at least in symbolic terms. Part of this, of course, is the luck and discipline of physical health. He took good care of himself. But so did Mae West. Reagan, however, was not seen as pampering himself, pickled in adulation for what he did before. He directed his and others' attention from himself to the principle of America as a politically rejuvenating phenomenon. This was accomplished by a mysterious access of Reagan's believing self to our own springs of belief and desire to believe. That is: no one has undergone a more thorough initiation into every aspect of the American legend than Reagan has, and no one has found so many conduits— so many channels, open and indirect, associative, accumulative—for bringing that legend to us in the freshest way. He is the perfect carrier: the ancient messages travel through him without friction. No wonder he shows little wear or tear.

Much of this access derives from Reagan's long familiarity to us in radio, movies, television, and then again on the radio. This is both an obvious and an unexamined fact about Reagan's political life. Early attempts to dismiss him as "just an actor" misfired so badly that more thoughtful attention has not been given to the fact that he *was* indeed an actor, along with everything else. His own first handlers tried to minimize the importance of his Hollywood days, and so have later analysts of his policies. Reagan, with surer instinct, cheerfully emphasizes what others feared to bring up. He understands that a show-business background is part (though only part) of his political resonance. He was never a boy genius, but he was in the place where legends of boy geniuses were fabricated. He was dying as the Gipper while Mickey Rooney played young Edison.

He is an icon, but not a frail one put away in the dark, not Norma Desmond gone brittle on celluloid, her reality decomposing. He is a durable daylight "bundle of meanings," as Roland Barthes called myth. Reagan does not argue for American values; he embodies them.... His approach is not discursive, setting up sequences of time or thought, but associative; not a tracking shot, but montage. We make the connections. It is our movie.

4. THE 1984 ELECTION: REAGANISM AT FULL TIDE

Reagan's campaign for a second term in 1984 provided an occasion for his supporters and detractors to sum up their positions. In a fervent campaign speech published in Fortune, *Texas oil tycoon T. Boone Pickens praised Reagan for singlehandedly reviving the Horatio Alger vision of America as a free-enterprise Utopia where success could come to anyone. John McLaughlin, meanwhile, was assuring* National Review *readers that Reagan—with an assist from the 1984 Los Angeles Olympics—had brought a revival of national pride and patriotism: flag sales were soaring to unheard-of levels. From a radically different ideological perspective, Andrew Kopkind in the* Nation *offered a thoughtful assessment of the cultural and social sources of Reaganism, a movement, he conceded, "as effective as anything seen in American politics since the early days of the New Deal."*

In his second inaugural address, delivered inside the Capitol rotunda because of bitterly cold weather, Reagan again struck a note of soaring optimism and unblushing patriotism, evoking a mythic American past peopled by praying generals, singing pioneers striding into the wilderness, and other sturdy individualists. Reagan mirrored for Americans what they wanted to believe themselves to be: "hopeful, bighearted, idealistic, daring, decent, and fair."

Of the hundreds of newspaper editorials on the inaugural, two may stand as representative: the Cleveland Plain Dealer's *cool analysis of the hard underside of the Reagan message, and the* Washington Post's *positive assessment of the speech coupled with a call for Reagan to make better use of his fantastic popularity. In a more extended commentary on the inaugural address published in* Harper's, *Rutgers political scientist Benjamin Barber noted the paradox of Reagan as "a conservative who revels in dreams"—but private dreams, offering no common vision around which Americans could rally.*

T. BOONE PICKENS, JR.

My Case for Reagan

[*Fortune*, October 29, 1984]

When businessmen consider why they should support President Reagan's reelection, their analysis should come down to two important questions: What has allowed their companies to grow and prosper? What makes business opportunities in America different from those in any other country?

The answer is free enterprise. Our economic system is what keeps Americans employed, clothed, housed, and nourished. That system makes it possible for every American to attain his or her dream of material or spiritual wealth. It truly makes ours the land of opportunity. This year voters will have a clear choice between a President who believes in retaining the maximum amount possible of the nation's wealth in the private sector and a challenger who supports a greater role for government.

More than any other President in the last 30 years, Ronald Reagan understands the importance of free enterprise. He knows that this country's markets should be allowed to operate freely and competitively. That's the philosophy he brought to the White House in 1981, and we've seen how beneficial the results are. Since President Reagan took office, inflation has dropped from nearly 14% to approximately 4%, and the prime rate has fallen from 20% to 13%.

By reducing government intervention, Reagan has injected a new competitive spirit into the marketplace. There is now an atmosphere that encourages business efficiency. For example, merger and acquisition activity, properly undertaken within the constraints of antitrust laws, has allowed companies and even entire industries to restructure and become more efficient and financially sound. Shareholders have reaped the rewards of their investments, and the government has received additional revenues as taxes are paid on those gains. . . .

The cheapest, most effective way to create jobs is to encourage business growth, not to devise complicated and costly federal programs. Ronald Reagan has proved that. His policies have invigorated the market and put more Americans to work. Economic recovery is the best jobs programs this country has had. A record 107 million people are currently employed, five million more than when the Carter-Mondale Administration left office.

But Reagan has done even more for the average worker than stimulate employment. Through his tax policies, Americans are now taking home more pay. They have more money for their children's education, a new home, retirement, and investments. Some 42 million Americans have invested in shares of publicly owned companies, either directly or through mutual funds, compared with 30 million in 1980.

We've seen tangible evidence that Ronald Reagan's policies are working for America. That's important for everyone in this country. The health of U.S. business is critical to our nation's survival. We do, indeed, have a responsibility to support candidates who understand that principle—a responsibility not just to ourselves but to all citizens.

I am frequently asked by high school and college students how they can attain success from modest beginnings. My answer is simple. Like many business executives, I owe my success to the free enterprise system. I started with a good education, $2,500 in capital, and an opportunity to do something—the sky was the limit, and fortunately the same opportunity still exists.

The American free enterprise spirit is something we will be able to maintain only under a Reagan Administration. While Walter Mondale tells us that his plan for this country is better, we've seen what better means: Mondale's recent speeches have promised increased government intervention in the market and our lives and disincentives in the form of higher taxes.

The ill effects of the Carter-Mondale Administration were far-reaching: double-digit inflation—the worst since 1946—unemployment, skyrocketing interest rates, and a crumbling economy. There is no reason to believe that a Mondale-Ferraro Administration would be any different in philosophy or outcome. . . .

America need not take that chance when it is blessed with an incumbent President who has proven leadership qualities. Ronald Reagan has been able to instill a new sense of pride and confidence in our nation. Gone are the days of Carter-Mondale defeatism and national malaise.

In 1980 the American people realized the disastrous economic brink on which this country teetered. They wanted a change for the better, and they chose a President who accomplished that goal. On November 6, Americans will once again ask themselves if a change is in order. I think the resounding answer will be that they wish to stay the course Reagan has charted. We're no longer on the brink of disaster; both feet are planted firmly on solid ground, and the future looks bright.

I'm supporting President Reagan and Vice President Bush for those reasons, and I unabashedly ask others to support them as well. I make no apology for political participation. At stake in this election is the future of the free enterprise system. A commitment from the business community, not just a check, is required to prevent another give-away-now, pay-later disaster. And that commitment will mean for future Americans a vigorous free market, the opportunity to succeed, and an attainable American Dream.

JOHN MC LAUGHLIN
The New Nationalism
[*National Review*, September 21, 1984]

There's a fresh reason to vote for Ronald Reagan this year, and it's neither the economy nor national defense. It's pride. The country is on a patriotic ego trip, proud of itself and unself-consciously enjoying the nationalistic binge. "I've never felt so good about the country in my life," a delegate told me in Dallas. George Bush put it well: "This sure beats that Democratic Temple of Doom in San Francisco." Kay Ortega, the convention keynoter, defined the genesis of this new "Era of Good Feeling": Ronald Reagan has "restored America's faith in itself," she said. Jeane Kirkpatrick also limned the new national high, seeing in Ronald Reagan's Presidency "a reaffirmation of historical American ideals" and a restoration of "confidence in the legitimacy and success of American institutions." The ambassador later repeated the same note a few octaves down when she so unforgettably burlesqued the "San Francisco Democrats" who always want "to blame America first." And Howard Baker continued the theme by remarking that when Walter Mondale holds office, "he creates misery, and when he's out of office, he invents it." The Dallas Convention gave expression to what the nation at large feels as it rides a tidal wave of nationalistic energy and conviction.

The U.S. Olympic athletes have helped create this surging uplift. Campaign insiders say the games increased Mr. Reagan's popularity by as much as 5 per cent. For some reason, Americans tie their septuagenarian President to the flower of their youth, perhaps because Reagan himself is a kind of *aeternus puer.* Does this explain why people between the ages of 18 and 39 prefer Reagan over Mondale, 58 to 37 per cent (*Los Angeles Times*)? If you narrow the bracket, to the 19 to 25 age group, the preference for Reagan stretches to an astonishing 69 to 28 per cent (*U.S.A. Today*). The film *Red Dawn*, featuring young Americans fighting Communists, an unblushingly patriotic salute, is a box-office smash despite harsh critical notices. The military services enjoy greater respect today than at any time since Vietnam, as evidenced by the current re-enlistment rates and by the quality of enlistees, despite an ongoing economic expansion. On college campuses, the ROTC is back in vogue, with both programs and enrollments on the upswing.

But the binge is not only a young people's thing. Convention delegates reported record turnouts all around the country this year on Flag Day and the Fourth of July. The Freedom Festival in Evansville, Indiana, played host to a record-busting quarter of a million people in the last week of June and first week of July. In Washington, the Architect of the Capitol says the number of requests for flags flown over the cupola is expected to climb to 112,000 this year, as against 84,000 requests last year.

Is Ronald Reagan responsible for this emotional high? Or was it a case of being at the right place at the right time? True, the book has been closed for some time on the Vietnam War and Watergate. Also, the USSR's invasion of Afghanistan and its threat against Poland are both now almost five years old. Everything was in place for a U.S. President to open the spigot and let the pent-up pride burst forth.

The release of the American hostages on the very day of Mr. Reagan's inauguration was the first patriotic lightning-bolt to strike the populace. Then the President's economic program came along, with a gathering wave of optimism in its wake. This was followed by the successful military intervention in Grenada (as contrasted with the Iranian captivity and aborted rescue). And, let's face it, the Soviets have also helped to feed nationalistic sentiment in the United States. Their abstention from the Olympic Games, their treatment of Sakharov, their refusal to talk disarmament, their current stiffing of Mr. Reagan all spur the American people to rally round their Commander-in-Chief.

Reagan appeals to this hunger for self-respect through both his programs and his personality. Despite all the charges of unfairness, Reagan retains a populist look—especially as compared to Walter Mondale or Geraldine Ferraro. He is seen as a power-to-the-people, shrink-big-government President who wants to slash taxes, cut spending, and redirect money outward and downward (federalism). Mr. Reagan has "a democratic personality," as Richard Wirthlin has appositely noted, with his geniality, wit, and obvious enjoyment of the job; he is more reminiscent of FDR or JFK than of Herbert Hoover or Calvin Coolidge.

All of which might be viewed as respectable Sunday-supplement fare, and that only, until you recall that nationalism is the greatest single determinant of modern history. It makes leaders well-nigh invincible if it is on their side, permitting them to fashion the organization, structure, and expression of public life. So, as happened with President Eisenhower when Americans were on another nationalistic high, the people seem to have committed themselves to Ronald Reagan already (witness his uncanny strength in the opinion polls). And they have developed a taste for the Reagan nationalism, with its emotional buoyancy and exhilaration. As Kay Ortega observed, if (as now appears likely) Mr. Reagan receives a powerful mandate, he will be seen less as the communicator and more as the leader, reforging America and sinking the roots of his conservatism deeper.

ANDREW KOPKIND
The Age of Reaganism
[*Nation*, November 3, 1984]

Not since the era of the late junior Senator from Wisconsin has an American political figure given this country an eponymous ism. Reaganism is now an established movement and an important historical event. Its roots can be discerned in periods long past, and its consequences will carry beyond the Presidential tenure, and perhaps the earthly existence, of the man who gave it a name. In the coming few years, at least, it will surely engage and dramatically alter the institutions and activities of American civic culture.

Like other native American movements—Populism, Progressivism and the various "new radicalisms" of this century—Reaganism lacks sharp ideological definition and programmatic coherence. It has not yet produced a unitary creed to resolve the differences among its components: the Moral Majority, the corporate class, blue-collar ethnics and the country-club set. The contest between monetarists and supply-siders is still undecided. Reaganism seems vague, trendy, spontaneous, opportunistic, impressionistic and contradictory. But not always: those who are making the movement have a precise idea of their goals and a fair sense of the strategies to achieve them. They have located a social base to support their campaign; they have developed an institutional network to maintain it; they are fashioning an economic system to feed it; and they have invented educational policies to supply it with manpower for generations to come. However amorphous any of those elements may look at the moment, the whole Reaganist project has the spin, the feel, the significance of a force of history.

The rise of Reaganism is focused in the electoral arena this year, but it is not primarily a phenomenon of political campaigns, public office or even Republican Administrations. A landslide victory for Reagan and his allies next week would certainly advance the movement, but a good Democratic showing would not stop or reverse it. For power is already in place to continue the movement's mission in the coming years. The first targets of choice are clear: all those liberal institutions that have defined and shaped American culture for fifty years or more—the press, the churches, unions, academia, local public education, urban government, philanthropic foundations, the artistic establishment, Hollywood, publishing, Federal service, the liberal professions and their organizations. They will come under increasing pressure to redirect their orientation along lines that have already been drawn, to change their social roles, to reassess their values. Even the term "liberalism" has been dropped from polite political discourse. A major ideological conflict is under way....

Reaganism underscores the issues and subsumes the symbols of the electoral debate. Grenada, Central America, the Pentagon budget, taxes and deficits, school prayer, abortion, family values, patriotism, leadership—those words have specific referents, and in an ordinary campaign they would acquire no larger meaning. But this is no ordinary election. Its ideological character makes a sensible pattern of disparate factors. And that, of course, is what ideology is for; it creates a consciousness that can be laid over random subjects as an outline traced on paper assembles scattered dots into a picture. Grenada, then, is no isolated adventure but a tactic in the strategy of rollback—Reaganism's long-term policy of destroying socialism and preventing revolution in the Third World (and that is only the beginning). Defense spending is not a set of figures but a way of increasing militarization of America's political economy, and its cultural life as well. Taxes and deficits are tools for increasing the power and enriching the coffers of the corporate class. Family values refer to more rigid social controls, leadership means authoritarianism, school prayer and support for religious education are means of hastening the privatization of American society—a key strategy.

The unusual level of polarization that most political commentators noticed in the campaign earlier this year was a symptom of its ideological nature. It is a truism of political science that candidates move to the middle to maximize their appeal as the voting day approaches. But Ronald Reagan and his allies around the country have been different. For the most part, they have sharpened rather than leveled debate, hardened rather than softened positions, divided rather than merged constituencies and generally occupied extremes rather than the center of the spectrum. For a moment it seemed that Reagan was bidding to become the peace candidate, but he used his *pro forma* meeting with Andrei Gromyko to emphasize his toughness.

The ideological thrust comes almost entirely from the Reagan side. . . . His purpose is not simply to win votes but to organize and train the movement. Reaganism feeds on divisiveness, pitting fundamentalist and orthodox religions against liberal ones, whites against blacks, the Sun Belt against the Rust Belt, the service and technological industries against primary and manufacturing sectors, the upper classes against the lower, men against women, families against the unwed, individuals against the state. As Reaganism articulates those values it moves its constituencies—perhaps already the new majority—toward an ideological pole. That is not coalition making but movement building, and it has been as effective as anything seen in American politics since the early days of the New Deal.

Reaganism has developed from the several trends and transient phenomena that followed the convulsive social activity of the 1960s. It takes ideas, energies and some personnel from such varied elements as the George Wallace movement, neoconservatism, the New Right, neoliberalism, fundamentalism, post-feminism, the ''back to basics'' movement in education, the ''return to roots'' trend in Judaism, Catholic orthodoxy, the white backlash to integration and affirmative action, the straight-male hostility to women's liberation and gay rights, the Anglophone aversion to bilingualism. It also draws on historic American Populism, especially its racist, nativist and regionalist themes. It twines with some curiously contradictory threads in Progressivism: America Firstism and moral imperialism, a distrust of politics and politicians, an antagonism to Wall Street and monopolies. For its personal values it draws on social Darwinism, but its economic vision looks quite the other way, to a heavenly city of corporate control. Chronologically, Reaganism belongs to the late period of America's imperial drama, as fear of impending doom and a sense of inevitable loss prepare the actors for unwonted roles.

Many people or groups of people feel that they lost something, or lost out, in the Vietnam era and after. It is among those who see their power diminished, their profits dissipated, their mobility curtailed and their security endangered that Reaganism finds its social base. Included are whites in general and men in general; conservative political figures of both parties; the military and defense community; some Jews, most European ethnics and entry-level yuppies. They all have different reasons to resent the old liberal order. There's simple, straightforward racism and male chauvinism, to begin with, and it would be hard to underestimate the strength of those factors in Reaganism's support. Anyone who probes the political consciousness of white American males usually finds that what they like most about the Reagan Administration is the way it puts blacks and women in their places. . . .

At the cornerstone are the fundamentalist churches and their rapidly growing school system, which threatens the health and even the life of public education; about a thousand new religious elementary schools were opened this year. Alongside are the foundations and think tanks, the military and militaristic institutions, sports and celebrations, broadcasting and publishing, volunteer and charitable institutions and a new breed of ideologically oriented businesses. Amway sales agents are Reaganist cadre; so are R.O.T.C. trainees, weekend "survival game" players, religious disk jockeys and Bible salesmen, and certain professional athletes. Everyone who watched the World Series heard that the San Diego Padres' pitching staff is stuffed with John Birchers. The Olympics became a Reaganist spectacle, and the chant "U.S.A.! U.S.A.!" was appropriated for Reagan-Bush rallies.

The Administration actively supports institutions that promote its designated values. It wants to give tax credits to private schools, it encourages private patriotic displays (such as the Statue of Liberty extravaganza which promises to be next year's Olympics), it places ideologues in key positions (such as in the National Endowment for the Humanities and the Federal Communications Commission), it gives government access to Reaganist organizations like Accuracy in Media. Such support makes perfect strategic sense. Institutions teach people to think in specific ways. Private institutions teach "private" values: competitive enterprise over collective endeavor, the family unit over the heterogeneous community, male authority over sexual democracy, patriotism over internationalism, selfishness over altruism, having over sharing. There is nothing new or inherently sinister in the *process* of ideological institution building. Liberals did a good job of it for many decades and succeeded in creating a liberal value system for the whole country. Radicals made a stab at the same thing in the 1960s. Underground newspapers and FM stations, "new age" restaurants and businesses, noncompetitive sporting events, rock concerts, the many expressions of a new feminist culture, black studies programs and gay organizations all were designed to give their participants an opportunity to reorient their individual values and social consciences. If history is a question of consciousness, the way to transform the world is to change people's minds. Reaganism grasps that simple and profound reality, and is taking appropriate measures.

As Reaganism was gathering steam, liberalism began looking for the proper response, a way to recapture the terms of political debate, to re-enter the social discourse, to gain the moral high ground or the upper hand of power. Simple right-baiting would not work. The day has passed when just the "conservative" label was enough to discredit its bearer. Nowadays it is worn proudly, while "liberal" has become the pejorative of choice.

For a long time liberals carried on a painful search for "new ideas," a self-defeating maneuver which merely confirmed the popular impression that the liberal intellectual and political program was finished. Next, liberals began adopting Reaganist constructs—family values, national security, patriotism— and attempted to give them progressive content. Gov. Mario Cuomo's wildly applauded speech to the Democratic Convention in July represented a bid to capture the family issue. Mondale has tried to appropriate the security issue by announcing his plans for humane, safe and cheap interventionism: a quarantine of Nicaragua rather than an invasion, military expeditions to save American lives rather than to topple governments, a leisurely advance in the arms race rather than a blitzkrieg dash to global supremacy. Various leftists and liberals keep insisting that the flag belongs to everyone and that patriotism is the first refuge for citizens of all creeds and colors; they rarely speak of internationalism. . . .

Culturally, Hollywood has responded by dishing up the new themes with the old humane details thrown in for filler. The clutch of new films set in the country defer for atmosphere to the Reaganist nostalgia for a mythic American heartland, but the people brim with liberal values of racial integration, collective struggle against greedy profiteers, and kindness toward the handicapped. For the first time some out-and-out examples of Reaganism are creeping into Hollywood (the premise, if not the conclusion, of *Red Dawn*), and the struggle is heating up on television, where the value systems are locked in nightly combat.

Since Reaganism sets the terms of the debate, it need not be overly concerned about the details. It holds the high ground; what happens at the lower levels is curious but not crucial. Reaganism can live with ideological pluralism, but it still will strive for the upper hand.

What is the Reaganist project? It begins with the idea of rollback: not only in international affairs, where it is directed against revolution in the Third World and, finally, against Communist Eastern Europe, but also in domestic matters, where it aims to repeal the progressive developments of a century of liberal action. If that seems farfetched, conjure a more radical fantasy: Turn-of-the-century America has a politically active military establishment directing a militarized economy in a Christian nation. Civil rights and civil liberties are subject to circumscription by a Supreme Court whose members are vetted by religious leaders and ideological overseers. Foreign adventures arouse little opposition because the pool of potential protesters has shrunk with the degradation of democratic education and the repression of radical and liberal institutions. All but the most pliant labor unions are decertified. The old middle class has vanished and a Reaganist class of service managers, franchise owners and venture capitalists sits on a huge underclass of burger wrappers and security guards. The press is assiduously neutral, the airwaves are full of hymns and sermons, and libraries are divided into a section of dog stories and Gothic romances for the public and locked stacks of books with more controversial subjects for expert eyes only.

If that seems unlikely, as it certainly is, the reason is contained in the contradictions within Reaganism as well as in the opposition. The divisions between the fundamentalists and the corporatists; the ethnics and the yuppies; the blue-collar workers and the technocrats; the Northeasterners and the Southwesterners, could be glossed over this year, while electoral triumph was in sight, but those conflicts of interest must sooner or later erode the strength of the movement. Although Reaganism is wider and deeper than Reagan himself, his presence and performance hold the abrasive elements together.

It is the dual nature of Reaganism's strength—its personal and ideological character—that offers the best opportunity for opposition from the outside. The political fight against the Reagan Administration, primarily but not exclusively in the electoral arena, can be transformed into the fight against the ideology. Just as the liberal and left attack on McCarthyism was waged largely against Joe McCarthy, so this battle must take advantage of the organizational symbol. Beyond that, Reaganism's social and political system is bound to produce specific counterattacks. The conditions that produced revolution in the Third World, the black struggle at home, the women's movement and the demands for economic and social equity only a few years ago have not essentially changed. Reaganism cannot work quickly or efficiently enough to alter the consciousness that developed then, nor can it effectively remove the conditions or erase the demands. It will have to rely on repression and neglect to maintain its forward motion and, finally, its stability. And we all know what happens then. It's not too soon to start thinking about the heady days to come as the age of Reaganism begins to darken.

RONALD REAGAN
Second Inaugural Address
[January 21, 1985]

There are no words adequate to express my thanks for the great honor that you've bestowed on me. I'll do my utmost to be deserving of your trust.

This is, as Senator Mathias told us, the 50th time we the people have celebrated this historic occasion. When the first President—George Washington—placed his hand upon the Bible, he stood less than a single day's journey by horseback from raw, untamed wilderness. There were 4 million Americans in a union of 13 States. Today, we are 60 times as many in a union of 50 States. We've lighted the world with our inventions, gone to the aid of mankind wherever in the world there was a cry for help, journeyed to the Moon and safely returned.

So much has changed. And yet, we stand together as we did two centuries ago. When I took this oath 4 years ago, I did so in a time of economic stress. Voices were raised saying that we had to look to our past for the greatness and glory. But we, the present-day Americans, are not given to looking backward. In this blessed land, there is always a better tomorrow.

Four years ago, I spoke to you of a new beginning, and we have accomplished that. But in another sense, our new beginning is a continuation of that beginning created two centuries ago, when, for the first time in history, government, the people said, was not our master, it is our servant; its only power that which we the people allow it to have.

That system has never failed us. But, for a time, we failed the system. We asked things of government that government was not equipped to give. We yielded authority to the national government that properly belonged to States or to local governments or to the people themselves. We allowed taxes and inflation to rob us of our earnings and savings and watched the great industrial machine that had made us the most productive people on Earth slow down and the number of unemployed increase.

By 1980 we knew it was time to renew our faith; to strive with all our strength toward the ultimate in individual freedom, consistent with an orderly society. . . .

We are creating a nation once again vibrant, robust, and alive. But there are many mountains yet to climb. We will not rest until every American enjoys the fullness of freedom, dignity, and opportunity as our birthright. It is our birthright as citizens of this great republic. And, if we meet this challenge, these will be years when Americans have restored their confidence and tradition of progress; when our values of faith, family, work, and neighborhood were restated for a modern age; when our economy was finally freed from government's grip; when we made sincere efforts at meaningful arms reductions and by rebuilding our defenses, our economy, and developing new technologies, helped preserve peace in a troubled world; when America courageously supported the struggle for individual liberty, self-government, and free enterprise throughout the world and turned the tide of history away from totalitarian darkness and into the warm sunlight of human freedom. . . .

At the heart of our efforts is one idea vindicated by 25 straight months of economic growth: Freedom and incentives unleash the drive and entrepreneurial genius that are a core of human progress. We have begun to increase the rewards for work, savings, and investment, reduce the increase in the cost and size of government and its interference in people's lives.

We must simplify our tax system, make it more fair, and bring the rates down for all who work and earn. We must think anew and move with a new boldness, so every American who seeks work can find work; so the least among us shall have an equal chance to achieve the greatest things—to be heroes who heal our sick, feed the hungry, protect peace among nations, and leave this world a better place.

The time has come for a new American emancipation—a great national drive to tear down economic barriers and liberate the spirit of enterprise in the most distressed areas of our country. My friends, together we can do this, and do it we must, so help me God.

From new freedom will spring new opportunities for growth; a more productive, fulfilled, and united people; and a stronger America—an America that will lead the technological revolution and also open its mind and heart and soul to the treasures of literature, music, and poetry and the values of faith, courage, and love.

A dynamic economy, with more citizens working and paying taxes, will be our strongest tool to bring down budget deficits. But an almost unbroken 50 years of deficit spending has finally brought us to a time of reckoning. . . .

We must act now to protect future generations from government's desire to spend its citizens' money and tax them into servitude, when the bills come due. Let us make it unconstitutional for the Federal Government to spend more than the Federal Government takes in.

We have already started returning to the people and to State and local governments responsibilities better handled by them. Now there is a place for the Federal Government in matters of social compassion. But our fundamental goals must be to reduce dependency and upgrade the dignity of those who are infirm or disadvantaged. And here a growing economy and support from family and community offer our best chance for a society where compassion is a way of life, where the old and infirm are cared for, the young and, yes, the unborn protected, and the unfortunate looked after and made self-sufficient.

There is another area where the Federal Government can play a part. As an older American, I remember a time when people of different race, creed, or ethnic origin in our land found hatred and prejudice installed in social custom and, yes, in law. There's no story more heartening in our history than the progress that we've made toward the "brotherhood of man" that God intended for us. Let us resolve there will be no turning back or hesitation on the road to an America rich in dignity and abundant with opportunity for all our citizens. . . .

Though our heritage is one of bloodlines from every corner of the Earth, we are all Americans, pledged to carry on this last, best hope of man on Earth.

I have spoken of our domestic goals and the limitations we should put on our national government. Now let me turn to a task that is the primary responsibility of national government—the safety and security of our people.

Today we utter no prayer more fervently than the ancient prayer for peace on Earth. Yet history has shown that peace does not come, nor will our freedom be preserved, by good will alone. There are those in the world who scorn our vision of human dignity and freedom. One nation—the Soviet Union—has conducted the greatest military buildup in the history of man, building arsenals of awesome offensive weapons.

We've made progress in restoring our defense capability. But much remains to be done. There must be no wavering by us, nor any doubts by others, that America will meet her responsibilities to remain free, secure, and at peace.

There is only one way safely and legitimately to reduce the cost of national security, and that is to reduce the need for it. And this we're trying to do in negotiations with the Soviet Union. We're not just discussing limits on a further increase of nuclear weapons. We seek, instead, to reduce their number. We seek the total elimination one day of nuclear weapons from the face of the Earth. . . .

Since the turn of the century, the number of democracies in the world has grown four-fold. Human freedom is on the march, and nowhere more so than in our own hemisphere. Freedom is one of the deepest and noblest aspirations of the human spirit. People worldwide hunger for the right of self-determination, for those inalienable rights that make for human dignity and progress.

America must remain freedom's staunchest friend, for freedom is our best ally. And it is the world's only hope to conquer poverty and preserve peace. Every blow we inflict against poverty will be a blow against its dark allies of oppression and war. Every victory for human freedom will be a victory for world peace. . . .

History is a ribbon, always unfurling; history is a journey. And as we continue our journey, we think of those who traveled before us. We stand again at the steps of this symbol of our democracy—well, we would have been standing at the steps if it hadn't gotten so cold. Now we're standing inside this symbol of our democracy. And we see and hear again the echoes of our past.

A general falls to his knees in the hard snow of Valley Forge; a lonely President paces the darkened halls and ponders his struggle to preserve the union; the men of the Alamo call out encouragement to each other; a settler pushes west and sings a song, and the song echoes out forever and fills the unknowing air.

It is the American sound. It is hopeful, big-hearted, idealistic, daring, decent, and fair. That's our heritage, that's our song. We sing it still. For all our problems, our differences, we are together as of old. We raise our voices to the God who is the Author of this most tender music. And may He continue to hold us close as we fill the world with our sound—in unity, affection, and love. One people under God, dedicated to the dream of freedom that He has placed in the human heart, called upon now to pass that dream on to a waiting and a hopeful world. God bless you, and may God bless America.

CLEVELAND PLAIN DEALER
A More Subtle Tune for Old Lyrics
[January 22, 1985]

It wasn't just the cramped, indoor setting that muted President Reagan's second inaugural address yesterday. Rather, after four years the president apparently has come to realize that trivial anecdotes, combative anti-government phrases and strident partisanship are not enough to bring about the revolution he wants.

Reagan has talked often of arms control, but achieved little until the final month of his first term. He railed against big government, but managed to oversee more deficit spending than any other president before him. He talked about the inequities of the tax system, but only now is getting serious about substantive changes. His frequent discussion of constitutional amendments—to promote school prayer, to further restrict abortions and to require a balanced federal budget—remain as so much rhetoric.

The president during his first term did renew a spirit of confidence in the country's future. He financed his way out of a recession. But after four years much of his agenda remains unfulfilled. So it was that on one of the coldest days of the coldest season of the year, Reagan offered an appeal for bipartisanship.

Don't be misled; the president remains as committed as before to the basic tenets of his presidency. And he still seems enamored more by the sound of soothing words than he is accepting of the realities of life in less insulated cities like Cleveland and Detroit. For him it is nice to say that "there are no limits to growth and human progress, when men and women are free to follow their dreams." It is something else to walk through urban ghettos where cynicism has replaced hope, and where the only laws are the laws of self-preservation.

"You elected us in 1980 to end this prescription for disaster. I do not believe you re-elected us in 1984 to reverse course," the president said yesterday. If that can be taken at face value, it means blacks will fall further behind the mainstream. It means more frustration for women, particularly single mothers. It means loose interpretation of the law for those with means, and a strict interpretation of the laws for those without.

The tone of yesterday's address might be viewed as signaling a change, or at least a willingness of the president to make bipartisan tradeoffs, to discuss the protection of some social programs in return for congressional support for the high priority items of the next term—arms control, deficit reduction and tax reform. More likely, however, it means the president has chosen a more subtle tune for his old lyrics portraying congressional Democrats as the bad guys who deserve to be thrown out of office if they fail to join in his initiatives.

[Reprinted courtesy *The Plain Dealer.*]

WASHINGTON POST
And Now the Party's Over
[January 22, 1985]

There was, we thought, a certain rare dignity and beauty to the inaugural proceedings held in the Rotunda of the Capitol, rather than in the customary outdoor setting. Sorry about those people who, holding prime grandstand seats for the event, weren't able to be crammed into the Rotunda, but the indoor hall seemed to us a perfectly fitting backdrop for the president's swearing-in. Inside the Capitol, looking at the assemblage of people gathered there, as distinct from peering down the vista toward the White House, was where this particular president should have been yesterday. Much of what he was committing himself to will depend on good relationships within that Capitol building. And there was no more suitable background for his remarks about the necessity of healing bitter divisions and working together.

Clichés? Well, of course there were a fair number. But we would say that by the standards set in the past for these speeches Mr. Reagan stayed pretty much on the scant and unflamboyant side. Some of the prose was resonant. It soared—especially the part about the "American sound," as he called it. That sound "is hopeful," the president said, "big-hearted, idealistic, daring, decent and fair. That is our heritage. That is our song."

Those critics of Mr. Reagan who are not inclined to grant him an inaugural amnesty (or themselves a temporary rest) will point out that much which went on in the president's first term by no stretch of the imagination could be made to fit that description. Yet even the most committed sourpusses should be willing to concede that this president has given tens of millions of people in this country a feeling that safe, stable times are returned and that fundamental values they hold dear are back in vogue and unashamedly so. He has also given them a sense of possibility that seemed to have been entirely wrung out of our politics in the grim decades that preceded his first term. Mr. Reagan doesn't tell the people they are bad or neurotic or doomed each time a particular problem arises. For that they are duly grateful—who wouldn't be?

Is there justification for this upbeat message? Can the optimism be even partially fulfilled? We will spare you (for today) yet another warning about what is waiting in the economic wings unless the president takes some steps he thus far seems disinclined to. We will even forbear to pursue our customary argument against the fatuous balanced-budget amendment—at least for 24 hours. We will note instead that there were passages in Mr. Reagan's speech—. . . the strong words on the necessity of racial justice in American life, the stress on emancipation of the individual spirit in our society—that are full of promise if Mr. Reagan cares to follow their implications.

The president will have his share of opposition in both houses of Congress— some of it will comprise resistance he *should* encounter. But by and large he has a freer hand and a freer field than any president has enjoyed since the late 1950s. The opposition party is in a shambles. His majority is huge. His personal popularity is even huger than that majority of voters. Mr. Reagan has tremendous opportunities just now to act on the more inspired parts of his inaugural pledge.

BENJAMIN R. BARBER

Celluloid Vistas

[*Harper's*, July 1985]

America's future rests in a thousand dreams inside your hearts . . . and helping you make those dreams come true is what this job of mine is all about.
—President Ronald Reagan

Our President, Ronald Reagan, is a puzzle: the optimistic conservative. The optimistic conservative, by the traditional standards of ideology and party politics, is an oxymoron. Historically, optimism has been the currency of liberals and radicals. The conservative has been a realist, a skeptic, a cynic. He has cautioned against the dreams of those who think man and nature malleable, perfectible. He has learned the lesson of limits. Men disappoint; found government on laws. Government corrupts; divide and limit its powers. Necessity governs human affairs; acknowledge its boundaries.

In light of this, what in the world are we to make of President Reagan? What are we to make of this, from his second inaugural address?

We believed then and now that there are no limits to growth and human progress when men and women are free to follow their dreams.

The true conservative resists dreams, knowing that they are on a collision course with reality. Not our President. He dreams. He is drawn to other dreamers, like John Kennedy and Franklin Roosevelt. He wants to help make *your* dreams come true.

The puzzle: the conservative who revels in dreams. The solution? For that, we must look beyond the boundaries of ideology and politics. We must look west, to where the President's political disposition took form, and where so many American dreams have been engendered. *Hollywood.*

Hollywood dreams are picture-show dreams. What kinds of aspirations and desires do we find in the movies? Whose dreams? Hollywood movies tend to star solitary heroes; they rarely offer communities or civic bodies as protagonists. They tend to dramatize the struggle of individuals *against* something large, complex, and unspecified. Simplicity is the hallmark of these stories of hope and desire. They have endings, tidy and happy; there is no hint of the ambiguities of a morally messy world—no Bitburgs, half neutral, half Nazi. Film, all light and shadow, loathes gray.

President Reagan's second inaugural address was punctuated by allusions to memorable Americans. These allusions were not historical in the scholarly or textbook sense. They were more like film stills.

A general falls to his knees in the hard snow of Valley Forge; a lonely President paces the darkened halls and ponders his struggle to preserve the Union; the men of the Alamo call out encouragement to each other; a settler pushes west and sings a song. . . .

The speech lauds "We the People," but its heroes are men alone (no women are mentioned). In the President's script, Washington leans on no comrade in arms, Lincoln consults no cabinet. The defenders of the Alamo call out to one another as if crouching far apart in anticipation of a lonely battle, and only a single settler is conjured for us—his family wagon and the long train of Conestogas that must surely have accompanied it are kept out of sight (and out of mind). Hollywood heroes realizing celluloid dreams: all burdens and all rewards belong to the individual.

The election of a Hollywood dreamer to an office so badly tainted has been a balm to the troubled American spirit. And the President has reminded Americans of the place of dreams in the American heart. The nation was founded on dreams: the belief in a new Eden, in the shining city on a hill (the President was quick to borrow John Winthrop's phrase). Recent polls suggest that even those most hurt by Ronald Reagan's policies are beginning to share in the vague but buoying spirit of hope and self-confidence that springs from his Hollywood reveries. Hope is a precious and necessary commodity in a democracy; if it takes a Hollywood dreamer to revive it for us, so be it.

But are President Reagan's dreams the American dream? What is disturbing about them is not that their flicker and glow are best appreciated in the semi-light, or that they are tainted with Hollywood escapism, but that they are wholly *private* dreams. They are dreams of, by, and for solitaries: John Waynes and Horatio Algers, prospectors and entrepreneurs, Olympic speedsters and venture capitalists, do-it-yourselfers and me-firsters. The talk at the White House is of liberty; liberty, however, is mistaken for the private market and personal ambition.

Emancipation has historically been the achievement of communities. No one knew better than Lincoln that while one man's courage could be an emblem for the Union, its survival depended on anonymous armies of bluecoats, workers, and citizens. The Union in whose name Lincoln risked all—even the dream of the emancipation of the slaves—represented to him the greater dream of a national community that would bring together countless individuals who, locked into their regions or parties or interest groups, were radically incomplete.

The lone settler celebrated by Reagan pushed west into a land of lawlessness and anarchy. His true emancipation would come only with the building of local schools, local courts, local town halls—a body politic capable of ensuring his rights. The true individualists back then were the outlaws, who turned the new lands into badlands and killed and died for Hobbes's "liberty": the war of all against all, a life poor, nasty, brutish, and short. Liberty came only with social cooperation and government; justice had to await the law. The dream of liberty is not a dream against government but a dream *of* government.

In truth, the great American dream has always been a *public* dream. The tired and the poor who swarmed ashore in the New World came in search of private liberty and personal fortune, to be sure, but they came above all in search of a form of government that would give them the right to create a common destiny for themselves and their children. Before they dreamed of waving greenbacks, they dreamed of waving citizenship papers.

Entrepreneurs may make money, but only citizens can make justice. The struggle for common goods—clean air, justice, peace—is a common struggle in which democratic government is our only ally. President Reagan asks much of individuals but nothing of citizens; he burdens the market with demands for progress and prosperity, but of the community and the government that is the community's instrument he asks nothing.

What have we dreamed for ourselves and our children and our neighbors? To be a land open to private dreams, America must itself be a public dream. And what is this dream made of? Democracy, precarious in the few places where it has taken root, unknown to most of the world; racial and sexual and economic justice, mocked by most systems, aspired to but hardly achieved in ours; mutualism, that is, defining our power and dignity as individuals by what we do together; citizenship, through which women and men dare to transcend themselves and become neighbors, and shapers of a common destiny.

This dream is the dream of "We the People." It does not now have a persuasive political spokesman. Until it does, it will remain a dream in search of dreamers.

The American Scene

1. ECONOMIC AND TAX POLICIES

The Early Years

We shift now from general assessments of Reagan and Reaganism to specific policy debates of the Reagan years, beginning with Reagan's economic program, called by some "Reaganomics" and ridiculed by George Bush (before he became Reagan's vice president) as "voodoo economics." Addressing a Chicago business group during the 1980 campaign, Reagan laid out the central elements of his economic vision: ruthless cuts in "runaway federal spending" (except for the military budget); a three-year, 30 percent cut in personal income taxes; and sharp cutbacks in the federal regulations supposedly strangling American business. Evaluating this program, Fortune *complained that business taxes were not being slashed as much as personal taxes, and presciently warned that the combination of tax cuts and increased defense spending could produce dangerous deficits.*

Once elected, Reagan set about to translate campaign oratory into policy. The result was dissected in a November 1981 Nation *article by Martin Carnoy and Derek Shearer (professors at Stanford University and Occidental College, respectively), challenging the assumptions of Reaganomics and predicting that its failure would lead to renewed interest in the use of federal programs to promote the economic well-being of all, especially the poor.*

By 1982 inflation had cooled, but the nation was mired in recession, and the deficits predicted by Fortune *had become a reality. When Reagan's 1983 budget projected a $91.5 billion deficit, the St. Louis Globe-Democrat (a staunchly Republican paper despite its name) loyally praised it as "a courageous document" by "a man of great resolve." Others, however, were dismayed. University of Pennsylvania economist Sidney Weintraub, in a gleefully polemical* New Leader *article, sardonically tore apart Reagan's "guns up/people down" budget proposals and proclaimed him "king of the deficit makers and undisputed master of the national debt mountain."*

RONALD REAGAN
Five-Year Economic Program for the U.S.
[Speech Delivered Before the International Business Council, Chicago, September 9, 1980]

I'd like to speak to you today about a new concept of leadership . . . based on faith in the American people, confidence in the American economy, and a firm commitment to see to it that the Federal Government is once more responsive to the people.

That concept is rooted in a strategy for growth, a program that sees the American economic system as it is—a huge, complex, dynamic system which demands not piecemeal Federal packages, or pious hopes wrapped in soothing words, but the hard work and concerted programs necessary for real growth.

We must first recognize that the problem with the U.S. economy is swollen, inefficient government, needless regulation, too much taxation, too much printing-press money. . . .

Our country is in a downward cycle of progressive economic deterioration that must be broken if the economy is to recover and move into a vigorous growth cycle in the 1980's.

We must move boldly, decisively and quickly to control the runaway growth of Federal spending, to remove the tax disincentives that are throttling the economy, and to reform the regulatory web that is smothering it.

We must have and I am proposing a new strategy for the 1980's.

Only a series of well-planned economic actions, taken so that they complement and reinforce one another, can move our economy forward again.

We must keep the rate of growth of government spending at reasonable and prudent levels.

We must reduce personal income tax rates and accelerate and simplify depreciation schedules in an orderly, systematic way to remove disincentives to work, savings, investment and productivity.

We must review regulations that affect the economy and change them to encourage economic growth.

We must establish a stable, sound and predictable monetary policy.

And we must restore confidence by following a consistent national economic policy that does not change from month to month. . . . We must balance the budget, reduce tax rates and restore our defenses. . . .

Let us look at how we can meet this challenge.

One of the most critical elements of my economic program is the control of government spending. Waste, extravagance, abuse and outright fraud in Federal agencies and programs must be stopped. Billions of the taxpayers' dollars are wasted every year throughout hundreds of Federal programs, and it will take a major, sustained effort over time to effectively counter this.

Federal spending is now projected to increase to over $900 billion a year by fiscal year 1985. But, through a comprehensive assault on waste and inefficiency, I am confident that we can squeeze and trim 2 percent out of the budget in fiscal year 1981, and that we will be able to increase this gradually to 7 percent of what otherwise would have been spent in fiscal year 1985.

Now this is based on projections that have been made by groups in the government. Actually I believe we can do even better. My goal will be to bring about spending reductions of 10 percent by fiscal year 1984. . . .

I already have as part of my advisory staff a Spending Control Task Force, headed by my good friend and former director of the Office of Management and Budget, Caspar Weinberger, that will report on additional ways and techniques to search out and eliminate waste, extravagance, fraud and abuse in Federal programs.

This strategy for growth does not require altering or taking back necessary entitlements already granted to the American people. The integrity of the Social Security System will be defended by my administration and its benefits will once again be made meaningful.

This strategy does require restraining the Congressional desire to "add-on" to every old program and to create new programs funded by deficits.

This strategy does require that the way Federal programs are administered will be changed so that we can benefit from the savings that will come about when, in some instances, administrative authority can be moved back to the states.

The second major element of my economic program is a tax rate reduction plan. This plan calls for an across-the-board, three-year reduction in personal income tax rates—10 percent in 1981, 10 percent in 1982 and 10 percent in 1983. My goal is to implement three reductions in a systematic and planned manner.

More than any single thing, high rates of taxation destroy incentive to earn, to save, to invest. And they cripple productivity, lead to deficit financing and inflation, and create unemployment.

We can go a long way toward restoring the economic health of this country by establishing reasonable, fair levels of taxation.

But even the extended tax rate cuts which I am recommending still leave too high a tax burden on the American people. In the second half of the decade ahead we are going to need, and we must have, additional tax rate reductions. . . .

Another vital part of this strategy concerns government regulation. The subject is so important and so complex that it deserves a speech in itself—and I plan to make one soon. For the moment, however, let me say this:

Government regulation, like fire, makes a good servant but a bad master. No one can argue with the intent of this regulation—to improve health and safety and to give us cleaner air and water—but too often regulations work against rather than for the interests of the people. When the real take-home pay of the average American worker is declining steadily, and 9 million Americans are out of work, we must carefully re-examine our regulatory structure to assess to what degree regulations have contributed to this situation. In my administration there should and will be a thorough and systematic review of the thousands of Federal regulations that affect the economy.

Along with spending control, tax reform and deregulation, a sound, stable and predictable monetary policy is essential to restoring economic health. The Federal Reserve Board is, and should remain, independent of the Executive Branch of government. But the President must nominate those who serve on the Federal Reserve Board. My appointees will share my commitment to restoring the value and stability of the American dollar.

A fundamental part of my strategy for economic growth is the restoration of confidence. If our business community is going to invest and build and create new, well-paying jobs, they must have a future free from arbitrary government action. They must have confidence that the economic "rules-of-the-game" won't be changed suddenly or capriciously.

In my administration, a national economic policy will be established, and we will begin to implement it, within the first 90 days.

Thus, I envision a strategy encompassing many elements—none of which can do the job alone, but all of which together can get it done. This strategy depends for its success more than anything else on the will of the people to regain control of their government.

It depends on the capacity of the American people for work, their willingness to do the job, their energy and their imagination.

This strategy of economic growth includes the growth that will come from the cooperation of business and labor based on their knowledge that government policy is directed toward jobs, toward opportunity, toward growth.

We are not talking here about some static, lifeless econometric model—we are talking about the greatest productive economy in human history, an economy that is historically revitalized not by government but by people free of government interference, needless regulations, crippling inflation, high taxes and unemployment....

When such a strategy is put into practice, our national defense needs can be met because the productive capacity of the American people will provide the revenues needed to do what must be done.

All of this demands a vision. It demands looking at government and the economy as they exist and not as words on paper, but as institutions guided by our will and knowledge toward growth, restraint and effective action....

The time has come for the American people to reclaim their dream. Things don't have to be this way. We can change them. We must change them. Mr. Carter's American tragedy must and can be transcended by the spirit of the American people, working together.

Let's get America working again.

The time is now.

FORTUNE
President Reagan's Economic Program
[December 1, 1980]

Soon after he takes office next January 20, President Ronald Reagan will have the pleasure of performing two simple acts of some practical and much symbolic importance. With a stroke of the pen, he will abolish wage and price guidelines. With another stroke, he will impose a federal hiring freeze. So much for dramatic openers, which will sustain for a while the contagious enthusiasm that is sweeping the American business community about Reagan's program to "put America back to work."

The more substantive parts of that program, involving as they do a profound change in the scope and direction of the federal budget and the government's role in the economy, can't begin to pay off in faster growth and lower inflation anytime soon. Reagan will need all his notable inspirational skills to convince the millions who voted for change that they will have to be patient about results.

The first major challenge for Reagan is the budget for fiscal 1981, which began October 1. He can hardly wait to tear into the $650-billion spending total that he inherits. His presumptive chief of staff, Edwin Meese III, has already announced that Reagan's department heads will be required to cut by 2% across the board—a saving of about $13 billion. That is probably doable, though Reagan may be accused of "impounding" appropriations, a charge that is hard to prove given the erratic pace of federal outlays. Lately they have been exceeding the budget at a $15-billion annual rate—and there lies the real difficulty for Reagan's budget cutters. One big item is higher interest costs, and another is defense, which Reagan wants to increase. So the outlook is that after vigorous pruning, spending in 1981 will end up only slightly below 1980 levels.

Reagan could compensate for that overrun by scaling down his tax cuts—as some of his advisers have urged him to do. But he is firmly committed to lopping personal rates by 10% next year. This . . . plus a modest $4-billion improvement in depreciation allowances for business, would cost $22 billion. In its election-year effort to achieve a more or less balanced budget, Congress hadn't allowed for any fiscal 1981 tax cuts, but it got a strong message from the voters. The likelihood is that Congress will give Reagan as big a reduction as he has asked for in personal taxes, without necessarily shaping the rate structure just as he would want it. Congress might actually sweeten the cuts for business, a proposition Reagan could find hard to refuse. Instead of the $18 billion Congress had planned on, the deficit will probably swell to at least $44 billion.

Given the already severe pressure on the financial markets, that seems clearly excessive. One hope for fiscal restraint is prolonged wrangling in the new and transformed Congress; if the tax cut doesn't pass until spring, the costs might be felt for only six months of fiscal 1981.

Reagan is counting on the Federal Reserve to bring the big guns to bear in the fight against inflation. Paul Volcker has already proved that he has the heart for the fight. In fact, he seems likely to push interest rates higher than business would like. The post-election spurt in rates mostly reflected pressures that were already at work in the markets, but even if rates should fall back for a while now, they will move up again as the Treasury weighs in with its huge credit demands.

In the short run, Reagan's budget package may worsen the outlook for inflation. The largest share of the tax cut goes to consumers, who are supposed to salt it away in savings. People in the upper-income brackets might do some of that, but the University of Michigan's Thomas Juster, the leading expert on consumer behavior, says that there won't be any sustained pickup in the savings rate until inflation subsides.

More consumer spending will be offset to some extent by the dampening effect of higher interest rates on housing and capital goods. Even so, the prospect is for somewhat stronger economic growth in the second half of 1981 than *Fortune* had expected—and somewhat more pressure on prices.

The basic inflation rate is already very high, driven by unit labor costs that have increased at a double-digit rate for the past year and a half. A main culprit driving up labor costs has been those steady declines in productivity. *Fortune* has assumed some productivity growth over the next year from a slowly improving economy, but strong gains will be a good while in coming, even if the new group of theorists are right in what they think a smaller government and less interference can do.

Meanwhile, the pace of hourly compensation could pick up. The guidelines have held wage rates down—perhaps by a percentage point, perhaps less, depending on which experts you believe. COLA [cost of living] adjustments were fattened in several big contracts this year, and on top of that, the January increases in Social Security taxes and the minimum wage will add nearly 1% to total compensation. So nothing looks likely to keep the hourly rate from moving up 10% again next year, and inflation nearly as much.

In fairness, no President could do much very soon about an inflation so deeply ingrained. Reagan, like Carter before him, will be pointing past the bad news to a bright longer term when his basic economic philosophy will turn things around. How valid is that promise?

As caricatured by his opponents, Reagan's approach is to shovel out money in tax cuts and wait for the sounder economy that will magically result. The Reagan program does assume some extra receipts generated by the economic effects of lowering taxes, but the growth dividend built into the projections is of modest and defensible proportions.

It should also be recognized that *any* U.S. President would be shoveling out tax cuts in the first half of the Eighties. If the tax law were left unchanged, that huge "windfall" bite on oil, plus the effects of bracket creep on personal taxes, would send a tidal wave of revenues to Washington. Without spelling out just how it would spread the blessing around, the Democratic Congress had projected cuts totaling $145 billion by the end of fiscal 1985 (that's in constant 1980 dollars). Reagan's program, to be sure, makes Congress look like a bunch of tightwads. He plans $375 billion in cuts.

Whether that is irresponsible and inflationary, as President Carter charged, depends on what happens on the spending side of the ledger. Reagan plans to increase defense outlays by at least 5% a year, and he has come out for weapons programs that would cost much more than that. Even if defense is held to a 5% real rise, nondefense spending would have to be pared back to 1975 levels in real terms to accommodate all the tax cuts and achieve a balanced budget. Reagan showed no taste for such Draconian measures when he was governor of California, and it is doubtful that he will hit his targets. Presumably, however, if he cuts spending less, he will also cut taxes less.

The other basic question concerns the very odd way Reagan would parcel out his cuts. No one has given more lip service than Reagan to the idea that business needs a break. But he would cut personal taxes $320 billion and business taxes by only $55 billion over his four-year term. Reagan's advisers say they aren't counting on the now suspect Keynesian notion that boosting consumption is the best way to get business to spend more on plant and equipment. Rather, by tilting personal tax cuts toward higher-income families, they hope to encourage savings, which in turn encourages capital investment. But in a period when the U.S. is saddled with a lot of antiquated plant and is having trouble competing in the world market, there is room to wonder whether the odd shape of this tax package will stand the test of time.

That same observation applies to Reagan economics as a whole. His program represents something of a compromise between the tax cutters like Arthur Laffer and the traditionalists like Alan Greenspan—both of whom had the candidate's ear. Presumably, the cheers that went up last week from the business community were for the general direction of the program toward less government and a stronger private economy—not for the fine print of a long-term budget that will be subject to change.

MARTIN CARNOY AND DEREK SHEARER
Reaganomics: The Supply Side of the Street
[*Nation*, November 7, 1981]

In one year, the Reagan Administration and a compliant Congress have legislated the most significant income redistribution since the 1930s. This time, however, the shift was from the poor and the working class to the rich. The redistribution has been accomplished by transferring resources from the public to the private sector. Thus, Reaganomics does not really mean getting the government off people's backs; it means repealing the hard-won social gains of the past fifty years and using the government to transfer money to large corporations, high-income earners and military contractors....

Women, minorities and poor people have a different view of Reaganomics.

Military spending is being increased to "restore" American power abroad and to create jobs at home. The Administration claims that the planned elimination of 300,000 Federal jobs will be offset by 1984 through an increase in private-sector employment in the defense industry. Yet the people who stand to lose their jobs are not the ones who will be hired by industry. Government employment primarily benefits professional women (both white and black) and professional minority men (about 50 percent of these two groups worked at all levels of government in the 1970s). Indeed, since 1950, increased public spending has been the single most important impetus behind the greater economic mobility of women and minority men. Defense contractors will hire some women and minorities, but few of them at the professional level. Large corporations have a dismal record on this score. They are dominated at the highest echelons by white males, and there is no reason to believe that, in the current political atmosphere, this will change. Not only will the budget cuts directly affect poor women, blacks and Hispanics but they will slow or halt their long-term economic advancement. Instead, white male skilled workers, engineers and executives will benefit, especially those working for large corporations in the Sun Belt.

If the trade-off of fewer social benefits for more corporate profits is to be made palatable to the majority of Americans, they must gain increased purchasing power. If this does not happen, Reagan's program will be politically bankrupt, and the question he asked in the 1980 Presidential debates—"Are you better off now than you were four years ago?"—will return to haunt him in 1984.

American workers' real wages have declined by 12 percent between 1978 and 1980 and by 18 percent since 1973.... Adding to the average family's economic woes are continuing high interest rates, which have undermined the American dream of owning a home and buying a new car every year or so. If the erosion of real income goes on, the short-term outlook for most Americans' standard of living is bleak.

According to supply-side economics, the problem with the economy is that people are not saving or investing enough. Furthermore, productivity is not rising because of government intervention in the economy. Finally, people don't want to work because of high taxes, and inflation is rampant because of too much public spending. The supply-siders claim that redistributing income upward will induce more saving, more investment and greater productivity, all of which will lead to higher growth rates, increased wages, lower inflation and a balanced budget.

Unfortunately for those with dreams of a Republican dynasty based on permanent prosperity, the economic problems are real, but the supply-side assumptions are illusory.

The supply-side hypothesis that lower income taxes will induce people to work harder, produce more and save more is not supported by the facts. For instance, a family making $25,000 a year will be entitled to a $400 tax refund in 1982 and one of about $800 in 1984. But since real wages will continue to decline, this family will probably use their tax savings to maintain their current standard of living. . . .

The supply-siders' theory that tax savings will be plowed back into productive, job-creating activities is also not supported by the facts. Many corporations are currently using their anticipated savings from the new rules on depreciation to establish new lines of credit to acquire other companies. Oil companies, which account for more than one-quarter of all private profit, are seeking to monopolize other resources by buying into coal, copper and shale. Consolidation rather than expansion is the dominant corporate strategy. Capital flight continues as manufacturers move abroad. The major source of new capital is public investment in defense industries.

Also implicit in the supply-side recipe for economic abundance is the proposition that corporations will pass on lower costs from lower taxes and improved productivity to the consumer rather than increase their own profits. That prospect is unlikely, however, since any savings from lower taxes will be offset by high interest rates. But even if interest rates should fall, many businesses would like to return to "normal" profits of 16 percent to 18 percent, which they made during the 1960s, as opposed to the 11 percent to 13 percent rate of the 1970s. Re-establishment of high profits is the heart of Reaganomics, and it can only mean continued "profit-push" inflation.

The final article of faith in the supply-side creed is that large private corporations are fundamentally efficient. Once government regulations are lifted and taxes lowered, the line goes, they will expand sales, hire more workers and beat their foreign competitors. Reaganomics is based, in large part, on the belief that only the large corporations can revitalize the American economy. Yet costly mistakes by the managers of some of these large corporations—for example, in the tire, automobile and steel industries—have been a major cause of the nation's economic decline. . . .

Supply-side measures will create an economy heavily weighted toward military production, turning out goods that cannot be consumed. The well-paid workers in defense industries will create inflationary pressures. As a result, overall real wages must continue to fall so that total demand is held in check. This means squeezing unions and forcing workers to accept lower wage settlements.

President Reagan has said that anyone who has a better plan should step forward. . . . There is a workable alternative. . . . To check inflation, at least in the short run, wage and price controls should be imposed on the largest corporations. Welfare expenditures could be reduced by planning for full employment and a strong defense without massive spending for elephantine carrier fleets, outdated bombers and unnecessary missile systems. Energy costs could be contained by establishing a government-run corporation with complete control over oil imports—a kind of national oil purchasing firm—and by aggressive conservation measures combined with a search for renewable energy sources. Health-care costs could be stabilized through a comprehensive national health insurance plan coupled with tough oversight procedures. Public funds could be channeled into the construction of nonluxury housing, schools, roads, bridges and railroads.

Banks should be directed, through selective credit controls, to invest in those sectors where the ratio of capital investment to job creation is the most favorable. Tax reform should close such loopholes as the deductions on interest taken by speculators in real estate and commodities. Sensible tax reform should actually increase taxes on high incomes. State and local governments, as well as the Federal government, should play a more *direct* role in expanding employment through the purposeful use of public funds, particularly pension funds, to launch new public enterprises.

The failure of Reaganomics will show that far from being the cause of our economic difficulties, government is the last best hope for a democratic revival of the economy—one that will make it both more equitable and more productive.

ST. LOUIS GLOBE-DEMOCRAT
The 1983 Budget: A Courageous Document
[February 9, 1982]

In assessing President Reagan's proposed 1983 budget, it is essential to understand much more than the actual numbers involved.

Contrary to what certain Democrats are saying, Reagan has presented a well thought out proposal. It is a courageous document in that the president is sticking to his course of cutting back the growth in federal spending, reducing taxes, trimming the regulatory burden, and rebuilding the nation's defenses.

Proposed spending for fiscal 1983 is $757.6 billion, which is only about 4.5 percent above the $725 billion for 1982. This is a marked improvement over budgets during the Carter administration that soared each year by more than 10 percent.

If this is so, why is the projected deficit $91.5 billion?

There are a number of factors responsible for this.

First is the recession which is reducing revenues. This recession was not of Reagan's making. It stemmed primarily from double-digit inflation, excessive government growth, overtaxing, excessive money creation and overregulation that his administration inherited after a generation of deficit spending.

Second is Reagan's program for reducing taxes (which includes a 10 percent rate cut for individuals starting July 1) and providing other incentives for restoring badly needed economic growth. If he was not a man of great resolve who believes his supply-side program will work, Reagan might have buckled and called for a delay or elimination of the planned tax cuts. But the president knows that it will take time for the tax-incentive program to take effect, and he is holding to his course.

Third is the need to greatly strengthen the Armed Services that were badly neglected for more than a decade prior to Reagan's arrival. Reagan is calling for a 10.5 percent increase in defense spending (after adjustment for inflation) that will strengthen the military in four primary areas: Strategic forces, combat readiness, force mobility and general purpose capabilities.

It addresses many dangerous deficiencies. It calls for major improvements such as: A much greater ability to fight sustained conflicts; a big increase in naval power to make up for years of attrition; new flexibility and mobility of all the services, including development of a Rapid Deployment Force; much improved communications and warning systems; construction of new strategic weapons such as the B-1 bomber, MX missile system, and deployment of cruise missiles on bombers and attack submarines. All the elements are aimed at offsetting an enormous Soviet buildup in huge ICBMs, missile-launching submarines, and long-range bombers.

Basically, Reagan should get the essential elements in this defense package. But, like all other programs in the budget, defense spending should be closely examined for possible elimination of unnecessary or wasteful programs.

While the $91.5 billion deficit is large it may not be nearly as inflationary as such a deficit might have been under previous policies. The reason for this is that the Reagan policy of encouraging greater savings and profits probably will make it possible to finance virtually all of this deficit from the private sector, obviating the necessity of the Federal Reserve creating large amounts of new money to cover the deficit as it has in the past when federal policies actually discouraged savings and profits.

Thus while Reagan's policy of encouraging economic growth by reducing taxes has added to the short-term deficit problem, this policy coupled with his program of reducing the growth of federal spending should pave the way for a strong economic expansion and the long-sought balanced budget.

It is a departure from the perennially unsuccessful short-term gimmickry under which Democrats tried year after year to create jobs and bolster the economy by pouring out tens of billions of dollars for make-work projects and new welfare programs, inducing the Federal Reserve to unleash a flood of fiat money to pay for a great part of this inflationary binge.

SIDNEY WEINTRAUB
The [1983] Budget: Guns Up, People Down
[New Leader, February 22, 1982]

Thumbing his nose at his own long and uninformed babbling about the economy, Ronald Reagan is destined as President to become king of the deficit-makers and undisputed master of the national debt mountain. John Wayne and Bela Lugosi, in their respectively macho and fiendish movie incarnations, would have undoubtedly applauded the "Guns Up, People Down" Reagan budget for fiscal 1983....

The main features of the budget were spread in the press two days before their transmittal to Congress ... [but] what the press has missed are the absurd ideological fantasies interred within the so-called Budget Message. Truth-shading abounds; the Presidential ghosts have an extraordinary aptitude for overlooking facts, with the technical advisers craven enough to inject outrageous rhetoric on issues where reasonable judgments can differ. The clear flip-flop on deficits was manifestly too big to hide; intellectually distressing, however, are the self-serving assertions on the merits of fiscal shortfalls under Republican auspices and the demerits in Democrat hands. Those passages are not merely partisan by-play, they are malodorously deceptive. The expenditure centerpiece tots up to $757.6 billion, . . . while revenues weigh in at $666.1 billion, a very exact number likely to have little relation to the actual tax-take. That will depend upon the start of the economy in 1983, and the foreshadowed course of interest rates indicates the recovery will be anemic, not robust, compelling higher unemployment and welfare outlay plus slenderized tax collections.

The discrepancy between the expenditure and revenue figures translates into the $91.5 billion deficit that has traumatized the conservative Reagan Regulars. Of course, the President extols his deficits as an act of statecraft, strutting out on the hustings to challenge others ''to put up or shut up.'' Obvious alternatives that occur instantly are to defer some tax cuts for his cronies, alter some of the queer corporate investment-credit tax rules, and install an Incomes Policy to ease the monetary stand-off that is taking us down disaster road and, among other things, ensuring a massive future housing shortage. Only Hollywood speech writers could inject so sterile a platform ploy into presumably substantive Presidential remarks.

Our never wasteful, never extravagant military—tell that to anyone who has served in our Armed Forces—is slated to grab $216 billion, an increase of 18 percent. Between military and interest outlays, given the incredible Reagan interest rate mismanagement, 42 per cent of the budget sums is absorbed, with the military taking 29 and interest charges 13 per cent. The interest statistic is understated, based as it is on the ''assumption'' that short-term Treasury bills, will yield about 10.5 per cent despite the present 14.5 per cent range. Don't wager more than a penny on this calculation, for this Administration's predictions have been as shrewd as those of the man who continually bets that temperatures in Buffalo will be lower in July than in January.

Other budget allotments follow the Reagan non-compassion pattern: Education, down nearly 15 per cent (on top of the inflation erosion); mass transportation lopped by 38 per cent, highway funds out 21 per cent, Amtrak 30 per cent. Reagan never rides trains and his limos avoid potholes. This is a magnificent example of a ''think-small'' aldermanic approach to a great country's potential. Reagan's New Old Federalism involves a vision of a public sector about the size of a Mom and Pop store. Up with bigger Duponts, Mobils, IBMs, United States Steels, and other sprawling corporate giants to safeguard the public interest. One has to wonder how conservatives can call this theology a realistic political philosophy.

Housing and Urban Development and the Labor Department would be chopped by 10 and 17 per cent, respectively; apparently our cities are already flourishing. Food stamps, which always make Reagan choleric, would drop by 10 per cent; perhaps the President has found a new cheater in Chicago—or is it in Orange County this time, among his rich friends? Welfare payments down, to $5.4 billion from $7.8. Drawing on the experience of his arduous work life as a sports announcer, movie actor and TV hawker, states would be required to exact work from welfare recipients. Shades of the WPA under FDR! Will we see news clips of leaf raking?...

To accompany these joyous tidings for the underclass, the Stockman office has provided tables and charts on GNP, consumer prices and budget sums way out to 1987. That may be a good year for California wine but the projections are a hoax, wholly wasteful of taxpayer money. Who, in the entire Stockman office, can predict a single stock on Wall Street that will rise, say, 3 points this afternoon? Yet this garbage gets "debated." Econometricians thrive on the nonsense—and charge while they change their predictions almost daily.

Presidential pronouncements notwithstanding, there is certain to be "tampering" with the sacrosanct Reagan-Stockman-Regan numbers. They will bear faint resemblance to the final facts, because the sums just don't add up. They are based on optimistic forecasts for inflation, for production and job growth, for interest rate declines. One statement in the purported "serious" Budget Message is enough to discredit them: Referring to the present recession, the President claimed "this factor alone accounts for nearly all of the difference between the $45 billion 1982 deficit we projected last year and our current estimate of $98.6 billion." So after going astray by 120 per cent in last year's forecast, Reagan wants us to take the new "document" as gospel, and to serve as starch for his fund-raising electioneering tour. The Great Communicator has no conception of his abject confession of blundering. . . .

In one of his TV spectaculars, the President gains much mileage by scaring us with a tale on the dizzy heights reached by a stack of $1 bills depicting the $1 trillion dollar debt. He could have made the pile more than 100 times higher by using pennies, or brought the heap closer to earth by borrowing $1,000 or $10,000 bills from his rich cronies. But no matter. The point is that "this President," as the new pomping has it, will go down as doing more to enlarge the national debt than any President in our history.

FDR was a piker by Deficit-Ronnie standards. Between 1933-40 the New Deal spender added about $20 billion to the national debt. Including World War II, the ascent was about $235 billion. Reagan will dash ahead by $350 billion on the Regan-Stockman estimates, and by about $650 billion according to the CBO figures. Either way, Reagan will stand out luminously in our debt annals—if he is given his head.

Obviously Democratic administrations have tolerated deficits, and it would be hypocritical of liberals to contend that the sky is falling because of the renegade Reagan's numbness on numbers. Yet there is a difference that can be profound, even if a full analysis must be deferred. In most of the Democratic instances, the deficit was run in concert with a stimulative and expansionary monetary policy to increase jobs and production, and at very low interest rates compared to today's legalized loan-sharking. Moreover, in the 1930s and the 1960s the inflation ingredient was absent, and during the War years wage and price controls prevailed.

The Reagan deficits, in contrast, collide with a monetary policy designed to *prevent* strong economic recovery. The Federal Reserve's keeping interest rates near historic highs will block jobs and output, and maintain the housing, steel and auto industries in their current state of shambles—or at best allow a modest uptick....

Reagan further declares that "the inflation spiral has been broken." Of course, on the backs of the jobless. He could go all the way by creating a Great Depression. Herbert Hoover was expert in bringing down prices, too. Republicans have a knack for enduring pain inflicted on plain folks. On inflation, Reagan has clambered to the other end of the stagflation teeter-totter; nevertheless, prices are still rising too fast.

To justify his approach, Reagan chatters away about his "mandate," meaning his squeaky 51 per cent vote margin over the combined Carter-Anderson 49 per cent. Skeptics will not see this as a blank check. Nor will they be deluded by his harping on the fact that "it is impossible in a short period of time to correct the mistakes of decades."

Since the close of World War II, beginning with Truman in 1948, we have had eight Presidential terms. Four of them were Democratic, four Republican. Is Reagan denouncing Eisenhower and Nixon-Ford? Or is this just Hollywood speaking, without concern for the facts? Many of us see most of the period, until about 1967 or so, as an era of spectacular growth to affluence—until the blight of the Republican Nixon epoch, nudged on by Ford and propelled by Carter into the stagflation ordeal. Rhetoric comes easy, and facts seem out of style in the Reagan White House....

The Reagan yearning for pony express politics in the computerized nuclear age is bound to muddle the dialogue over the next few years. Quips will fool some of the people some of the time, but in the end good ideas are unlikely to be denied by the demagogic uses of the TV screen. Faith in the good sense of the American people has seldom been misplaced, despite frequent lapses in political judgment.

[Reprinted with permission of *The New Leader.* Copyright © 1982 the American Labor Conference on International Affairs, Inc.]

The Later Years

As Reagan's term ended, observers and economic analysts assessed his economic impact one last time. Concluding that Reagan's 1988 budget perpetuated the doubletalk and faulty assumptions of its predecessors, the Democratic Kansas City Times *wrote a terse epitaph for his annual budget exercises: "disgraceful." Princeton economist Uwe Reinhardt, in a 1987* New Republic *piece, pointed out that the spending binge that gave the Reagan years a glow of prosperity had been built on the back of a massive trade deficit, and thus had been financed by a vast outflow of I.O.U.s. Future generations, Reinhardt warned, would ultimately have to pay the bills for the festival of consumer spending in the 1980s.*

A detailed article in the business magazine Forbes *in October 1988 employed a question-and-answer format and a mass of statistics and charts (not reproduced here) to examine the performance of the U.S. economy in the Reagan years. Federal budget deficits, the national debt, and private debt had all increased markedly during Reagan's watch, it concluded, but not so alarmingly when viewed relative to the gross national product and to the experience of other industrialized nations in the same period. The trade deficit, too,* Forbes *acknowledged, had bulged in the 1980s, but "trade deficits come and go"; when Americans had had more experience in world trade, it suggested, short-term fluctuations might not loom so large. As for Reagan's pledge to reduce government regulation, a matter of such concern to business,* Forbes *resorted to counting pages in the Federal Register (a compilation of all rules and notices issued by federal agencies) to argue that regulation had indeed declined in the early 1980s, but then had stabilized at about the level of 1975. Overall, this* Forbes *assessment pictured an economy far less influenced by Reagan than the missionary zeal of his rhetoric would have suggested.*

KANSAS CITY TIMES
Happy Talk
[January 8, 1987]

President Reagan has long treated his annual budget proposal to Congress as nothing more than a cynical exercise in public relations. He has sought to duck blame for huge deficits by repeatedly proposing the reduction or elimination of federal programs both popular and necessary. Meanwhile, administration officials have employed as many accounting gimmicks and bogus economic projections as necessary to make their plans seem reasonable.

There had been hopes that this year would be different. Some thought that Reagan, with an eye toward history, might be different. No such luck.

He has made a few concessions to fiscal and political reality. The president still wants defense to get a hefty increase over inflation, but it is the smallest such increase he has ever sought. He also has proposed billions of dollars in what amount to tax increases for certain individuals and corporations.

But the only real point of disagreement in Washington seems to be whether this budget is a carbon copy of its predecessors or "a badly smudged Xerox." Either way, lawmakers are dismissing it as unrealistic.

Contrary to popular belief, the president is a big spender, and not just on defense. This week he approved pay raises ranging up to 16 percent for federal officials. His budget calls for more money for AIDS research. Reagan wants more money for law enforcement and science programs. He wants hundreds of millions of dollars for a new program to help American workers who have lost their jobs. During his tenure in the White House, the budget has grown by hundreds of billions of dollars; this latest budget punches through the $1 trillion mark.

Much of this spending is worthwhile. But the problem is the president's refusal to pay for either new programs or the ones already in place. Far from raising the money to do so, he has played the demagogue, hounding Congress for income tax cuts year after year.

It has been a disgraceful performance for a national leader, mitigated only by the willingness of lawmakers to pass income tax cuts. Everyone in Washington gives lip service to the deficit, of course. Congress weeps regularly over it. Reagan's budget message acknowledges that the deficit remains "a major threat to our future prosperity."

But the White House answer is happy talk. As Reagan sees it, there's no need to worry about the next recession because he thinks—incredibly—that there will not be another one in the foreseeable future. As for the deficit, he said, "this year there appears to be a major turn for the better." How many times have we heard that before?

The answer is not further cuts in programs for the less fortunate members of society. Federal cuts have already devastated them, and forced state and local governments to increase their taxes to take care of the resulting problems.

To make the numbers meet Gramm-Rudman deficit reduction targets, the administration is relying increasingly on proposed sales of federal assets. Such sales, which Reagan once opposed, are one-time shots in the arm, some of which may cost the government money in the long run.

The only real answer is an income tax increase. But that's the one thing

Reagan refuses to even discuss, no matter how gently more responsible national leaders try to broach the subject. This refusal makes a mockery of his professed willingness to work with Congress.

[Reprinted courtesy *The Kansas City Times.*]

UWE E. REINHARDT
Reaganomics, R.I.P.
[*New Republic,* April 20, 1987]

As the Congressional Budget Office observes in its latest *Economic and Budget Outlook,* published in January, a verdict on Reaganomics boils down to the question of justice between generations. Our fiscal policy since 1981 has allowed people living today to enjoy higher consumption at the expense of those who will be living tomorrow.

It is not clear whether President Reagan actually meant to throw this party or whether things simply got out of hand, as seems to happen so often in his reign. He achieved the presidency through eloquent denunciations of "big-spending government," while more sophisticated Reaganites attacked decades of "Keynesian demand management." By "demand management" they meant federal policies that sought to tease added employment and economic growth out of the economy through added government expenditures, or through transfer programs that channeled income from well-to-do individuals who would have saved and invested it to lower-income groups who spent it on consumption. That fiscal policy, it was argued, treated much too cavalierly the supply side of the economy whence economic growth actually springs.

In 1979, when these "supply-side" complaints were reaching a crescendo, about 62.8 percent of America's total national output was absorbed by personal consumption. About 18 percent went for private investment. About 19 percent was spent by all levels of government to run their operations. Finally, a very tiny sliver—0.1 percent of real GNP—represented the excess of investments of Americans abroad over investments by foreigners made here.

Only 18 percent for private investment is low by international standards. In fact, it is the lowest in the industrialized world. Nations enjoying more rapid growth set aside a much larger proportion of their GNP for the replacement and enhancement of their capital stock. In Japan, for example, the percentage has tended to be in the mid-30s; in West Germany it has tended to be in the mid-20s.

The key element of any supply-side strategy, therefore, must be to reduce the share of GNP going to consumption and government, in order to increase the share set aside for capital formation—a set-aside also known as gross domestic saving. A second element is encouragement of the nation's entrepreneurs to avail themselves of these savings and to invest them wisely. A third and much overlooked element ought to be developing an accounting system that splits the government's share into expenditures that are truly in the nature of consumption and those that are truly in the nature of long-term investments—for example, the building of a physical infrastructure or the education and training of the nation's future labor force, a process properly labeled by economists as "human-capital formation." Reaganite propaganda encourages us to think of all government spending (except for defense) as consumption, or simple waste. It is an expensive mistake, as our aging public infrastructure demonstrates.

By the nature of the task, any true supply-side strategy will be multifaceted and complex. Unfortunately, in the late 1970s, and in the presidential campaign of 1980, that task was depicted as child's play in the alluring teachings of a new cult led by the economist Arthur Laffer, its affable and verbally facile guru. The cult's message was spread by an equally facile troop of proselytes, some of whom had developed both their verbal skills and the requisite hauteur as writers for the *Wall Street Journal*'s supercilious editorial page.

To accomplish the desired shift of resources from consumption into capital formation, the Laffer cult offered a simple and politically appealing strategy: an across-the-board cut in federal income tax rates. The cut in income tax rates would lead to such outbursts of added taxable economic activity that tax revenues would actually increase. American entrepreneurs, enticed by the prospect of higher after-tax rewards, would employ new armies of workers, themselves enticed to work (or to work longer hours) by higher after-tax wages. For capital, the reborn entrepreneurs could count on massive infusions of new savings. These savings would come from American consumers, encouraged by higher after-tax interest rates to cancel planned dinners and vacations for the sake of saving for a better future. (Some members of the cult talked of a doubling of savings as a share of disposable income.) The capital pool would be supplemented by higher business savings made possible by higher after-tax profits.

And, finally, there would be positive government savings at long last. Because the cut in tax rates would raise total federal revenues, the cult assured us, the federal budget would be balanced by 1984. Along with the traditional surpluses of state and local governments, a balanced federal budget would make for a positive contribution to the pool of savings by government as a whole.

Five years later, the sad conclusion of the story can be read right off the many tables included in the *Economic Report of the President*, delivered to Congress in January. Did the pent-up economic energy gush forth as President Reagan and his supply-side cultists had predicted? Did Americans save and invest a larger slice of their GNP? Did legions of hitherto slumbering American entrepreneurs crawl out of the woodwork? And were new jobs created in unprecedented numbers?

Let's begin with a look at the federal budget. Reagan's record can fairly be described as replacing the much-derided policy of "tax and tax, spend and spend" with a policy of "spend even more and just borrow." Combined with an inexorable upward drift in federal spending, the 1981-83 tax cut triggered federal budget deficits that now exceed $200 billion a year. This deficit grew even as the economy recovered from the deep recession of 1982-83. To hope that it will gradually melt away without either substantial tax increases or painful reductions in federal expenditures—spending cuts of a size that Reagan himself has never even dared to propose—is a pipe dream.

It has been suggested that the administration deliberately triggered the large deficits to pressure Congress into overall spending cuts. If that was the strategy, it failed. To be sure, some federal outlays were curbed. There have been cuts in federal support for students and for research, for example, and near-poor working mothers lost their food stamps, welfare, and Medicaid. But for every dollar thus saved, several new dollars were spent. Outlays on national defense almost doubled from $157 billion in 1981 to $273.4 billion in 1986. Interest on the federal debt doubled from $68.7 billion in 1981 to $136 billion in 1986.

Instinctively reluctant to take on any politically powerful group, the president capitulated pre-emptively to the aged, promising rich and poor alike that their path to the federal treasury would remain unobstructed. That promise was kept. Between 1981 and 1986, Social Security benefits increased from $138 billion to almost $200 billion, while outlays on Medicare almost doubled from $41 billion to $74 billion. . . . The president capitulated pre-emptively to the farm lobby as well. In the late 1970s the federal farm-price support program absorbed about $4 billion. By 1986 that figure had risen to $26 billion and was heading higher.

A theme vigorously marketed by the president and by his political allies, such as the editors of the *Wall Street Journal*, is that Congress bears sole responsibility for the inexorable upward march of federal expenditures. . . .

In fact, as the *Wall Street Journal* itself reported in January, Reagan asked Congress to approve expenditures of $4.307 trillion for fiscal years 1982-86 and Congress actually approved $4.342 trillion—only some $35 billion more over five years. In other words, those "big spenders on the Hill" spent less than one percent more than Reagan himself wanted to spend. To be sure, Congress and the president differed over the allocation of the total, as might be expected in a democracy. But the overall budget record demolishes the fantasy of a president valiantly seeking to control a big-spending Congress.

What of that proverbial national pie, the GNP? Did Reaganomics realign the slices in the manner envisaged by the Laffer cult? . . . Let's compare the pie of 1979—the depths of Carterite malaise—with the pie of 1986. The slice of GNP going to personal consumption has *increased* by three percentage points, from 62.8 percent in 1979 to 65.8 percent in 1986. The government's slice also has increased, by 1.3 percentage points, from 19.1 percent to 20.4 percent. The only slice that hasn't increased is the "supply-side" slice—gross private domestic investment.

How could two slices increase, the third not change, and the whole thing still add up to one whole pie? It doesn't. In 1986 total domestic spending by Americans on personal consumption, private investment, and government operations added up to 104 percent of GNP. That is, what we spent on goods and services in 1986 exceeded by four percent (or $150 billion in constant 1982 dollars) what we produced. The extra four percent came from the oft-vilified Japanese, and from the Canadians, Germans, and other nations with whom we are running a trade deficit. . . . The foreigners exported us machine tools, Walkmans, BMWs, and fine wines, and we exported to them in return American-made IOUs (bonds and notes) or simply legal titles to American assets (real estate or stock certificates). Unhappily for our children, they will have to redeem these pieces of paper with goods and services some time in the future. Should our children refuse, we shall then redeem the IOUs by simply transferring to foreigners legal title to real assets our kids would otherwise have inherited.

There is nothing wrong with importing capital. Foreign capital helped develop this nation in the last century, and it can help us now. If we had avoided huge government deficits and increased our domestic investment beyond the traditional 18 percent, our children would have plenty of extra money to service the foreign debt and to be better off themselves. But we used the foreign capital to increase our consumption and government spending, not our investment. . . .

Meanwhile, what of America's entrepreneurs? Has our festival inspired them to new achievements? Reliable data on the penchant for entrepreneurship are not easily had. The president's report to Congress does contain a table on business formation and failures. It shows that between 1980 and 1986 there were actually fewer new business incorporations each year than in 1976-80. Business failures, on the other hand, increased each year during the 1980s. In the late 1970s the annual rate of failure decreased. The Index of Net Business Formation (1967 = 100) ranged in the high 130s during the late 1970s; it stood at only 121 in 1984-85.

In 1980 the civilian unemployment rate stood at 7.1 percent. In 1986 it stood at 7.0 percent. Now, it has been argued that the unemployment rate is too negative a concept, because it obscures the astounding number of new jobs created during the Reagan era. Was the number really astounding? According to the president's report, total civilian employment stood at 100.4 million in 1981 and at 109.6 million in 1986, a gain of 9.2 percent or 9.2 million jobs. During the preceding five-year period total civilian employment grew from 88.8 million to 100.4 million—a gain of 13 percent, or 11.6 million new jobs. . . .

Not all facets of the president's economic program have been equally dubious. Inflation has been soundly licked, thanks in part to President Carter's wisdom in appointing Paul Volcker as chairman of the Federal Reserve Board, but also thanks to Reagan's steadfast support of brother Volcker. President Reagan continued the program of deregulation already set in motion by his predecessor in energy and transportation, and he extended it to the financial markets. And Reagan has given strong rhetorical support to the principles of free trade, although the actual share of our imports that are affected by some sort of trade restriction has doubled from 1980 to 1986, from 12 percent to 22 percent.

The peculiar free-lunch populism sold to the nation as "supply-side economics" may be summarized in the following flaky propositions: (1) cutting tax rates increases (government) revenue; (2) inflation can be reduced without a transitional period of unemployment; (3) government expenditures can be greatly reduced without sacrifice of anything by anyone except bureaucrats and welfare queens. The Republic won't collapse because our leaders sold the public on these transparently false propositions—and possibly even believed them themselves. We will simply be left a little poorer in the long run than we could have been under less myopic stewardship. For, whatever Reaganomics may have been, it was not supply-side economics. It was politics as usual, practiced to please or at least not to offend powerful political constituencies, and pushed just one step further in the direction of irresponsibility.

Will the party soon have to end? Actually, we may go on for a while. As long as other nations are willing to add dollar-denominated American IOUs to their portfolios, we can continue to live happily beyond our means. After all, what do we really mean by "means"? Like many spendthrifts, our means include wealth as well as income. And we remain a wealthy country. Should foreigners tire of holding our IOUs, they might still be happy to take legal title to our income-yielding real assets—as they already are busily doing. And we've got plenty of those. Even sections of Hawaii still remain on our books, and there's Fifth Avenue in New York, and the whole state of Oregon. Why not liquidate some of these assets and live it up a little longer?

An alternative would be to go back to square one and to balance the government's books. During 1980-86, net private savings—roughly, the amount of investable funds available after replacement of worn-out capital— has averaged 6.2 percent of GNP (down from 8.1 percent in 1970-79). Savings by state and local governments brought the total available savings pool to 7.5 percent of GNP. The federal deficit alone drained 4.1 percent of GNP from the pool—that is, more than half of it—leaving only 3.4 percent of GNP for net private capital formation beyond the replacement of worn-out capital. We did, as noted, supplement that meager pool by tapping the savings of foreigners through borrowing and the sale of real assets. If that is to cease, we must either bring the federal budget closer into balance or start saving a lot more—that is, start consuming less—as individuals.

PETER BRIMELOW WITH LISA SCHEER
Is the Reagan Prosperity for Real?
[*Forbes*, October 31, 1988]

There are lies, damned lies and statistics, said British Prime Minister Benjamin Disraeli. Many American voters would heartily endorse his sentiment in this year of electoral econobabble. . . . To help clarify matters, FORBES offers the following . . . , designed to answer the important question of how the American economy has performed during the Reagan era, and to shed light on various popular perceptions and myths. . . .

Why did the federal deficit increase during the Reagan years?
The answer is instantly obvious: Tax revenues were not significantly cut—spending rose. Total federal government receipts were 19.4% of GNP in 1980, and they are expected to be 19.3% in 1988, toward the high end of their historic range. But federal spending reached a peacetime peak of 24.3% of GNP in the postrecession year of 1983 and will probably still be about 22.4% in 1988. Despite the alleged Stockman slashes, federal spending remains above its 1946-80 levels even though there's no Korean or Vietnam war going on. Reagan has not decisively reversed the drift to bigger federal government that emerged in the mid-1970s.

Note that despite all the hoopla about tax cuts, federal revenue from taxes on individual income is still undulating gracefully in its post-World War II range of 8% to 9% of GNP. Income tax revenue did briefly swell up to 9.6% of GNP in the pre-tax-cut year of 1981 because of "bracket creep"—unlegislated tax increases as inflation propelled millions into higher tax brackets without increasing their purchasing power. But this level of income tax revenues was exceptional, the highest since 1944. . . .

Defense spending, which includes pensions and benefits to retirees, is not the key factor in federal expenditure growth: It has indeed risen post-Carter as a percentage of GNP, but it remains far below its Eisenhower-Kennedy peacetime peaks.

So what about those Reagan deficits? Measured against GNP, they are broadly comparable to the deficits of the Depression. But of course they are nowhere near as large relative to the federal budget, since the federal government was so much smaller in the 1930s. And neither set of deficits is anywhere close to those run during World War II, which peaked at 31.6% of GNP in 1943.

Placing the federal deficits in the context of overall GNP reduces them to scale. Thus in 1988, when the federal deficit-to-GNP ratio is expected to be 3.1%, GNP itself seems likely to grow about 4% and inflation is running at 4.1%. So, if federal spending were merely held constant in nominal terms for just over two years, the deficit could be wiped out.

How serious is the deficit problem?

The U.S. federal deficit alone is a misleading number. In many countries, central governments perform many functions, such as education, that in the U.S. are devolved to the state and local levels. To get a true picture of the deficit problem, all these levels should be added together to produce the "general government" budget. Since state and local governments tend to run surpluses, the U.S. general government budget can be in balance overall even with a deficit at the federal level.

Which has happened as recently as 1978. This was a sharp recovery from 1975, when the general government deficit of 4.1% of GNP was noticeably higher than the peak Reagan general government deficit of 3.8% in 1983. Even as far back as 1958 the U.S. general government deficit reached 2.8% before rebounding to a surplus in 1960.

And despite continual loud harrumphs of disapproval from the other major industrialized countries, the U.S. general government deficit relative to GNP does not actually appear to be much out of line with their own performances. . . .

Has the government role in the U.S. economy been reduced?

The answer here is stark: Far from being rolled back during the Reagan era, government spending appears to have consolidated its share of GNP at a point even higher than the gains it achieved in the Carter years. In 1986, the last year available, it amounted to a record 36.9%.

This is an important unreported story. There has been a very modest reduction in the federal government's share of GNP since the peak year of 1983, although it is still higher than in 1980. But this reduction has been more than counterbalanced by growth in state and local spending.

Of course, the total government role in the U.S. economy is still low compared to the situation in most other industrialized economies. In 1986 government in the welfare states of Western Europe took as much as 46.6% (Germany), to say nothing of Italy's 50.5%. But government in Japan takes significantly less than in the U.S. (33.1%).

Still, it should perhaps be noted that even the formidable Margaret Thatcher hasn't made much headway in reducing government share of GNP in the U.K. At 46.2% in 1986, it was only slightly below its peak of 48%, which it reached in the high-unemployment year of 1984.

Something else is clear: New spending programs in Washington would not be a mere matter of restoring cuts in government expenditure made during the Reagan era. They would boldly expand the government share of U.S. GNP into territory where no politician has been except in time of war.

How burdensome is the U.S. national debt?

Gross federal debt—the "national debt"—has more than doubled in the Reagan years, to a mind-boggling $2.6 trillion.

Charting the national debt relative to GNP over time unboggles the mind to some extent. Because, whereas the debt ratio has risen, from 34.2% in 1980 to an estimated 54.9% in 1988, it's still only in the range experienced during the Kennedy Administration. And of course it's far lower than the levels reached during and immediately after World War II, when national debt peaked at 127.3% of GNP in 1946.

The fact is that national debt relative to GNP goes both up and down. It has already done this several times in U.S. history. The national debt ratio reached peaks of 26% in the 1870s, after the Civil War, and about 30% after World War I. Subsequently, it was reduced to lows of 2% in 1916 and 16% on the eve of the Depression.

And it should be noted that the steady decline in the national debt ratio after 1946 is not entirely an indicator of economic virtue. The ratio can be reduced in three principal ways: The federal government can run surpluses; the economy can grow faster than federal government deficits—or inflation can reduce the real value of debt denominated in nominal terms. Increasingly after World War II, the third method was employed.

Maybe this will be a consolation if inflation returns.

Despite the recent expansion of the U.S. national debt, the international comparison chart reveals it is still not particularly out of line with those of other major industrialized economies. Nor has its growth been exceptionally fast.

Is the Reagan prosperity just a matter of borrowing from foreigners?

The U.S. government, at least, has not financed itself in the Reagan years by unusual borrowing abroad. The proportion of the national debt held by foreigners is lower now than it was under President Carter.

The U.S. government is arguably in a uniquely strong position vis-à-vis foreign creditors: Its foreign debt is denominated in its own currency, so that it can always be inflated away. Still, for what it's worth, it appears that at least some of the governments of the other industrialized countries have financed themselves with foreign debt to about the same extent as the U.S. West Germany has 20.8% of its government debt held by foreigners, Canada some 14.7%.

Foreign loans to the U.S. private sector are the result of a market process, with the domestic borrower judging his ability to repay and the foreign creditor taking the risk. By contrast, government obligations are assumed as the result of a political rather than an economic decision. Foreign loans to the U.S. private sector did rise to 4.48% of GNP in 1986, up from 1.3% in 1980 and an acceleration of a rising trend stretching back to the 1960s. But foreign loans remain a small fraction of total private sector debt, which in 1987 amounted to 124% of GNP.

What about the trade deficit?

Because the world no longer has fixed exchange rates, worrying about the trade deficit appears at first to be rather paradoxical. After all, inflows, outflows and the floating exchange rate must equilibrate by definition. And central governments no longer have to be concerned that the reserves they needed to defend their currencies' value are being eroded.

Still, the trade deficit relative to GNP appears here by popular demand—the media have made a mighty issue of it. And it does show a Reagan number that is actually out of line with U.S. post-World War II norms. The 1987 deficit was 3.6% of GNP; estimate for 1988, 2.9%.

The U.S. has the largest trade deficit of the major industrialized countries, although booming Britain has also developed a substantial deficit, running at 2.5% of GNP in 1987. In other respects, however, international experience is comforting. It teaches that trade deficits come and go. Japan regularly ran merchandise trade deficits from the end of WWII to 1963—at times up to 1% of GNP—before turning the trade balance positive and becoming the Japan we know and love today. South Korea has since followed a similar pattern. It may be that Americans have not had enough experience of what it feels like to be involved in international trade. Total U.S. merchandise trade was 14.7% of GNP in 1987, almost double the levels of 20 years earlier.

Okay, but what about private debt—consumer and corporate?

The number that has gotten most out of line in the Reagan years is debt. However, relative to GNP as far back as Federal Reserve Board numbers go, the trend looks slightly less alarming. The debt buildup also seems to predate Reagan, beginning in the mid-1970s.

In principle, market forces should determine the appropriate level of debt for the U.S. economy. This is what happens for individual industries, whose levels of leverage vary widely and fluctuate over time. And some observers argue strongly that what is now going on in the U.S. economy overall is nothing to worry about. They say debt is not excessive relative to other measures, such as total assets, corporate equity and corporate cash flow, or when allowance is made for financial innovation—more corporate debt today is "securitized," repackaged and sold in the public marketplace, and hence is less of an open-ended threat to the issuer's financial health. Furthermore,

Japanese and West German corporations are said to be far more leveraged than their American counterparts.

Still, the debt question clearly merits further, calm, investigation. . . .

Has the economy been sweepingly deregulated?

The extent and effectiveness of government regulation of the economy is of course inherently difficult to measure. But one accepted way is to count the number of pages in the Federal Register, which records all rules and notices issued by federal agencies. This is supposed to be a proxy for the intensity of regulatory activity from year to year.

Clearly visible in such a page-counting exercise is the flurry of activity associated with World War II—and the tidal wave of regulation under Presidents Nixon, Ford and Carter in the 1970s. The Reagan years do seem to have brought an ebbing, although things have basically churned since 1984. But note that, at least as measured by pages in the Federal Register, there appears to be about as much regulation going on in the economy as in 1975.

Another approach, adopted by the Center for the Study of American Business, at Washington University in St. Louis, is to track the administrative costs of regulatory agencies. The theory is that, since the regulators are presumably not just sitting there, money spent to support them reflects regulatory impact in the economy as a whole.

This measure shows an even smaller reduction in regulation. Relative to GNP, the rise in regulatory spending was halted and even reversed until 1983. After that, it kept pace with GNP growth, which is currently estimated at 4%.

In real terms, regulatory spending first decreased and then began to recover after 1983 at a rate comparable with the Carter years. The startling result: By 1987 Reagan Administration regulatory spending was higher than at the end of the Carter Administration. Regulatory staffing levels followed a similar path, although their recovery to Carter highs is not yet complete.

A popular book on Reagan Era deregulation described it as "the dismantling of America." On the evidence of this chart, America has survived. Or at least the federal regulatory apparatus has. . . .

What's the economic bottom line on the Reagan years?

On the basis of these figures, it seems safe to conclude that the prosperity is not hollow—or at least not much more so than previous post-World War II expansions. The economic phenomena discussed here are not radically out of line with both past experience and international comparisons—with the debatable exception of private-sector debt, which has little to do with government policy.

Whether the stagflation Reagan found on taking office was sufficiently serious to merit running Depression-level deficits is, perhaps, ultimately a matter of judgment. In Britain, Margaret Thatcher dealt with a similar situation without quite such heavy recourse to deficits (although they were closer to U.S. levels than is generally realized). In the American political system, without Mrs. Thatcher's total control of the legislative branch for five years before any election, this would probably have spelled suicide.

In retrospect, the Reagan Administration was a conservative revolution in a very specific sense. It was more cautious, seen in perspective, than either friends or foes appreciated. Its achievements were not so much what it actually did, but what it prevented from happening.

In the final years of the Carter Administration, there were powerful trends at work in the economy, ranging from bracket creep to rising federal spending. During the Reagan Administration, these trends have to some extent been slowed, stopped and even—in the case of federal spending only recently—reversed.

In addition, of course, Reagan presided over a very strong expansion that, unlike the 1970s, has not been accompanied by rising inflation.

There was a price to all this. Reagan accepted a recession in 1982 and also the notable, if not unprecedented, developments outlined in this article.

Any future President will have to decide if this price is worthwhile—and whether the trends Reagan opposed are to reverse or resume.

[Reprinted by permission from *Forbes Magazine.*]

2. WELFARE POLICY AND THE POOR

No Reagan administration policy aroused a more passionate response from journalists and political writers alike than its spending cuts and tightened eligibility rules for some domestic social programs. For Reagan's critics, the administration official who recommended that ketchup be counted as a vegetable in the federal school-lunch program epitomized the callousness they saw as the stone-cold core of Reaganism. This critical perspective is reflected in the 1981 article by Frances Fox Piven of Boston University and Richard Cloward of Columbia University, arguing that the cuts in social programs for the jobless reflected less an effort to trim federal spending than to make the unemployed more willing to accept low-paying or otherwise undesirable jobs.

But Reagan's social policies had able defenders as well, including the skillful polemicist Michael Novak. Writing in the neoconservative journal Commentary *in 1983, Novak rejected the prevailing perception that Reagan's tax cuts favored the rich or that his social program "hurt the poor." In fact, Novak declared, overall spending on social programs went up in the early eighties while the cuts and tighter eligibility requirements affected only those who were not truly needy. Novak challenged Reagan's critics to come up with proposals of their own to deal with the widely admitted shortcomings of the welfare system.*

But the perception of Reagan's insensitivity to the poor persisted, and when he implied in 1986 that the hungry were to blame for their plight, many newspapers echoed the Burlington Free Press *in taking him to task. Another seasoned polemicist, the liberal economist John Kenneth Galbraith, writing in the* Humanist *in 1985, summed up the ways Reaganite social theorists avoided confronting the reality of poverty.*

FRANCES FOX PIVEN AND RICHARD A. CLOWARD
Keeping Labor Lean and Hungry
[*Nation,* November 7, 1981]

Almost immediately upon taking office, President Ronald Reagan asked Congress to slash billions of dollars from Federal allocations for social programs. Aid for the unemployed and the poor was the primary target, while spending for defense remained sacrosanct. But the all-out assault on social programs, many of which date back to the New Deal, was launched for reasons that had little to do with defense, tight money or even the New Federalism.

The White House, of course, cited the need to reduce budgetary deficits as the primary reason for the cuts in spending for social programs. Its spokesmen also interpreted the 1980 election as a "mandate" for shrinking the size of the Federal government, especially the part of it that is concerned with social welfare.

But neither of these rationalizations will wash. Even if we accept the need for budget cuts, and even if we buy the unsubstantiated claim that "the electorate" wants less government, we are left with a case for overall reductions in Federal spending—not a license to sock it to the poor.

Actually, the progressive philosophy behind the programs—the idea that government should help the poor and the unemployed—was the real target of the Reagan budget ax. Programs that do not require the applicant to demonstrate need or submit to a means test, like Social Security, Medicare and a variety of veterans' benefits, were left relatively unscathed, while most of the cuts were made in funding for public-service jobs, unemployment insurance, Medicaid, welfare, low-income housing, workers' compensation and food stamps. A reason other than fiscal prudence was the motivating force; conservatives believe that, in an industrial society, aid to the needy reduces business profits by enhancing the bargaining power of the labor force.

The nexus between social programs and the labor market is to be found in the relationship between unemployment and wage levels. A large number of unemployed workers exercises a downward pressure on wages because people who need work will generally accept wages below the going rate. A large pool of unemployed people also acts as a check on the pay and benefit demands of those who have jobs, because the latter, aware of the long line of applicants at the factory gate, are reluctant to jeopardize their own positions. When the unemployed are absorbed by an expanding job market, however, worker demands increase and cut into profits. This, some analysts say, is what happened in the late 1960s, when the long post-World War II boom reached its crest.

Manipulating the relationship between unemployment and wages has been an objective of economic policy in the United States since the Great Depression. Government planners used fiscal and monetary policies that raised or lowered aggregate demand to smooth out the business cycle. Instead of being allowed to swing from trough to peak to trough again, it was regulated. Moderate recessions were induced every few years, however, to increase unemployment without driving it to dangerous levels. The large number of people looking for work lowered wage demands. The promotion of limited unemployment became a major tool for stabilizing the economy and controlling inflation. . . .

In the two decades following World War II, the strategy worked. Cyclical increases in the unemployment rate produced the expected fall-off in the rate of wage increases. By the 1960s, however, the relationship was beginning to weaken, and by the early 1970s it no longer existed. According to Barry Bosworth, head of President Jimmy Carter's Council on Wage and Price Stability from 1977 through 1979, an unemployment rate of 6 percent failed to curb inflation following the recession of 1969-71. . . .

The new element in the picture was the expansion of social welfare benefits, which undermined the historic relationship between unemployment and wages. It is not difficult to see how this happened. If the desperation of the unemployed is reduced by the availability of benefits, there is less pressure on them to take the first job they can find, something that economists quickly realized. . . . As Edgar R. Fiedler, Assistant Secretary of the Treasury for Economic Policy in the Ford Administration, explained:

> A change has taken place in the unemployment-inflation trade-off since the mid-1950s. . . . [One reason] is the unemployed today are subject to less economic pain than used to be the case, because of the development of more generous income-maintenance programs. . . . Consequently, most people who lose their jobs today are under less

pressure to accept the first offer they get regardless of the pay and working conditions.

Slashing social programs will reinstate the terrors of being without a job. Unemployment benefits will be limited to twenty-six weeks unless joblessness reaches "catastrophic" levels nationwide; moreover, fewer of the unemployed will be eligible for either food stamps or medical benefits. Pressures on the unemployed will be enhanced by adding to their numbers. The dismantling of the jobs programs started under the Comprehensive Employment and Training Act added 350,000 people to the labor market. It has already been announced that 400,000 households receiving money under the Aid to Families with Dependent Children program will be declared ineligible. The Social Security Administration has accelerated a review, begun under the Carter Administration, of Federal disability payments. Initial reports on 1,300 cases in New York State showed that 38 percent of the aid recipients were not entitled to benefits. The agency expects that 25 percent of the 500,000 cases reviewed nationwide during the next fiscal year will be found to be ineligible. And if the partial Social Security benefits at age 62 are reduced, or if the retirement age is raised to 68, millions of people will be compelled to remain in the labor force. The number of people looking for work will be further enlarged by reductions in housing subsidies, food stamps and Medicaid for the working poor.

Moreover, under the New Federalism, the Reagan Administration is moving to make many income-maintenance programs the responsibility of the states. Food stamp allotments are only the beginning. If this effort succeeds, it will eliminate the equalizing effect of national standards. Benefit levels will be driven down, since state governments are vulnerable to threats from industries to relocate to places where taxes and wages are lower. The decentralization of income-maintenance programs will also antagonize local taxpayers, especially the working poor, who bear the brunt of regressive state sales taxes.

Reagan's "reforms" will thus exert a powerful pressure on people to undersell one another, to take any job at any wage and under any conditions. The effects will be felt by a broad spectrum of people, especially those in the rapidly expanding service sector. Three out of four of those losing benefits will be women, most of them unskilled. They will be hired by the fast-food chains, hotels and offices to cook, serve and clean in competition with the existing low-wage work force, which is already largely female.

At bottom, the Administration holds a two-class view of human nature; it assumes that the rich are very different from the poor and that they require different kinds of incentives. The rich exert themselves for rewards; increase profitability by lowering taxes, for example, and they will step up socially useful investment. The poor, on the other hand, respond to fear and punishment; they must be goaded by hunger, and economic misery makes them more industrious.

In simple and human terms, the welfare state has reduced some of the hardships generated by a market economy that sloughs off the people it no longer needs as it does any other surplus commodity. People have resisted being treated as commodities, believing they had a right to subsistence. And they sometimes fought for that right. The programs of the welfare state were the fruits of those struggles. Moreover, the programs did more than merely protect those with the least power. They grew to a point where they enabled workers to improve their bargaining power. And that is why they are the target of a concerted attack by the privileged and the powerful, with Ronald Reagan serving as chairman of the board.

MICHAEL NOVAK
The Rich, the Poor, and the Reagan Administration
[Commentary, August 1983]

According to a recent Gallup poll, 82 percent of the American people hold that President Reagan's domestic programs "help the rich" and 75 percent hold that they "hurt the poor."

In one respect, this Gallup finding may seem understated. For so insistently have the major news media harped upon the alleged hard-heartedness of the Reagan administration, from the night of the first inauguration ball to the present day, and so emphatically has every Democrat, from "Tip" O'Neill to Tom Hayden, made this the central item in his political bill of indictment against the present administration and against the Republican party in general, that one is surprised to learn that 18 to 25 percent of Americans do not immediately agree.

Still, the fact that the "fairness" issue has been made the single determining focus in assessing the domestic record of the administration does not mean that it has itself been considered fairly, on its merits.

Indeed, when one tries to establish what is "fair," problems arise immediately. In 1976, Jimmy Carter campaigned on the claim that the tax system of the U.S. was so unfair as to constitute "a disgrace to the human race." By 1980, no one thought that Carter, as President, had made it less so. As he departed office, Carter also left behind an annual rate of inflation of 13 percent, 7.5 percent unemployment, interest rates at 22 percent. No one then claimed that Carter was helping the poor. By his own description, the country was suffering a broad "malaise." It is by no means obvious, then, that Reagan's programs are any more unfair than Carter's.

What is obvious, however, is that the Reagan administration's critics have more exalted standards in mind. Some judge fairness by the degree of "redistribution" effected in society. In their eyes, an administration would be fair if it took from the rich and gave to the poor. Yet as Bertrand de Jouvenal long ago pointed out, this dreamy ideal can never be fulfilled literally, for the simple mathematical reason that there are too few rich and that, even in the aggregate, they have too little income. . . . To confiscate the entire remaining after-tax income of every U.S. citizen earning over $200,000 and give it all to the poor, whatever one might say about the "fairness" of such a measure, would result in under $850 for each individual officially counted as poor.

Do those who advocate redistribution believe, then, in taking from the *middle class* and giving to the poor? This the Democrats do not say. And one cannot, in any case, really credit most of President Reagan's critics with an honest belief in equality of income, if only because so many of them are themselves very well paid and have shown no discernible movement toward taking less, in the name of fairness, or in any other name for that matter. . . .

So if fairness does not mean doing as Democrats did from 1976 to 1980, and does not mean redistribution from the middle class to the poor, . . . what does it mean? Perhaps it signifies, as some have put it, that there should been no cuts in tax rates for the rich and no welfare cuts for the poor. But even this turns out, theoretically and practically, to be problematical. . . .

II

As the records of tax payments to the IRS suggest, those Americans who earned more than $50,000 in 1980—the top 3 percent—remitted 31 percent of all income taxes paid, or $79 billion of the total $250 billion collected by the IRS from individual income taxes. In 1980, the bottom 50 percent, or those who made $12,000 or less, paid $14 billion in income tax (or only 6 percent of all taxes paid). Thus, the top 3 percent paid five times more in taxes than the bottom 50 percent combined.

For the top 3 percent to carry the bottom 50 percent seems highly admirable. What one cannot say is that those in the top layer "benefit" unduly from a cut in tax rates that is of the exact proportion granted to every other taxpayer. For by saying this one would simply be calling attention to the far greater proportion of taxes such persons are now paying. The Reagan tax cuts of 1981 were, by design, one and the same for all, at every income level. In fact, as the independent Congressional Budget Office has noted, under the Reagan program "the largest tax cut in dollar terms" has gone not to the very rich but to the "$10,000 to $40,000 middle-income group, which as a group also has the most households and the most income." . . .

Not only have high-income persons not benefited disproportionately from the cut in tax rates but the gross amounts they are paying are, if anything, greater than before the cuts went into effect. If that were not true—if, instead of paying $79 billion in taxes, as in 1980, the 3 percent at the highest income in 1982 were paying, say, $71 billion (a 10-percent cut) or 67 billion (a 15-percent cut)—then the IRS would be receiving less in 1982 than it had received in 1980, and this might be considered "unfair" in its consequences for federal expenditures. But such a supposition is false. Although the final figures are not in, it is almost certain that the top 3 percent of income earners in 1982 had by April 15 of this year paid *more* than $79 billion in taxes. The rate at which they were taxed went down, but the amount of taxes they paid appears from early signs to have gone up. . . . So did the economy, whose growth was stimulated by new funds made available for private investment.

Is this unjust, unbeneficial, or unfair? It seems, on the contrary, wise policy. . . .

III

If the "rich" side of the so-called "fairness" issue seems to have less in it than meets the eye, what about the "poor" side? Is President Reagan's program hurting the poor?

In one area—employment—the obvious answer is yes. Although one cannot blame Reagan for an unemployment rate already going up well before his tax and welfare programs went into effect, the fact that unemployment rose by a full 3 percent during Reagan's first two years in office means that some 3 million families experienced real hardship. Savings were wiped out; lifetime projects were grievously interrupted or destroyed; fears spread; some factory doors clanged shut forever.

Yet when people say that Reagan's programs are hurting the poor they have in mind not so much the number of the unemployed as the condition of the welfare programs sustaining the poor. Quite apart from the increase in the numbers of the poor because of unemployment, the poor are said to be getting poorer.

President Reagan is alleged to be cutting benefits to the poor. But what does "cutting" mean? One can cut a benefit in three ways: (a) by inflation; (b) by providing less funding; (c) by curbing a projected growth in funding. For Democrats, the classic way of cutting benefits has been to give with one hand (in appropriations) while taking away with the other (through inflation). This was President Carter's way. During his four years in office, inflation raged almost at double-digit levels for three years, devastating individuals and families with low income or fixed income. Inflation is the cruelest tax, although the easiest one for the "party of compassion" to levy. . . .

In this respect, Reagan has done more to *help* the poor than Carter. Inflation has come down more quickly, more steeply, and (so far) more steadily than anyone dared to hope on inauguration day. Whatever dollars the poor receive under Reagan, they are more honest dollars than they were under Carter, when even the practice of indexing welfare benefits to the rate of inflation could not prevent all other costs from leaping beyond reach.

As for gross expenditures on welfare programs, even adjusting for inflation, there are a few—but only a few—welfare programs on which the government is spending less in 1983 under Reagan than was spent in 1980 under Carter. In the aggregate, certainly, far *more* is being spent. Even in 1980, critics said welfare spending was "out of control." It still is. Mercilessly, and most often without commensurate benefit, it just keeps going up, automatically. President Reagan deserves little "credit" for this; on the contrary, he has tried desperately to control it. Yet his efforts to make deep cuts have by and large failed.

To be sure, if we were to ask poor and unemployed Americans, one by one, whether their present condition under Reagan is worse than, better than, or the same as under Carter, I would expect Reagan to score lower than Carter. Such persons are the best judges of their own circumstances. But on the level of federal social policy—which has to do with appropriations, expenditures, programs, line budgets, and year-end reports—it is impossible to sustain the accusation that Reagan is spending less on welfare programs than Carter did.

Take the three biggest items, the so-called "middle-class" social programs which actually benefit the poor even more significantly than they benefit others: Social Security, Medicare, and Medicaid. (Poverty was not long ago a problem predominantly of the elderly; these three programs have virtually ended that.) On these three programs Reagan is indisputably spending more than Carter did:

OUTLAYS FOR THREE BASIC SOCIAL PROGRAMS
(millions of dollars)

	1980	1983
Social Security	117,117	168,267
Medicare	35,033	57,262
Medicaid	13,956	19,326
TOTAL:	166,106	244,855

Source: Office of Management and Budget

Thus, the sharpest accusations about "hurting the poor" cannot plausibly be aimed at these three fundamental welfare programs. But what about the relatively minor programs designed especially for the poor: Aid for Families with Dependent Children (AFDC), food stamps, housing assistance, rent supplements, Small Business Administration minority loan programs, Head Start, and the long list of other agencies, programs, and benefits? These amount, in aggregate, to about 10 percent of all federal spending, or some $70 billion. And it is on these that the case against Reagan rests.

This case is built principally on the contention that the administration has not merely cut the rate of increase of the programs in question, but has also made actual inroads into their funding. The particulars, which tend to bear out the President's frequent assertion that virtually every program has been budgeted for more in 1983 than in 1980, speak for themselves:

OUTLAYS FOR SOCIAL PROGRAMS
(millions of dollars)

	1980	Estimated 1983
Unemployment Benefits	18,029.2	36,855.0
Housing Programs	5,353.6	9,325.0
Food Stamps	9,117.1	12,045.1
Child Nutrition	3,377.1	3,196.5
Women, Infants, Children	716.7	1,117.7
AFDC	7,308.4	7,766.8
Supplemental Security Income	6,411.5	8,845.3
Earned Income Tax Credit	1,265.2	1,205.0

Source: Office of Management and Budget

These figures are not adjusted for inflation (which has been reduced but not eliminated). In a time of recession, moreover, one would expect to see a gross increase in social spending to ease the burden of the poor and near-poor. Just such an increase is patent in these figures. Still, some categories show only a slight rise or, in two cases, a fall. The fact that the Reagan administration has tightened eligibility requirements for these programs just at this precise moment is the most plausible reason for saying that Reagan's program is unfair.

On whom did these cuts fall most heavily? Not on the poorest of the poor. By all evidence, the poorest, who have benefited the most from the reduction in inflation, have also been the least affected by the Reagan cuts. In every category, those cut have been at the *top* of the relevant criteria for eligibility. . . .

It is thus a portion of the borderline poor who have felt the pain. Within those programs which have been cut, or whose growth has been cut, the Reagan policies have consistently aimed at removing from the rolls those with higher incomes. Ironically, these are the very ones among the poor likely to have voted for Reagan in 1980, and presumably likely to do so again in 1984, in numbers much greater than the poorest of the poor, whose eligibility has been entirely protected. As Roosevelt is sometimes referred to as the liberal who saved capitalism, Reagan may some day be known as the conservative who saved the welfare state intact for the very poor.

IV

If, however, the Reagan administration has neither helped the rich nor hurt the poor in the blatant way that has been charged by its critics, it *has* failed to address meaningfully the larger question posed by the continuing existence of a welfare population whose ranks are not diminishing but appear rather to be swelling. . . .

The American people have been exceedingly generous in the amounts of money they have assigned for the elimination of poverty; yet, despite this expenditure, poverty seems not on the way to being eliminated but rather to be growing. Surely, therefore, it is incumbent on all of us—but especially on those who accuse President Reagan of "hurting the poor"—to think of alternatives. . . .

As a Democrat, I hope that my own party will devise a new approach to the problem of eliminating poverty. A promising direction would seem to be the suppression of the present multitude of minor programs in favor of a package of direct cash payments and in-kind benefits designed to place every family above the official poverty line *tout court.* The cost of such a radical redesign would appear to be no more, and perhaps considerably less, than the present burden. Such a design—which has, in one form or another, been endorsed by Milton Friedman and Senator Daniel P. Moynihan—would eliminate at one stroke both the perverse incentives of current programs and a huge amount of regulatory apparatus. Should the Democrats propose it, a Republican administration would be hard-pressed to oppose it; and a Democratic administration might achieve it. As a strictly monetary matter, poverty would cease to exist.

In the meantime, intellectual fairness is not being served by allowing partisan passion to inflate and to obfuscate the "fairness" issue.

BURLINGTON (VERMONT) FREE PRESS
There He Goes Again
[May 23, 1986]

There he goes again.

In a press conference with high school students, President Reagan declared that anyone who was hungry in America simply did not know where to turn for help. Because of their lack of knowledge "as to what things are available," the hungry, he intimated, must share the blame for their plight.

Such statements speak volumes about the compassion and understanding of an administration which pretends to be aware of the problems of the nation's poor. Yet Reagan's "shining city on the hill" is populated by a citizenry that is comfortably middle class. The plight of the less fortunate does not fit into that scheme of things. That his vision falls considerably short of reality is testimony to his inability to perceive the complexities of the situation. Perhaps it is because of the fact that he does not wish to acknowledge the existing disparities between the poor and the affluent in the nation.

But it is a fact that American society is divided into two diverse groups: one made up of an affluent middle class and the other of the poor. Because they are politically powerless, the needy often are the first to feel the slash of the budget-cutting knife. While horror stories abound about abuse of the nation's welfare system, few similar stories are told about cheating by the middle class.

Reagan's tendency toward oversimplification, however, cannot obscure the fact that his administration has consistently demonstrated an insensitivity to the needy. Saying that they could get help if only they knew the right strings to pull more often than not becomes a convenient excuse for doing little or nothing to help them. And shifting the responsibility for caring for the poor to private charitable organizations is to deny that government has an obligation to assist them in meeting their needs.

It is indeed a sad commentary on a government's priorities that millions of its citizens are homeless, that children are underfed and that adequate housing is beyond the reach of the working poor.

What is worst, however, is that a president who should be aware of the problem can blithely misstate the facts without offering any evidence to support his views.

And it creates the impression that Reagan really believes in the fantasy he has created in his own mind.

[Reprinted courtesy the *Burlington Free Press.*]

JOHN KENNETH GALBRAITH

How We Get the Poor Off Our Conscience

[*The Humanist*, September/October 1985]

. . . The first of the current ways we get the poor off our conscience proceeds from the inescapable fact that most of the things that must be done on behalf of the poor must be done in one way or another by the government. It is then argued that the government is inherently incompetent, except as regards weapons design and procurement and the overall management of the Pentagon. Being incompetent and ineffective, it must not be asked to succor the poor; it will only louse things up or make things worse.

. . . We do ourselves and public servants an extraordinary disservice by this design for denying help to the poor. There is, of course, always opportunity for improvement in public administration. My generation, when urging welfare action, was too inclined to think that it had accomplished the task when it passed the legislation; we didn't sufficiently contemplate the problems of administration involved. But we must see that the present condemnation of government and government administration is really part of the continuing design for avoiding responsibility for the poor.

The second . . . is to argue that any form of public help to the poor only hurts the poor. It destroys morale. It seduces people away from gainful employment. It breaks up marriages, since women can seek welfare for themselves and their children once they are without their husbands.

There is no proof of this—none certainly that compares that damage to the damage that would be inflicted by the loss of public assistance. Still, the case is made—and believed—that there is something gravely damaging about aid to the unfortunate. It is perhaps our most highly influential piece of fiction.

Third . . . is the argument that public assistance measures have an adverse effect on incentive. They transfer income from the diligent to the idle and feckless, thus reducing the effort of the diligent and encouraging the idleness of the idle. The modern manifestation of this is supply-side economics. Supply-side economics holds that the rich in the United States have not been working because they have too little income. So, by taking money from the poor and giving it to the rich, we increase effort and stimulate the economy. Can we really believe that any considerable number of the poor prefer welfare income to a good job? Or that business people—corporate executives, the key figures in our time—are idling away their hours because of the insufficiency of their pay? This is a scandalous charge against the American businessperson—notably a hard worker. Belief can be the servant of truth—but even more of convenience.

The fourth . . . is, of course, the presumed adverse effect on freedom of taking responsibility for them. Freedom consists of the right to spend all of one's own money—a maximum by one's own choice, a minimum for government programs. (Again, expenditure on national defense is excepted.) In the enduring words of Professor Milton Friedman, people must "be free to choose."

This is possibly the most transparent of all the designs; no mention is ordinarily made of the relation of income to the freedom of the poor. (Professor Friedman is here an exception; through the negative income tax, he would assure everyone of a basic income.) There is, we can surely agree, no form of oppression in our society that is quite so great, no constriction on thought and effort quite so comprehensive, as that which comes from having no money at all. Though we hear much about the limitation on the freedom of the affluent when their income is reduced through taxes, we hear nothing of the extraordinary enhancement of the freedom of the poor from having some money to spend. Yet the loss of freedom from taxation to the rich is, we can only conclude, a small thing as compared with the gain in freedom from providing some income to the impoverished. Freedom we rightly cherish. Cherishing it, we should not use it as a cover for denying help to those in need.

Finally... we resort to simple psychological denial. This is a psychic tendency that in various manifestations is common to us all. It causes us to avoid thinking about death. It causes a great many people to deny thought of the arms race and the consequent rush toward a highly probable extinction. And by the same process of psychological denial, we decline to think of the poor.

[Reprinted by permission of *The Humanist.*]

3. REAGAN AND BLACK AMERICA

Of the traditional components of the Democratic coalition, only blacks continued to vote overwhelmingly Democratic during the Reagan years. Nevertheless, in a speech to the National Black Republican Council in September 1982, Reagan vigorously made his pitch for black support. Not only had inflation been licked, helping blacks and other poor Americans, the President insisted, but his administration was vigorously enforcing civil-rights laws and promoting "enterprise zones," offering tax breaks and other incentives to U.S. corporations to open plants in urban ghettos. A few days later, however, the Roanoke Times and World-News *sharply challenged Reagan's claim that his administration was taking the lead in civil-rights activism.*

Despite Reagan's appeals, most blacks continued to oppose him. In the October 1984 issue of Essence, *a magazine for black women, a number of well-known blacks vented their unhappiness with Reaganism. One of these, Mary F. Berry, a black historian and member of the U.S. Civil Rights Commission, accused Reagan of trying to turn the commission from a "watchdog" into a "lapdog" by replacing its most activist members with Reaganites.*

A more sustained summation of the black case against Reagan was offered in a 1986 address by John E. Jacob, president of the National Urban League, a major black organization, who charged the administration with turning its back on black America and instead adopting policies that had "intensified the problems facing black and poor people." One of the bitterest attacks on Reagan came from Roger Wilkins of the Institute for Policy Studies, a liberal Washington think tank. Beneath the soothing rhetoric and the shrewdly chosen "photo opportunities" with blacks, charged Wilkins in the Nation *in 1984, the President had in fact prettied up racism and made it tolerable for the 1980s.*

RONALD REAGAN
Address to National Black Republican Council
[September 15, 1982]

There are those who have accused the Republican Party of writing off the black vote. Well, I'm here to tell you that we're not writing off anyone. Maria Montessori once said that if she were trying to climb a ladder and a dog was snapping at her heels, she could stop and kick the dog or climb the ladder. And you have encouraged Nancy and myself to keep on climbing the ladder.

I'm sensitive to the unique and sometimes difficult position in which you often find yourselves as black Republicans. What you're doing takes great vision and true courage. Black Republicans have been performing above and beyond the call of duty. The rest of us in the GOP are grateful for your commitment and deeply impressed by your tenacity.

For too long now, black Americans seem to have been written off by one party and taken for granted by the other. And for the vast majority of black Americans, that's been a strictly no-win situation. Changing it will require a commitment from all of us. So, tonight I want you to know that the Republican Party stands ready and willing to reach out to black Americans. . . . While there's been a certain lack of communication on our part over the years, the other party seems to have capitalized on the rhetoric of compassion. They don't accomplish much, but they sure do talk about it.

It's time to set the record straight. When I first ran for Governor of California, I ran against an incumbent with impeccable liberal credentials. And then I was elected and discovered that in 8 years, he had made only a handful, a tiny handful of minority appointments, all to relatively minor positions in State government. I figured it was time to play catch-up. I appointed more blacks and other minorities to executive and policymaking positions in State government than all the previous 32 Governors of California put together. And my continued commitment at the national level is no 11th hour conversion.

So far, we have placed blacks in over 130 top executive policymaking positions. But more important, these appointments are not on the basis of color. They have been made because of ability and skill, and they cover a wide range of responsibilities.

When it comes to improving the economic well-being and protecting the rights of all our citizens, our party doesn't play second-fiddle to anyone. When I entered office less than 20 months ago, we were in the midst of an economic catastrophe from which we're just now beginning to recover. All of us were suffering, especially the poor, the elderly, and the disadvantaged. Some of our political leaders were even saying that nothing could be done and that we had to accept a lower standard of living and that America's best days were behind us. Well, to those on the bottom end of the economic ladder, that kind of talk is disaster. It robs them of hope and condemns them to a life of dependency and deprivation.

Our economic hardship is not some kind of mysterious malaise suffered by people who have suddenly lost their vitality. The problem is that the liberal economic policies that dominated America for too long just didn't work. It was not that those in power lacked good intentions; in fact, most of the compassionate rhetoric I mentioned a moment ago was not about accomplishments—it was about the wonderful intentions of the costly liberal programs. Well, too often the programs didn't do what they were supposed to and in many cases, they made things worse. . . .

The record is there for all to see. This country entered the 1960's having made tremendous strides in reducing poverty. . . . True, the number of blacks living in poverty was still disproportionately high. But tremendous progress had been made.

With the coming of the Great Society, government began eating away at the underpinnings of the private enterprise system. The big taxers and big spenders in the Congress had started a binge that would slowly change the nature of our society and, even worse, it threatened the character of our people.

By the end of the decade, the situation seemed out of control. At a time when defense spending was decreasing in real dollars, the Federal budget tripled. And, to pay for all of this spending, the tax load increased until it was breaking the backs of working people, destroying incentive, and siphoning off resources needed in the private sector to provide new jobs and opportunity.

Inflation had jumped to double-digit levels. Unemployment was climbing. And interest rates shot through the roof, reaching 21½ percent shortly before we took office. Perhaps the saddest part of the whole story is that much of this Federal spending was done in the name of helping those it hurt the most, the disadvantaged. For the result of all that big spending and taxing is that, today, those at the lower end of the economic ladder are the hardest hit of all. . . .

In 1980 the American people sent a message to Washington, D.C. They no longer believed that throwing tax money at a problem was acceptable, no matter how good the intentions of those doing the taxing and spending. . . .

The signs that our program is working are just now on the horizon. Gross national product is up. The leading economic indicators are up. Inflation is down dramatically, and so are interest rates. Housing permits are up. The stock market is up and so, for the first time in years, is real income.

Yes, there have been other indicators saying the economy isn't well yet. But we've managed, despite all the gloom and doom spouted by our opponents, to instill a new spirit of confidence in the country.

Our critics to the contrary, the poor and disadvantaged are better off today than if we had allowed runaway government spending, interest rates and inflation to continue ravaging the American economy. A family of four, for example, on a fixed income of $15,000 would today be $833 poorer, that much weaker in purchasing power, if we hadn't brought inflation alone down as far as we have from the double-digit rates that we inherited. A similar family living at the poverty level would be $472 poorer if inflation had continued at the 12.4 percent rate. It's been 5.4 percent since January.

When one considers that the poor spend most of their family budgets on necessities—food, shelter, and clothing—leaving few ways to cut back to beat inflation, the importance of solving inflation is better understood.

We must remain firm and not be lured again into inflation-spending patterns. But let's be frank: The lives of those in the lower income levels are not what we'd like them to be. . . .

Since the end of the Second World War, too many of our major cities have become stagnant and depressed, enclaves of despair even when times were good. Federal spending programs didn't make a dent in the problem. For example, from 1965 to 1974, the Federal urban renewal program spent over $7 billion and ended an abysmal failure, destroying more housing units than it replaced. . . .

On March 23d of this year, I proposed a new, experimental approach to the problem—enterprise zones—which would harness the energy of the private sector and direct it toward providing economic opportunity for some of our most needy citizens. By removing regulations and offering tax incentives, we seek to accomplish what hundreds of billions of tax dollars and millions of hours of bureaucratic planning failed to do. . . .

Later this month, I'll announce a program which will promote minority business development. Of course, the most important item for minority businessmen, as with all small businessmen, is the tax and regulatory reforms we've instituted over the last 20 months. Yet beyond these, we've committed the Federal Government to promote an economic environment in which minority entrepreneurs can fully marshal their talents and skills to make a go of it in the marketplace.

There are many things that we can do to help minority business take root. Part of this administration's overall initiative for minority enterprise will include a plan for the Federal Government to procure substantial amounts of the goods and services during fiscal years '83, '84, and '85 from minority businessmen. . . .

Putting the American economy back on the right track has clearly been the top priority of this administration. But I think it's important for all of us to understand that at the same time we haven't forgotten the Federal commitment to civil rights. . . . Usually I try to ignore personal attacks, but one charge I will have to admit strikes at my heart every time I hear it. That's the suggestion that we Republicans are taking a less active approach to protecting the civil rights of all Americans. No matter how you slice it, that's just plain baloney.

There's no room in the Republican Party for bigots, and the record shows that we've been firm in protecting civil liberties ever since entering office nearly 20 months ago. . . .

In this administration, I've appointed individuals for whom I have the deepest trust and admiration to head the Department of Justice, the Equal Employment Opportunity Commission, and the Civil Rights Commission. They are committed, as I am, and as every other member of this administration, to protecting the civil rights of all Americans to the fullest extent of the law. Again I say, look at the record. The level of activity of this administration in investigating and prosecuting those who would attempt to deny blacks their civil liberties by violence and intimidation has exceeded the level of every past administration.

The Department of Justice has, since we came to Washington, filed 62 new cases charging criminal violations of civil rights laws and has conducted trials in 52 cases. And these numbers are greater than those in any previous administration. In addition, the Justice Department has filed nine new antidiscrimination cases against public employers and has reviewed more than 9,000 electoral changes to determine compliance with the Voting Rights Act. And that, too, is a higher level of activity that in any prior administration.

Consistent with this spirit, on June 29th of this year I signed into law the longest extension of the Voting Rights Act since its enactment. As I've said on many occasions, voting is the crown jewel of our liberties, and it's something that we as Republicans and Americans will never permit to be infringed upon.

The record of the Equal Employment Opportunity Commission, EEOC, is equally impressive. Under the first full year of this administration, the Commission dramatically increased its activity over the previous year. . . .

Now, no less important is this administration's first commitment to strengthening the historical black colleges, institutions which have played an important role in the progress of black America. More than 85 percent of black lawyers and doctors, for example, finished their undergraduate training at these schools. We have done our best to ensure that even in these times of necessary cuts, historical black colleges not only will survive but progress and will serve future generations of black Americans, as they have so faithfully for the last 100 years.

Now these are more than numbers. They represent this administration's solid, unshakable commitment to civil rights and human betterment. We Republicans are the hope for all those who seek expanded opportunity. You and I know that most of those trapped in welfare dependency would like nothing better than a chance for dignity and independence. . . .

What we've seen in too many cases in the inner city is the broken will of people who desire to be as proud and independent as any other American. And perhaps unintentionally, many government programs have been designed not to create social mobility and help the needy along their way, but instead to foster a state of dependency. Whatever their intentions, no matter their compassion, our opponents created a new kind of bondage for millions of American citizens.

Now, together, we can break this degrading cycle and we can do it with fairness, compassion, and love in our hearts. No other experience in American history runs quite parallel to the black experience. It has been one of great hardships, but also one of great heroism; of great adversity, but also great achievement. What our administration and our party seek is the day when the tragic side of the black legacy in America can be laid to rest once and for all, and the long, perilous voyage toward freedom, dignity, and opportunity can be completed—a day when every child born in America will live free not only of political injustice but of fear, ignorance, prejudice, and dependency. . . .

Let us prove again that America can truly be a promised land, a land where people of every race, creed, and background can live together in freedom, harmony, and prosperity. And let us proclaim for all to hear that America will have brotherhood from sea to shining sea.

ROANOKE TIMES AND WORLD-NEWS
Ronald Reagan on Civil Rights

[September 29, 1982]

Many people grow wary when a troubled President Reagan steps up to the podium and says he wants to set the record straight. In combating the negative images of his administration, the president often applies thinking that can charitably be called creative.

A recent illustration of this is his speech Sept. 15 to the National Black Republican Council. He said it "strikes at my heart" to hear charges that the administration lags on protecting civil rights.

"No matter how you slice it," declared Reagan, "that's just plain baloney." He cited statistics that he said demonstrate that his officials are more active than those of any previous administration in pressing cases against civil-liberties violators.

Others who have accepted the president's invitation to look at the record see a different picture.

Within the government itself, a document of the Equal Employment Opportunity Commission says that the number of job discrimination suits approved by EEOC has dropped sharply.

The independent Washington Council of Lawyers says that during its first 20 months, the administration filed only two new cases in the voting rights field. In its first 12 months, the Carter administration had filed nearly a dozen new cases. In one voting rights case that Carter's people won—in Lubbock, Tex.—Reagan's people asked that the judgment be vacated.

In claiming a higher level of enforcement, Reagan leaned heavily on the fact that the Justice Department had reviewed more than 9,000 electoral changes to determine compliance with the Voting Rights Act. But those are largely pro forma, not initiated by the administration. They're automatic whenever a state or local government changes its election law, and there have been many such changes because of voter redistricting since the 1980 census.

The administration's motives are further called into question by the fact that earlier this year, it fought an amendment to strengthen the Voting Rights Act. The resistance was led by William Bradford Reynolds, head of the Justice Department's Civil Rights Division.

Housing discrimination is another area where the Reagan administration has been reluctant to act. The Council of Lawyers report says that from 1978 to 1980, 19 new cases were filed yearly; in the Republican years 1969-76, there were 32 new cases a year. In the past 20 months, the Civil Rights Division has filed two new cases. The only area in which the Reagan administration has a definite statistical edge is in prosecuting police brutality and other violent denials of civil rights.

This is not to say that readiness to go to court is the only gauge of civil rights protection. Busing can be a blunt if not counterproductive instrument in desegregating schools. Voluntary programs for rooting out job discrimination can play a useful role. Overall policies need to be re-examined for usefulness, as the Reagan White House has been doing.

But in defending his administration's record—on civil rights as in several other areas—the president should not turn statistics upside down and flaunt meaningless records. He is still a supremely effective communicator with individual audiences and with the American public. He will lose much of that ability if suspicion grows among his listeners that they and the facts are being manipulated.

[Reprinted courtesy *Roanoke Times and World-News.*]

JOHN E. JACOB

The Government and Social Problems

[Lecture at John F. Kennedy School of Government, Harvard University, May 1, 1986]

America today is in the midst of a national debate on the proper role of government in dealing with social problems—chief among them the disproportionate poverty and social disorganization afflicting the black community.

During much of the post-war era that debate centered on how our institutional structures could secure civil rights for black citizens and help minorities enter the mainstream of American life.

In recent years, the terms of the debate have changed. Under the leadership of an Administration that labels government itself as "the enemy," the debate centers more and more on how government can effect a strategic withdrawal from social policy. . . .

To place the current debate in context, I would like to suggest several propositions:

One—that federal policies have historically promoted economic and social mobility.

Second—that federal policies have led to significant black advances.

Third—that current government policies have intensified the problems facing black and poor people.

American history shows the extent to which government policies shaped opportunities. From the institution of free public education to free land to subsidized railways, Washington's policies always served social ends. . . .

Given that record, the argument that government has no role to play in social policy rings hollow. Government policies created a large middle class and preserve the wealth of the affluent. Government should play an equally decisive role in providing opportunities for the poor.

When the federal government did intervene to protect black rights and to reduce poverty, its efforts were by and large successful. . . .

At a time when cutting such programs is becoming an article of faith among some who consider themselves "conservatives," we should recall that conservative columnist George Will wrote: "It is cheaper to feed the child than jail the man. Persons who do not understand this are not conservatives, just dim."

It is also dim to brand such programs as taxwasters. Evidence suggests they pay for themselves. . . .

The Reagan era has seen a reversal of federal policy—a shift away from intervention to neglect. The result has been to worsen the conditions of poor and black Americans.

Between 1979 and 1984 real dollar income for the poorest fifth of families with children declined by 24 percent, and the income gap between whites and blacks grew.

Overall, poverty rates rose by a third. More than a third of all black people—over 9 million—are poor today, 2 million more than in 1978.

But federal programs were severely cut. Between 1981 and 1984—years of deep recession and slow recovery—four million people lost welfare, Medicaid, SSI and food stamps. Benefits were reduced for millions more.

The deepest cuts came in programs that invest in education and employment skills, such as job training, which was cut by more than half.

There is a distinction among welfare programs between universal programs affecting everyone and means-tested programs designed for the poor. Universal programs like social security have not been touched for political reasons. Blacks are less likely to reap the benefits of such programs because they die too young or earn too little to fully share in the payoff.

But blacks typically account for 30 to 40 percent of participants in means-tested programs. And the cuts in those programs reduced the income of poor families by 7.5 percent and drove 2 million people into poverty. . . .

Everything we know about race and poverty in America suggests that unless the poor are given some extra help—in the form of social policies that enlarge their opportunities—they will not compete on equal terms with the affluent.

The results of the current economic recovery bear that out. We are in the longest sustained economic recovery in memory, and the results are barely perceptible in poverty communities.

Unemployment and poverty are far higher than they were before the recession. Jobless rates for every group, including white men of prime working age, are higher than they were in 1979.

Black unemployment, which was 6.7 percent in 1970, is stuck at fifteen percent—more than double the white rate. Black unemployment has been in the double digits since the mid-1970s—a 13-year Depression with no end in sight. . . .

Economic growth alone cannot create sufficient employment opportunities for the poor and the unskilled.

Some argue that even with supportive government policies, many will remain poor because they have neither the skills nor the attitudes to allow them to escape poverty. . . .

The rise in female-headed households is blamed for the rise in black poverty. It is further asserted that there has been a breakdown in moral values leading to family instability and welfare dependency.

Those assumptions are wrong.

The central cause of black poverty and black family instability is the lack of economic opportunity.

The rise in female-headed families is directly linked to the decline in black male employment.

In 1960 almost three-fourths of black families were intact and almost three-fourths of black men had jobs. In 1985 only half of black families are intact and only about half of black men have jobs.

Even as the economy successfully absorbed a massive influx of white females into the labor force, it failed to provide jobs for the black unemployed, with terrible results for black family stability. . . .

So while it is convenient to argue that family instability causes poverty, it is more accurate to say that *poverty causes family instability.*

The dependency issue is largely a sham. Some people may settle into long-term dependence on welfare, but most move in and out of the welfare system depending on circumstances. . . .

Over the past two decades . . . we have seen the systematic destruction of unskilled jobs, including high-paying jobs in auto factories and steel plants.

Today, blacks are concentrated in industries most affected by job losses and by competition from imports. They live in cities where low-wage manufacturing jobs were replaced by office and skilled service jobs.

Blacks didn't leave jobs—jobs left blacks.

So the real issue in public policy is not whether federal social programs encourage dependency, but whether they offer opportunities—opportunities to participate in the economy.

That does not exclude internal community efforts we often call "self-help." Blacks have been picking themselves up by their bootstraps ever since we've been here—even when we didn't have boots.

Today, that tradition continues. In literally hundreds of communities we see creative programs initiated and run by black community-based civil rights agencies and neighborhood groups, ranging from economic development to housing management to food banks. . . .

So blacks do not need any lectures about self-help. We *are* helping ourselves. And it is instructive that the people most deeply involved in those self-help efforts are often the same people who demand more positive national social policies.

Precisely because we are the poorest and most vulnerable part of our society, we know there is no substitute for policies that provide employment and training opportunities and create the conditions that make self-help efforts feasible. We know that *black poverty cannot be significantly altered without changes in social policies.*

Yes, there is much that black people can do—and are doing—for themselves, but the place of blacks in our society will ultimately be determined by national policies that provide opportunities and make full use of all of America's human resources.

I believe that such policies will eventually be adopted because they are in the national interest.

Changing demographics mean that a third of new entrants into the labor force are non-white. A severe labor shortage is predicted before the end of the century.

Unless we equip our neglected minorities with the education and the skills to fully participate in a post-industrial economy, America can expect second-class economic status, a weakened world position, and deep unrest at home.

Rather than commit suicide for the sake of antigovernment ideology, I believe America will return to a more activist social policy....I would suggest a targeted, sustained, three-part national effort. It would include:

One—a Universal Employment and Training System that ensures jobs and training for all. It would include private and voluntary sector participation and provide skills training for jobs that will be in short supply along with support services to reach and motivate participants.

Two—Education reforms that equalize opportunities for children in poor families, offer quality pre-school learning experiences, and ensure that students are equipped with employable skills and with the services to help them move from the world of school to the world of work.

Three—social welfare policies that stress human development and ensure decent living standards for all of the needy, while providing child care and support services that encourage work.

I believe such a national effort would go far to end poverty and dependency in America, secure social justice and launch our economy into the twenty-first century.

ROGER WILKINS
Smiling Racism
[*Nation*, November 3, 1984]

Pundits have offered a variety of explanations for Ronald Reagan's enduring popularity, but none of them encompass the whole truth. There is one explanation, though, that is rarely written about in the press or even discussed in polite company. Reagan's dirty little secret is that he has found a way to make racism palatable and politically potent again.

That his policies are not only unfair but also demonstrably racist is crystal clear. Early in the 1980 campaign when he spoke in Philadelphia, Mississippi, he sent out a signal. In the town where civil rights workers James Chaney,

Andrew Goodman and Michael Schwerner were murdered by Klansmen in 1964, Reagan told the South that he favored states' rights. When it was pointed out that he was glorifying a principle that had been used to fight the drive for civil rights, Reagan used the gambit that would become a trademark of his Presidency. He said that his words hadn't meant what they surely conveyed.

There is no need to recapitulate Reagan's civil rights record. It is enough to note two of the strongest signals he has sent out: support for tax exemptions for schools that discriminate on the basis of race, and opposition to busing and affirmative action. For Reagan, the facts don't matter, only the message does. Campaigning for Jesse Helms earlier this fall in Charlotte, North Carolina, he proclaimed that busing does not work. No matter that the experience of the city in which he was speaking directly contradicted him. *The Charlotte Observer* promptly published a stinging editorial pointing out his error and rebuking him for sullying an accomplishment of which the city is justly proud, but the message of where Reagan stood had already been flashed around the country on the nightly news shows.

Besides symbolically expressing a hostility to the aspirations of black people, Reagan has waged a cruel and successful war on their pocketbooks. True, his Administration's policies have hurt all poor people, without regard to color: the top 60 percent of Americans have benefited, while the bottom 40 percent have suffered. But blacks have been hurt the most. The Center on Budget and Policy Priorities recently reported that "the average black family in every income strata—from the poor to the affluent—suffered a decline in its disposable income and standard of living since 1980"; that the hardest hit were black families in which one parent works and the other takes care of the children, losing an average of more than $2,000 in disposable income from 1980 to 1984; that the poverty rate among blacks is almost 36 percent, the highest since 1968; and that while long-term unemployment among whites has increased 1.5 percent since 1980, among blacks it has increased by a whopping 72 percent.

For white audiences Reagan takes the rough edge off his policies by the adroit use of "photo opportunities." A few years ago, after reading that a cross was burned on the lawn of a black family in suburban Maryland, he helicoptered out to the house, with the White House press corps in tow, to say what a bad thing it was. Recently, he and Nancy Reagan went by motorcade along Martin Luther King Boulevard in southeast Washington to dine with the family of a black second-grade student with whom he had been corresponding. After he had shared a chicken dinner and delivered his gifts of jelly beans and tickets to the Jackson Victory Tour concert that night, Reagan posed for pictures with the boy and his parents. It was another example of Reagan's technique of denying the undeniable in order to dupe the gullible. How can a man who shows such concern and consorts so easily with blacks be a racist? It was a shrewd way of sending the message that unremitting opposition to the true interests of black people doesn't make one a mean racist.

Haynes Johnson of *The Washington Post*, one of the few journalists who has written about the political effectiveness of Reagan's approach, recently interviewed Merle Black, a political scientist at the University of North Carolina. After discussing several studies indicating that racism motivates some people to become Republicans, Black told Johnson:

> Race is very important, and especially for today's students. They've been to desegregated schools, and they've had some experience with affirmative action programs and they do not like them. Every one of them has a friend who didn't get into UNC who had higher board scores than blacks who did get in here. So a lot of their experience has made them very sensitive to racial things, and when Reagan comes out and says the things he says, boy, they like that.
>
> Reagan's kind of civilized the racial issue. He's taken what [Alabama Gov. George C.] Wallace never could do and made it acceptable. It fits in with their sense of perceived injustice, with what they see as the status of being a white person not being as high as it was 15, 20 or 30 years ago.

For the most part, Americans don't want to admit that they are racists and they certainly don't want to tell that to political journalists or pollsters . . . . So Reagan has unleashed an invisible monster on American politics in a way that makes him virtually unassailable.

Southern politicians used to promise their redneck constituents that they would "keep the niggers in their place," and when elected, they proceeded to do just that. It has been reported that after losing an early election to just such a politician, George Wallace vowed never to be "outniggered" again. Well, it is clear that Ronald Reagan is not going to be "outcolored."

[Reprinted with permission of *The Nation* Magazine/The Nation Co., Inc. Copyright © 1984.]

4. REAGAN AND WOMEN

In 1980, when 55 percent of male voters cast their ballots for Reagan, only 47 percent of women did—the widest gender discrepancy ever observed in a presidential election. This "gender gap" attracted much attention from journalists and political activists alike. Writing in Psychology Today *(November 1982), Zick Rubin, professor of social psychology at Brandeis University, suggested that the sources of the gap were partly psychological: men were more drawn than were women to Reagan's tough talk to the Russians and his "free and unfettered" outdoorsy image.*

The year 1983 was especially rough for Reagan on the gender front, as a series of episodes highlighted his "woman problem." At the National Women's Political Caucus convention in July, Reagan was roundly criticized—a signal of trouble ahead, warned the St. Louis Post-Dispatch. *Then, in early August, in apologizing to a group of business and professional women who has been denied a White House tour in a scheduling mixup, Reagan made matters worse by quipping ungrammatically that if it were not for women, "us men would still be walking around in skin suits and carrying clubs." The* Richmond Times-Dispatch *could see nothing wrong with the President's praise of women's "civilizing, humanizing qualities," but feminists found it patronizing.*

Later that month a Justice Department official, Barbara Honegger, resigned with a blast at the administration for dragging its feet on campaign pledges to eliminate sexually discriminatory federal laws. This fresh controversy led the U.S. News & World Report *to a careful examination of Reagan's record on women's issues. By the end of the year, Reagan's backing among women had slumped to 38 percent, while 53 percent of men continued to support him. Addressing the gender gap during the 1984 campaign, Reagan contributed an article to the* Ladies' Home Journal *heaping praise on his mother, his wife Nancy, and his two daughters Maureen and Patti, for their profound influence on his life. (First wife Jane Wyman went unmentioned.) The gender-gap issue eventually faded, but in muted form it dogged Reagan to the end of his term.*

ST. LOUIS POST-DISPATCH
President and Gender Gap

[July 13, 1983]

The National Women's Political Caucus convention in San Antonio over the weekend produced its share of rhetoric as well as the spectacle of eager candidates falling into the merciless trap of special interest semantics. It left, too, a host of questions for political reporters to chew over.

Was Bella Abzug right in declaring that "Women will decide who the next president of the United States will be"? Can John Glenn recover from his gaffe in referring to a married couple as "man and wife" instead of the approved "husband and wife"? Will women remember at the polls that Walter Mondale proclaimed that "I am a feminist"—and will it matter if they do? Can Ronald Reagan get even one woman's vote in 1984?

Mr. Reagan, in particular, took a terrific beating at the convention. He was described variously as "hopeless," "a dangerous man" and someone who at every turn is "guilty of some failure to understand how women live their lives." Those are harsh words but they are reflected in the public opinion surveys. One commissioned by *The New York Times* and CBS News found that 82 percent of the Republican men sampled think Mr. Reagan should be re-elected in contrast to 68 percent of the GOP women. That survey also found that, overall, only 33 percent of the women sampled believe that Mr. Reagan deserves another term.

At this point in the long election season, it is useful to bear in mind the warning of the Democratic pollster, Peter D. Hart, who points out that information gathered so early on is "written in the sand at the water's edge." Even so, the pattern of feminine disaffection with Mr. Reagan is such that Ms. Abzug's boast cannot be dismissed out of hand. If the president's standing with women, who make up 53 percent of the electorate, does not improve dramatically—and if his image with black Americans does not undergo a remarkable improvement—he could find himself in serious difficulty if he chooses to run, regardless of how well he is thought of by the white male electorate.

As the *Times*/CBS News poll shows, Mr. Reagan's approval among women—Republicans and Democrats—has tumbled precipitously since the spring of 1981. At that time, the gap between GOP men and women was only 9 percentage points on the question of Mr. Reagan's performance.

The NWPC chairwoman, Kathy Wilson, a Republican, suggested that Mr. Reagan could bridge the gender gap by reversing his position on such issues as abortion and the Equal Rights Amendment. The president's advisers reply that a switch like that is inconceivable, but that Mr. Reagan could improve his standing with women by sponsoring legislation on issues such as pension equity.

That cosmetic tactic may well be the best that Mr. Reagan has, but even it is unpromising. Equal political rights and abortion are only two issues on which Mr. Reagan's stands have cost him support among women—and women are scarcely united on those. His economic program that discriminates against the working poor and the elderly, his unrelenting emphasis on expanding the military and building up nuclear weaponry and his dangerous Cold War approach to the Soviet Union also are costing him with women. He cannot easily change policy on so broad a front.

There was a message, in short, from San Antonio. Beneath the rhetoric was a warning for Mr. Reagan—one that he cannot ignore and cannot respond positively to without repudiating much of his presidency.

[Reprinted courtesy *St. Louis Post-Dispatch*.]

RICHMOND (VIRGINIA) TIMES-DISPATCH
The Gender Trap
[August 5, 1983]

Twelve hundred delegates to a convention of business and professional women showed up at the White House Wednesday for a long-planned tour. They were not, however, "on the schedule" and they were turned away.

To make amends President Reagan asked to speak to their assembly—to bridge, as it were, the gender gap. Instead, he fell into it.

No snub was intended, he told the women, asking their pardon. But now, it seems, he has something else to apologize for. "I happen to be one who believes," the president said in the course of his remarks, "that if it wasn't for women, us men would still be walking around in skin suits and carrying clubs."

"Degrading," snapped the president of the women's group. "I thought it was inappropriate and I was offended." As were, apparently, others.

Well, pardon us, but we're having trouble crediting their offense. If anybody should be offended, it's men and grammarians.

These are, we must note, professional women who have come a long way, Ronnie, from the mere exercise of a civilizing influence on barbarians. They obviously do not appreciate their achievements being evaluated only in terms of their beneficent effect on men. It is a throwback to the very attitude that made theirs such a long, long way to come. It makes of them no more than adjuncts. That much we understand. Tie-straightener to mankind—this is not their mission in life.

But heaven help us if their mission in life is to make the civilizing, humanizing qualities of women as anachronistic and demeaning as dwelling in caves.

That sharkskin suits have replaced animal hides and hand-held computers have displaced clubs may be not the only, or even the most remarkable, testament to the capabilities of women and their contributions to society. But it is one, it's far from shameful, far more than cosmetic; and the so-called feminine qualities that contributed to it are not what women or the world need liberating from. The greatest contribution of women's lib is to demonstrate that women are not only capable of succeeding on virtually any turf traditionally reserved to men but are entitled to choose to do so. That can be demonstrated, and success can be achieved, without denigrating women's prehistoric or historical accomplishments and without disdaining femininity, which doesn't mean buttons and bows any more than it means bows and scrapes.

The most exasperating thing about these women's fury is that it blinded them to the one truly significant statement the president made. His "penance" for the scheduling snafu, he said, "is going to be that . . . I personally am going to read" a stack of computer printouts detailing statutes and regulations that discriminate against women. What can be amended by executive order will be, he promised, and what requires congressional action will be submitted for amendment to Congress.

"Trivial," pronounced the group's president. Only the Equal Rights Amendment will suffice, and since Mr. Reagan isn't for it, the group isn't for Mr. Reagan. Pity. Yes, the president has made that promise before; if held to it, he might learn something.

So might his opposition. It is the ardor of ERA's most vociferous advocates for axing all legislation that discriminates on the basis of sex, even legislation that discriminates in favor of women who choose "traditional roles," which gives many advocates of women's rights pause—and most opponents their ammunition. Had ERA proponents backed specific legislation to address specific grievances with all the time and energy they've expended on the blanket proscription of the ERA, women might be a lot closer to the legal and economic equality they are due without jeopardizing the legal protection they need.

[Reprinted courtesy *Richmond Times-Dispatch.*]

ROBERT A. KITTLE AND PATRICIA AVERY
Women's Issues—and the Reagan Record

[*U.S. News and World Report*, September 5, 1983]

As the first modern President to be markedly less popular among women than among men, Ronald Reagan finds himself increasingly on the defensive over his record on women's issues.

His struggle against the "gender gap" suffered a big setback in late August when a Justice Department official who said her job was to identify sexually discriminatory laws quit in protest. The aide, Barbara Honegger, labeled the project a "sham" and accused Reagan of reneging on promises to women. "He doesn't deserve loyalty, because he has betrayed us," she said.

The attack stunned presidential strategists, who had hoped that the White House was making headway against a problem that could be highly troublesome in the 1984 election. Reagan says, "I will match our record against any other administration."

What the debate is all about—

Ending legalized bias. In opposing ratification of the equal-rights amendment, the President pledged to advance women's rights by trying to eradicate federal and state laws that discriminate. Feminists complain that the task force reviewing federal laws has been at work almost two years and has found many discriminatory statutes, yet not a single one has been changed. They also allege that the effort to encourage states to overhaul discriminatory laws and rules has been given short shift.

After Honegger resigned, Reagan ordered the Justice Department and a cabinet council to accelerate their review and to propose recommendations by Labor Day.

Enforcing anti-bias laws. Feminists charge that the administration has weakened enforcement of such laws in important ways. They point to suggested easing of federal regulations that govern affirmative action in hiring and promotion. Another sore point: A pending Supreme Court case dealing with Grove City College in Pennsylvania, in which the administration seeks to narrow application of a law that bars sex discrimination in schools getting federal funds. "They are gutting the law," declares Kathy Wilson, head of the National Women's Political Caucus.

Reagan aides reject this. They note that in other instances government lawyers have sided with the feminists, such as in a case now before the Supreme Court in which a female attorney is challenging an Atlanta law firm's contention that decisions on naming partners are immune from sex-bias laws.

Economic issues. Women's organizations assert that it is women who have taken the brunt of Reagan's deep cutbacks in welfare programs, since females far outnumber male recipients in such programs as Aid to Families With Dependent Children, food stamps, medicaid, federally subsidized day care, family planning and legal aid.

Defending his economic record before Republican women in San Diego on August 26, Reagan said, "I believe the greatest contribution this administration can make to women is to get the economy moving and keep it moving."

The decline in inflation, White House aides emphasize, benefits women. "We need to let women know that we've given them more buying power," says a senior presidential adviser.

The President takes credit for enactment of other measures that help women: Near elimination of federal estate taxes that often forced widows to sell family farms and businesses; reduction of the "marriage penalty" that taxes working couples at a higher rate than single-income families, and an increase in child-care tax credits.

Feminists insist that most of these moves started in Congress and, in the words of Pat Reuss of Women's Equity Action League, "gathered cobwebs on White House desks" for a long time.

The White House is now backing bills to improve collection of child-support payments and outlaw sex discrimination in pension rates and is drawing up a proposal to boost tax-deductible contributions homemakers can make to IRA's—individual retirement accounts.

Social issues. The President's support for a constitutional amendment to ban abortions and for measures to restrict abortion funding are other major grievances of the feminists.

So is the administration's adoption earlier this year of the so-called squeal rule, requiring federally funded family-planning clinics to notify the parents of minors who receive contraceptives. The government is appealing a court ruling that overturned the regulation.

Female appointees. The Chief Executive has appointed about the same number of women to federal posts as Jimmy Carter. He is the first President to name a female Supreme Court Justice—Sandra Day O'Connor—and the first to have three women serving simultaneously in cabinet-level positions: Health and Human Services Secretary Margaret Heckler, Transportation Secretary Elizabeth Dole and U.N. Ambassador Jeane Kirkpatrick.

Reagan trails Carter in appointment of women to jobs requiring Senate confirmation. Carter by this point had named 113 to such posts, compared with 95 for Reagan. Women's-rights groups fault the President for appointing only 10 women to federal judgeships, compared with Carter's 18.

As charges and denials flew between the Reagan and feminist camps, the President installed his daughter Maureen as his adviser on women's issues.

"My father came to me and said, 'I seem to have this problem, and I don't think I'm such a bad guy,'" Maureen Reagan explained. She added, however, that it would take a speedup in action to convince many women that the President really is trying to help them.

[Copyright © 1983 *U.S. News and World Report.*]

RONALD REAGAN
In Praise of American Women
[*Ladies' Home Journal*, January 1984]

Women's lives have changed a great deal since this magazine began a century ago. I can see this evolution in the roles of women in my own family. My mother, my wife, my two daughters—these are the women who have had the greatest influence on me. Each is strong in her own way, in her own generation. I thought I might write today about these three generations of women who mean so much to me, because in their personal lives is the larger story of the changing role of American women over the past one hundred years.

My mother was named Nelle, a beautiful name from another time, and it fit her quiet determination and beauty perfectly. She was small with auburn hair and blue eyes, and she kept our family together, with deep-seated faith, through the Depression and through those ups and downs every family experiences. Her trust in God was absolute. My father was hard-working, had a sense of humor, and was more worldly than she. He also had a problem. He was an alcoholic. He would go months without a drink, and then with no warning become a different person.

As we grew up in that small town of Dixon, Illinois, her love and strength helped us understand our father. . . . The Depression forced her to work in a dress shop for $14 a week so that we could make ends meet. She kept us together emotionally and financially and provided stability for our family.

Her education took her through only elementary school, but she knew no diploma was needed for kindness, for love, for doing what was right. I could recall all day stories of her goodness. After my parents moved to California, my mother discovered a tuberculosis sanatorium for indigents and devoted many hours to the patients there. . . .

I know, even as I write this article, there are women in America just like my mother. They have hearts that carry without complaint the pains of the family. Perhaps the husband is troubled or out of work or even gone. Perhaps the children need special help or attention. They are women who seek to hold their family safe from alcohol or illness or crime or any number of possible threats, all the while working so that the family can survive economically. These women have my deepest respect and affection for what they are accomplishing. They are human treasures, and I hope their families love and cherish them for their goodness and strength. . . .

The women of Nancy's generation have probably had the most difficult time dealing with the changes that have swirled around us. Many of them grew up in a society that taught them to be one thing, only to arrive at a point in their lives when society began expecting something else. Nancy had a successful career as an actress. I would never have asked her to give it up for marriage, but she made that choice herself. She said she wanted marriage to be her full-time job.

Whatever the expectations of her, Nancy has always come through with flying colors. She has met challenges that take a great deal of inner strength. She married an actor, but as I became interested in politics, her life evolved into something much more complicated than she or I had ever imagined. In politics you gain a great deal, but you also lose some things. She lost part of her private life, and lost part of our family time together. I guess you might say Nancy is a nester. She loves home and family life, and public office has taken a major portion of that away—there are always obligations to meet and events to attend. . . .

When I was elected President, Nancy got a full-time job as well, the job of First Lady. And make no mistake, it is a job, a difficult and demanding one—and one, I might add, she never sought. But she had the desire and perseverance to succeed in this new role, and she is doing marvelously. I wish you could read all the letters from kids involved with drugs telling how much she has helped them and how she has changed their lives. And what really brings a lump to my throat are the letters about the lives she has saved.

I am so proud to be married to this woman. Nancy had the strength to give up part of herself for my career in politics, yet at the same time maintain who she is inside. She did it willingly and lovingly. Nancy is my partner in life. She makes the wonderful things worth sharing, and the harder, more painful things easier to bear. Nancy's love is the strongest part of her being and it gives me strength as well.

My daughters, Maureen and Patti, are women of a different era than either Nancy or my mother. They are new, modern women, and they are very independent. I am quite proud of them. I must admit when certain people, for political reasons, say I don't understand the modern woman, I am always very tempted to say, "Oh yeah? Then how come I have two of the most independent, accomplished, loving daughters a father could find?"

I think they are the kind of women who can do just about anything. Maureen has worked in radio and television, promoted overseas trade, run for political office; and now, on a parttime basis, she is giving her old dad advice on, believe it or not, how to communicate to women what the Administration is trying to accomplish. She is married to a very fine man, but one thing I know about Maureen is that she will always be able to take care of herself. She has what in the old days we would call spunk; today they call it assertiveness.

My younger daughter, Patti, is independent as well. She is a songwriter, a singer, an actress, and talented in each. She also has very much her own opinions. We two agree on the need to reduce nuclear weapons, but we have different ideas on how to go about it. And don't think there haven't been some animated discussions on that topic. She is the only person I can debate nuclear arms with who will then turn around and give me a kiss.

I not only love my daughters, I admire them. They are true individuals. Their outlooks and their lives are representative of the varied interests and varied futures women have today. Some seek to focus on the home and family. And some seek to do all these things.

My mother was basically a homemaker. Nancy filled the role of homemaker plus that of actress and public figure. My daughters are pursuing demanding careers. This to me is the story of women over the last century. No role is superior to another. The point is, a woman must have the right to choose the one role she wishes or to perhaps fill them all....

With the strength, love and intelligence America's women have always possessed, the future is not something to fear. I have great faith in the women I love, and I have great faith in all of America's women.

5. REAGAN AND RELIGION

Many Americans, particularly evangelical Protestants, hoped that Ronald Reagan would reverse what they saw as a rising tide of secularism and moral decay in America. These themes loomed large in Reagan's campaign and in his presidential rhetoric, as he spoke out on such emotionally charged issues as abortion, pornography, prayer in the schools, and the need for a strong military arsenal to resist the march of godless communism.

The issue of Reagan and religion moved to center stage early in 1983 when he addressed, first, the nation's religious broadcasters and then the National Association of Evangelicals meeting in Orlando. In the second speech (excerpted below), linking warm praise for religion with fervent anticommunism, the President proclaimed the Soviet Union "the focus of evil in the modern world." These speeches elicited a torrent of comment. While William F. Buckley, Jr., approved the Orlando speech and linked it to Abraham Lincoln's Civil War reflections on God's role in human affairs, other observers were sharply critical. Reagan's political sermonizing and his efforts to link communism abroad to "modern-day secularism" at home were deeply divisive, warned the New Republic. *The liberal Catholic publication* Commonweal *saw Reagan as spokesman for a "civil religion" that had taken many forms in American history, and argued that his pieties reflected the feelings of many Americans ignored by a secular media which often displayed "striking intolerance toward religious belief." But* Commonweal *agreed with the* New Republic *that Reagan's enthusiasm for a school-prayer amendment was politically mischievous and subversive of authentic religious faith.*

RONALD REAGAN
Address to National Association of Evangelicals
[Orlando, Florida, March 8, 1983]

The other day in the East Room of the White House at a meeting there, someone asked me whether I was aware of all the people out there who were praying for the President. And I had to say, "Yes, I am. I've felt it. I believe in intercessionary prayer.'' But I couldn't help but say to that questioner after he'd asked the question that—or at least say to them that if sometimes when he was praying he got a busy signal, it was just me in there ahead of him. I think I understand how Abraham Lincoln felt when he said, ''I have been driven many times to my knees by the overwhelming conviction that I had nowhere else to go.'' . . .

There are a great many God-fearing, dedicated, noble men and women in public life, present company included. And, yes, we need your help to keep us ever mindful of the ideas and the principles that brought us into the public arena in the first place. The basis of those ideals and principles is a commitment to freedom and personal liberty that, itself, is grounded in the much deeper realization that freedom prospers only where the blessings of God are avidly sought and humbly accepted. . . .

That shrewdest of all observers of American democracy, Alexis de Tocqueville, put it eloquently after he had gone on a search for the secret of America's greatness and genius—and he said: ''Not until I went into the churches of America and heard her pulpits aflame with righteousness did I understand the greatness and the genius of America. . . . America is good. And if America ever ceases to be good, America will cease to be great.''

Well, I'm pleased to be here today with you who are keeping America great by keeping her good. Only through your work and prayers and those of millions of others can we hope to survive this perilous century and keep alive this experiment in liberty, this last, best hope of man.

I want you to know that this administration is motivated by a political philosophy that sees the greatness of America in you, her people, and in your families, churches, neighborhoods, communities—the institutions that foster and nourish values like concern for others and respect for the rule of law under God.

Now, I don't have to tell you that this puts us in opposition to, or at least out of step with, a prevailing attitude of many who have turned to a modern-day secularism, discarding the tried and time-tested values upon which our very civilization is based. No matter how well intentioned, their value system is radically different from that of most Americans. And while they proclaim that they're freeing us from superstitions of the past, they've taken upon themselves the job of superintending us by government rule and regulation. Sometimes their voices are louder than ours, but they are not yet a majority. . . .

[In a section of the address omitted here, President Reagan discussed his opposition to abortion, his support for a constitutional amendment permitting prayer in the public schools, and other related issues.]

Now, I'm sure that you must get discouraged at times, but you've done better than you know, perhaps. There's a great spiritual awakening in America, a renewal of the traditional values that have been the bedrock of America's goodness and greatness.

One recent survey by a Washington-based research council concluded that Americans were far more religious than the people of other nations; 95 percent of those surveyed expressed a belief in God and a huge majority believed the Ten Commandments had real meaning in their lives. And another study has found that an overwhelming majority of Americans disapprove of adultery, teenage sex, pornography, abortion, and hard drugs. And this same study showed a deep reverence for the importance of family ties and religious belief.

I think the items that we've discussed here today must be a key part of the nation's political agenda. For the first time the Congress is openly and seriously debating and dealing with the prayer and abortion issues—and that's enormous progress right there. I repeat: America is in the midst of a spiritual awakening and a moral renewal. . . .

Now, obviously, much of this new political and social consensus I've talked about is based on a positive view of American history, one that takes pride in our country's accomplishments and record. But we must never forget that no government schemes are going to perfect man. We know that living in this world means dealing with what philosophers would call the phenomenology of evil or, as theologians would put it, the doctrine of sin.

There is sin and evil in the world, and we're enjoined by Scripture and the Lord Jesus to oppose it with all our might. Our nation, too, has a legacy of evil with which it must deal. The glory of this land has been its capacity for transcending the moral evils of our past. For example, the long struggle of minority citizens for equal rights, once a source of disunity and civil war, is now a point of pride for all Americans. We must never go back. There is no room for racism, anti-Semitism, or other forms of ethnic and racial hatred in this country.

I know that you've been horrified, as have I, by the resurgence of some hate groups preaching bigotry and prejudice. Use the mighty voice of your pulpits and the powerful standing of your churches to denounce and isolate these hate groups in our midst. The commandment given us is clear and simple: "Thou shalt love thy neighbor as thyself."

But whatever sad episodes exist in our past, any objective observer must hold a positive view of American history, a history that has been the story of hopes fulfilled and dreams made into reality. Especially in this century, America has kept alight the torch of freedom, but not just for ourselves but for millions of others around the world.

And this brings me to my final point today. During my first press conference as President, in answer to a direct question, I pointed out that, as good Marxist-Leninists, the Soviet leaders have openly and publicly declared that the only morality they recognize is that which will further their cause, which is world revolution. I think I should point out I was only quoting Lenin, their guiding spirit, who said in 1920 that they repudiate all morality that proceeds from supernatural ideas—that's their name for religion—or ideas that are outside class conceptions. Morality is entirely subordinate to the interests of class war. And everything is moral that is necessary for the annihilation of the old, exploiting social order and for uniting the proletariat.

Well, I think the refusal of many influential people to accept this elementary fact of Soviet doctrine illustrates an historical reluctance to see totalitarian powers for what they are. We saw this phenomenon in the 1930's. We see it too often today.

This doesn't mean we should isolate ourselves and refuse to seek an understanding with them. I intend to do everything I can to persuade them of our peaceful intent, to remind them that it was the West that refused to use its nuclear monopoly in the forties and fifties for territorial gain and which now proposes 50-percent cut in strategic ballistic missiles and the elimination of an entire class of land-based, intermediate-range nuclear missiles.

At the same time, however, they must be made to understand we will never compromise our principles and standards. We will never give away our freedom. We will never abandon our belief in God. And we will never stop searching for a genuine peace. But we can assure none of these things America stands for through the so-called nuclear freeze solutions proposed by some. . . .

A number of years ago, I heard a young father, a very prominent young man in the entertainment world, addressing a tremendous gathering in California. It was during the time of the cold war, and communism and our own way of life were very much on people's minds. And he was speaking to that subject. And suddenly, though, I heard him saying, "I love my little girls more than anything—" And I said to myself, "Oh, no, don't. You can't—don't say that." But I had underestimated him. He went on: "I would rather see my little girls die now, still believing in God, than have them grow up under communism and one day die no longer believing in God."

There were thousands of young people in that audience. They came to their feet with shouts of joy. They had instantly recognized the profound truth in what he had said, with regard to the physical and the soul and what was truly important.

Yes, let us pray for the salvation of all of those who live in that totalitarian darkness—pray they will discover the joy of knowing God. But until they do, let us be aware that while they preach the supremacy of the state, declare its omnipotence over individual man, and predict its eventual domination of all peoples on the Earth, they are the focus of evil in the modern world. . . .

Because [communist leaders] sometimes speak in soothing tones of brotherhood and peace, because, like other dictators before them, they're always making "their final territorial demand," some would have us accept them at their word and accommodate ourselves to their aggressive impulses. But if history teaches anything, it teaches that simple-minded appeasement or wishful thinking about our adversaries is folly. It means the betrayal of our past, the squandering of our freedom.

So, I urge you to speak out against those who would place the United States in a position of military and moral inferiority. . . . In your discussions of the nuclear freeze proposals, I urge you to beware the temptation of pride—the temptation of blithely declaring yourselves above it all and label both sides equally at fault, to ignore the facts of history and the aggressive impulses of an evil empire, to simply call the arms race a giant misunderstanding and thereby remove yourself from the struggle between right and wrong and good and evil.

I ask you to resist the attempts of those who would have you withhold your support for our efforts, this administration's efforts, to keep America strong and free, while we negotiate real and verifiable reductions in the world's nuclear arsenals and one day, with God's help, their total elimination.

While America's military strength is important, let me add here that I've always maintained that the struggle now going on for the world will never be decided by bombs or rockets, by armies or military might. The real crisis we face today is a spiritual one; at root, it is a test of moral will and faith.

Whittaker Chambers, the man whose own religious conversion made him a witness to one of the terrible traumas of our time, the Hiss-Chambers case, wrote that the crisis of the Western World exists to the degree to which the West is indifferent to God, the degree to which it collaborates in communism's attempt to make man stand alone without God. And then he said, for Marxism-Leninism is actually the second oldest faith, first proclaimed in the Garden of Eden with the words of temptation, "Ye shall be as gods."

The Western World can answer this challenge, he wrote, "but only provided that its faith in God and the freedom He enjoins is as great as communism's faith in Man."

I believe we shall rise to the challenge. I believe that communism is another sad, bizarre chapter in human history whose last pages even now are being written. I believe this because the source of our strength in the quest for human freedom is not material, but spiritual. And because it knows no limitation, it must terrify and ultimately triumph over those who would enslave their fellow man. For in the words of Isaiah: "He giveth power to the faint; and to them that have no might He increased strength. . . . But they that wait upon the Lord shall renew their strength; they shall mount up with wings as eagles; they shall run, and not be weary. . . ."

Yes, change your world. One of our Founding Fathers, Thomas Paine, said, "We have it within our power to begin the world over again." We can do it, doing together what no one church could do by itself.

God bless you, and thank you very much.

WILLIAM F. BUCKLEY, JR.

Reagan at Orlando

[*National Review*, April 15, 1983]

Although it sometimes seems as if everybody has commented on Mr. Reagan's speech in Orlando to the evangelicals, mostly to deplore it, it isn't by any means clear to the student who reads the entire text what exactly all the fuss is about. The columnist Anthony Lewis is so irate one fears for his health. Granted, if one could harness the day-to-day indignation of Tony Lewis one could solve the energy crisis. But he seems to be saying, in that dyspeptic blur, that President Ronald Reagan, on March 8, 1983, denounced as ungodly everyone who favors a freeze on nuclear armaments.

Well, if that's all there is to worry about, the remedy is simple. He didn't. Mr. Reagan did indeed say that "there is sin and evil in the world," a statement that, unhappily, deserves no headline. And he did say that "we are enjoined by Scripture and the Lord Jesus to oppose it with all our might." And that also is true. He did not, as Lewis insists, and as the eloquent Hugh Sidey of *Time* magazine suggests, go so far as to say that, in all matters, Americans are blameless. On the contrary, he followed the line above with the statement, "Our nation, too, has a legacy of evil with which it must deal." Did he then, as Mr. Sidey charges, act as one of those "self-anointed soldiers of God armed with unbending judgments about who and what are good and moral"? Yes, but surely Mr. Reagan did this in a way that not only is consistent with American tradition, but enhances that tradition, namely, by reaffirming our belief that some things are right, others wrong; that a decent respect to the opinions of mankind requires that we make clear why we think some things right, others wrong; and that we proceed, to continue quoting from the Declaration of Independence, "with a firm reliance on the protection of Divine Providence."

Mr. Reagan's speech touched on a number of matters, including prayer in the public schools, abortion, sex education, and other matters presumptively interesting to a gathering of evangelicals. On the matter of the Soviet Union he stressed a point of indispensable relevance at every level of current negotiations. If at West Point one half of the cadets asserted that there was no higher morality than getting back an examination with a good grade, the honor system would not work. Mr. Reagan, as leader of the Free World, does well to remind us that we are dealing with men explicitly bound to the proposition that the morality of advancing world revolution is superordinated to any other morality. Much flows from this, for instance the emphasis we need to place on verification in any move toward mutual disarmament. The notion, propagated by Anthony Lewis, that Reagan was in effect telling us that God prefers chocolate ice cream over tutti-frutti is, well, nutti.

There is, in fact, a noble analogue to what Mr. Reagan was attempting. Just after delivering his second inaugural address, Abraham Lincoln replied to an enthusiast that he did not expect that the speech would prove immediately popular. "Men are not flattered by being shown that there has been a difference of purpose between the Almighty and them. It is a truth which I thought needed to be told." The allusion was, of course, to those in the Union who believed in slavery, even as our opponents in the Soviet Union believe in slavery, although while the men around Jefferson Davis prayed to God for help, those around Andropov caught doing so would cease to be those around Andropov. But Lincoln's analysis, not unlike Reagan's, mutatis mutandis, alluded to "the progress of our arms, upon which all else chiefly depends." Reagan said that the survival of the Union for which Lincoln fought depends significantly on our being strong. Lincoln said that in the dispute in which we were involved, "Both parties deprecated war, but one of them would make war rather than let the nation survive, and the other would accept war rather than let it perish." So is it today, again, the necessary changes having been made.

And Lincoln said, "If we shall suppose that American slavery is one of those offenses which, in the providence of God, must needs come, but which, having continued through His appointed time, He now wills to remove, and that He gives to both North and South, this terrible war as the woe due to those by whom the offense came, shall we discern therein any departure from those divine attributes which the believers in a living God always ascribe to Him?"

And Reagan asks, If we shall suppose that the inhumanity of Communism is one of those awful blights that God has tolerated, let us accept the burdens and the sacrifices necessary to keep ourselves whole until the working of Divine Providence releases from bondage the peoples currently enslaved.

To the extent that we need to suffer in order to remain free, the lapidary resignation of Abraham Lincoln, inscribed on the wall of his memorial in Washington, would describe the resignation of Ronald Reagan in every respect: "As was said three thousand years ago, so still it must be said, 'The judgments of the Lord are true and righteous altogether.'"

NEW REPUBLIC
Reverend Reagan
[April 4, 1983]

When Ronald Reagan mentions "the phenomenology of evil," you sit up and listen. The President broached this, and other matters of great profundity, in his speech (more properly, his sermon) to the National Association of Evangelicals in Orlando. The speech deserves study. To date we have had no more comprehensive communication of the President's picture of American society, or of the moral ambitions he has for it. We have also had no more intellectual effort from this unintellectual (and uneffortful) President; he cited the Founding Fathers, Tocqueville, C.S. Lewis, Whittaker Chambers, Lenin, and, of course, the Bible. A major text, in short, of this conservative hour.

According to Ronald Reagan, history is reaching a climax. He portrayed his country as embattled, set upon by enemies from without and within, fighting for nothing less than its reason for being. The enemy without is Communism, which the President described as "the focus of evil in the modern world"; the speech left friends and foes around the world with the impression that the President of the United States was contemplating holy war. The enemy within is "modern-day secularism." With his implication that the two are working toward a single end, which is the weakening of America, Mr. Reagan insulted multitudes.

The President's larger point was that political struggles are spiritual struggles. The consequences of this point are many. The first is to raise the emotional pitch of politics in general. The President was not affable in the pulpit; he was apocalyptic. He thrilled his audience with the tale of a man who said that "I would rather see my little girls die now, still believing in God, than have them grow up under Communism and one day die no longer believing in God," as if this, in the area of foreign policy, is the question at issue. (That man had little faith in faith.) The West, the President warned, is in "spiritual crisis," which is graver and more grandiose than Jimmy Carter's "malaise." It is an emergency, in short, which requires not a politics of reason but a politics of the rod.

The second consequence of the President's spiritualization of politics is a staggering simplification of it. The slander of secularism—which, Mr. Reagan observed, on the authority of Whittaker Chambers, "collaborates in Communism's attempt to make man stand alone without God"—is bad enough. But there is more. The speech, in fact, is an orgy of cheap shots. Item: those who are in favor of the right to abortion must take responsibility for "infanticide and mercy killing," because they are all the result of the same "decline in respect for human life." Item: those who oppose the "squeal rule" necessarily believe that "something so sacred [as sex] can be looked upon as a purely physical thing with no potential for emotional and psychological harm." Item: those who support a mutual and verifiable nuclear freeze are not only politically but spiritually wrong, because they have yielded to "the temptation of pride—the temptation to blithely declare yourselves above it all and label both sides equally at fault."

Nowhere in the President's homily was there the hint of an understanding that all these positions originate not in sin, but in something much harder to fight—another point of view. This is not surprising, because Mr. Reagan's thesis was precisely that policy decisions must have religious reasons. "Is all of the Judeo-Christian tradition wrong?" he asked about the parents' right to know. Well, nobody said it was; the confidentiality of birth control counseling does not have a metaphysical basis. What has been offered on its behalf is a social consideration, not a spiritual consideration. But no social consideration has been offered for the "squeal rule," and society will pay dearly, with a new population of unwanted and unloved children, if the spiritual consideration has sway.

By what authority does this man claim to administer the Judeo-Christian tradition? We elected a President, not a priest. It is not arrogance, however, that is responsible for Mr. Reagan's sacerdotal conception of his role. That conception is based, rather, in a specific construction of the American political system. "When our Founding Fathers passed the First Amendment," the President explained, "they sought to protect churches from government interference. They never meant to construct a wall of hostility between government and the concept of religious belief itself." And he went on: "The evidence of this permeates our history and our government. The Declaration of Independence mentions the Supreme Being no less than four times. 'In God We Trust' is engraved on our coinage. The Supreme Court opens its proceedings with a religious invocation. And the Members of Congress open their meetings with a prayer."

This is very poor history. The author of the Declaration of Independence will offer small succor to a religious view of the Republic; the Supreme Being to whom Jefferson refers is a Deist deity, who made the world and left it to its devices. There is no more rationalist document of our early years, and no more strenuous plea for the strict separation of church and state, than Jefferson's draft for a constitution of Virginia, which was also written in 1776. (The President cited Tom Paine, too, which is exactly the opposite of the Devil quoting Scripture.)

The President was correct that "the Founding Fathers" did not design "a wall of hostility" between religion and politics. The spirit of the First Amendment is not anticlerical; although the differences in religious doctrine among the founders were considerable, almost none of them harbored a hostility to religion. But they designed a wall anyway. Perhaps the first to describe the nature of this wall was Tocqueville, an early sociologist of spiritual forms, whom the President misappropriated for his purposes. Tocqueville's problem was "to discover how [religions] can most easily preserve their power in the democratic centuries which lie before us." They can do so, he concluded, by "confining themselves to their proper sphere," which is not the sphere of politics. . . . Clearly things have changed. Priests now extend their ecclesiastical authority to affairs of policy, and the President extends his executive authority to affairs of the soul. "I think the items we have discussed here today," the President preached, referring to the religious analysis of abortion, school prayer, and parental notification, "must be a key part of the nation's political agenda." With these words he has set himself against the American political tradition.

"Neutrality" is how the Supreme Court has interpreted the First Amendment's attitude to religion; noting that "we are a religious people," the Court judged in 1963, that religion must nevertheless let government alone, so that "a majority [could not] use the machinery of State to practice its beliefs." Which is exactly what the President was recommending. . . .

President Reagan profoundly misunderstands the nature of secularism. He called secularism a "value system that is radically different from that of most Americans." Most Americans, he continued, believe in "families, churches, neighborhoods, communities—the institutions that foster and nourish values like concern for others and respect for the rule of law under God." But the rule of law need not be under God, as long as it is over man. Who are the secularists who are not committed to these institutions and values? Are the unchurched on the darkling American plain really against families and communities? There are precincts of sanctity in secular lives too. The President's rhetoric is deeply divisive. The moral and sociological reality of this country refutes his tidy and tendentious distinctions. Secularism is just as committed to what he called "the tried and time-tested values upon which our very civilization is based" as religion. Secularism simply has different reasons for its commitments. In a democracy, however, reasons cannot be ruled.

The President also misunderstands the profoundly secular character of democracy. This misunderstanding appears in the most ironic passage of his sermon. His argument for a religious conception of American citizenship ended with this evidence: "One recent survey by a Washington-based research council concluded that Americans were far more religious than the people of other nations. 95 percent of those surveyed expressed a belief in God and a huge majority believed the Ten Commandments had real meaning in their lives. And another study has found that an overwhelming majority of Americans disapprove of adultery, teenage sex, pornography, abortion, and hard drugs." Nothing could be more in the spirit of democracy and less in the spirit of religion than these remarks. Truth is indifferent to numbers. Politics is not. Priests do not take polls. Presidents do. Only in a political system in which legitimacy comes not from above but from below can public opinion become a form of bearing religious witness.

Obviously an overwhelming majority of Americans disapprove of adultery, teenage sex, pornography, and hard drugs. The study cited by the President proves only that the moral health of the public has not been impaired by the secularization of politics. Those who differ with the President in the matter of religion and politics do not do so because they approve of certain patterns of personal behavior, but because they disapprove of the idea that patterns of personal behavior require government approval.

The influence of religion upon the public life cannot be denied. In many instances it is salutary. The President does not want to divest the United States of this influence. He is not the first. The Anti-Federalists protested bitterly against the remorseless rationalism of the Constitution; the maintenance of republican institutions, they said, requires the persistence of religion. This was exactly the conclusion to which Tocqueville came, too; but religion in America, he wrote, bore not upon laws, but upon mores, where its function was to check the excesses of individualism and materialism. Mr. Reagan, it is plain, cannot have enough individualism or materialism. Still, he insists that religion is an instrument of improvement. It will not, however, improve politics.

The President should cease these celestial navigations. There is business on earth. He is not in the White House to save our souls, but to protect our bodies; not to do God's will, but the people's. Anyway, God will forgive— that, said Heine, is his profession.

COMMONWEAL

Mr. Reagan's Civil Religion

[September 21, 1984]

President Reagan has called for a rebirth of faith. But what faith? Right-wing Christian fundamentalism, say his critics. Not quite, although that is part of it. . . . What his opponents don't recognize is that he is not promoting religion in the sense of the many particular faiths that we know in America. He is preaching something else, and that something is *civil religion*. His own version of it.

The idea of civil religion—a generalized faith that binds together the nation and links the national purpose to some higher or deeper reality—has been batted about among observers of the American scene for some time now.

What they see has many ingredients: Protestant "civic piety," the Founding Fathers' belief in a somewhat Deist Providence, evangelical fervor and the democratic "faith in the common man," with its W.P.A. icons. Our civil religion has its rituals and obligations—on the Glorious Fourth, on Memorial Day, in presidential inaugural addresses. For some observers it is a necessary social glue that holds together a wildly disparate people; for others it is an authentic religious form that places the nation, for self-understanding and judgment, in a transcendental framework. For still others, it is a shallow celebration of the American Way of Life. We are among those who think it contains all these possibilities. It can be inclusive—providing a common language, part religious, part secular, so Americans of different outlooks can adequately voice their deepest convictions. And it can be exclusive, both of those Americans whose own languages it refuses to accommodate and of the rest of the world. It can be critical—as in the appeals of reformers from Thoreau to Martin Luther King, Jr. And it can be complacent—congratulating ourselves on material wealth or military might. It can be a vehicle for other faiths, assisting them into the public forum. Or it can be their rival, subverting their particular challenge in a miasma of "Americanism."

Civil religion has been transformed as new groups of believers and nonbelievers have claimed their rightful places in what was once a Protestant "overculture." The religion faded, and the strictly civic expanded. How many citizens could even understand the theological anguish of Lincoln's Second Inaugural today? JFK, at his inaugural, declared the nation's "belief that the rights of man come not from the generosity of the state but from the hand of God." Lyndon Johnson chose to declare the U.S. a "nation of believers" in more secular terms: "we are believers in justice and liberty and union. . . . And we believe in ourselves."

Not a few Americans have felt excluded by this shift. It seemed that their way of thinking and talking was no longer part of legitimate public discourse, at least on the national level. Unwilling to recognize how older forms of the civil religion were not, in truth, neutral but gave their own brand of Christianity a privileged status, they now found themselves frustrated by a secular "overculture" whose proponents were often equally unwilling to allow that it, too, might not be neutral but leave distinctly secular outlooks "more equal than others." The story is more complicated, of course; and the resolution not at all easy—or in sight. But the immediate fact is that President Reagan has understood this sense of grievance, as the Democrats have not, and exploited it. By appearing before sectarian groups, by announcing prayer weeks and Bible years, by endorsing an interpretation of recent history as enforced secularization, he has presided over the civil religion in such a way as to unmistakably give back to those Americans their share in it.

It is possible to see something inclusive and democratically healthy in this—and also much that is opportunistic and dangerously demagogic. Reagan's attribution of secularization to malign courts is a gross distortion of a process that has had numerous valid sources. His suggestion that all opponents of his version of civil religion are "attacking religion" and intolerant is shockingly unfair. Yet if one views the matter not from Smalltown, U.S.A., but from a cultural capital like New York, there *is* a striking amount of intolerance toward religious belief, and it is particularly frustrating because it is frequently displayed by those who hold themselves as models of tolerance and openmindedness. . . .

All this explains how it is possible to see something positive when Ronald Reagan sends the liberal editorialists into a dither. Something, maybe, but not too much. The destructive side of Reagan's forays into civil religion is revealed in its political centerpiece—"voluntary" organized prayer in the public schools. This proposal is simply double-talk and a real threat to conscience. It is, in our view, completely unlike questions about Christmas crèches, "equal access" for high-school religious groups, chaplains for state legislatures, religious themes on postage stamps, and a host of other issues about which we could live comfortably with considerable give-and-take. Why—besides the obvious political capital—cannot the president see this? . . .

At this point, whatever service the president's civil religion performs in reintroducing an alienated segment of believing Americans into public life is outweighed by the subversion it works on authentic religion—the kind that not only can celebrate family, hard work, and "strength and purposefulness in our foreign relations" but believes that even these things stand under God's judgment. There is something downright frightening about a civil religion in which the chant "U.S.A.! U.S.A.!" plays such a prominent part. Mr. Reagan's civil religion, self-congratulatory and sentimental, turns out not to be an umbrella under which our particular beliefs can flourish; it turns out to be the ardent elevation of the American Way of Life, of which our particular beliefs are presumed to be only superficial variations. We demur. We are ready to love and serve our nation but not worship it. Yes, ours is a jealous God.

6. THE REAGAN ADMINISTRATION AND THE ENVIRONMENT

While Reagan's position on black, feminist, and religious issues were of particular concern to specific groups, his views on the environment aroused widespread apprehension. A series of environmental studies and a spate of books beginning with Rachel Carson's Silent Spring *(1962), coupled with the energy crisis of the 1970s, had aroused deep fears about the exhaustion of natural resources and the pollution of America's land, water, and air. Many viewed Reaganism, with its free-enterprise rhetoric and its generic hostility to "big government," as seriously out of step with public opinion on this issue. Writing in the journal* Science *shortly after the election, Constance Holden conveyed environmentalists' fears and surveyed Reagan's mixed record on this issue. In a November 1981* Nation *article, James Ridgeway, author of several books on energy and the environment, reviewed the administration's assaults on the environment, including its efforts to weaken the Environmental Protection Agency and the Clean Air Act.*

As Reagan's term ended, Carl Pope, an official of the Sierra Club, a leading environmentalist lobby, evaluated the impact of the Reagan years. Despite the environmentalists' fears, he concluded, environmental awareness and activism had actually increased in the 1980s, in reaction to the administration's foot-dragging approach. Nevertheless, Pope's overall assessment was somber. Valuable time had been lost, he warned, in dealing with such urgent long-term issues as global warming, unhealthy air, industrial pollution, acid rain, and the exhaustion of the earth's fossil-fuel resources.

CONSTANCE HOLDEN
The Reagan Years: Environmentalists Tremble
[*Science*, November 28, 1980]

The environmental movement has had a nightmare and awakened to find it is true: Ronald Reagan is President-elect and the Senate is in Republican hands.

President Carter gave plum jobs to leaders of the environmental movement and supported many of their causes. Reagan, at least to judge by his rhetoric, could scarcely be less sympathetic. His hostility to government regulation has given rise to fears that the Environmental Protection Agency (EPA) may be severely restrained or even abolished. The Clean Air Act, without Edmund Muskie in the Senate to protect it, may be reduced in scope, along with much other environmental legislation. . . .

Reagan clings to the concept that environmental protection and economic growth are fundamentally incompatible, and commonly lumps environmentalists together with those who espouse a "no-growth" economy. He appears to regard environmental protection as a rather ephemeral value that may be attended to after the basic substantive matters—renewed economic growth and an all-out campaign to increase energy production—are well under way, environmentalists believe.

Environmental issues were discussed in the campaign not for their own sake but in the context of the Republican interest in cutting back federal regulations. According to a one-page environmental position paper, "We should return to the states the primary responsibility for environmental regulation in order to increase responsiveness to local conditions." Reagan's task force on regulation, headed by economist Murray Weidenbaum of the American Enterprise Institute, has fingered EPA as the main target. Reagan's people generally regard EPA as being in the hands of "environmental extremists"; they want to turn around the regulatory approach of that agency, as well as that of the Labor Department's Occupational Safety and Health Administration, so as to reflect much greater attention to the economic consequences of regulations and their effects on employment and the energy supply....

Reagan's environmental record as governor of California was "mixed," according to Michael McCloskey, director of the Sierra Club. McCloskey says Reagan "often ended up signing environmental legislation he had opposed if there was enough public interest and pressure." A rundown of his actions as governor, compiled by the Sierra Club Bulletin, reveals that Reagan tried to prevent the state from taking action to clean up auto emissions, resisted coastal zone management planning, fought government funding for mass transit, approved extension of the state highway system, and opposed expansion of the state parks system. (It was in 1966 that he made his famous remark—"A tree is a tree. How many more do you need to look at?"—in reference to the proposed expansion of Redwood National Park.) On the other hand, Reagan did sign California's water pollution law, said to be the strongest in the country.

In the years after being governor, Reagan, on his radio program and elsewhere, expressed what environmentalists regard as a fairly consistent anti-environmentalist line. He attacked the EPA's ban on DDT, and defended the baby seal killing program, saying it had been "unjustly maligned." He has complained that the wilderness system has protected too much forest from the timber industry. He is an ardent supporter of the Sagebrush Rebellion, which favors returning public lands in the West to private ownership.

Reagan has said that there are "no environmental problems" associated with nuclear energy. He wants to throw public lands open to oil shale exploration and go full speed ahead on offshore oil drilling. He has even cast energy conservation in a dim light, saying that "at best, it means we will run out of energy a little more slowly."

It is probably not Reagan's beliefs as much as his lack of intellectual sophistication and his willingness to embrace "facts" of indeterminate origin that unsettle environmentalists—as witness statements made in some of his few campaign references to the environment. Not only did Reagan tell Ohio miners that air pollution was "substantially" under control (a comment made during a 10-day smog crisis in Los Angeles), but he went on to state that 80 percent of nitrogen oxide pollution is caused by vegetation, and blamed Mount St. Helen's—in a statement containing multiple errors—for contributing more sulfur dioxide "than has been released in the last 10 years of automobile driving."

Another less publicized example of naiveté came in response to a question about the Administration's report on the year 2000. Reagan, averring that things probably weren't all that bad, claimed there were "farm studies, based on the tillable land on earth, and based on if they are farmed at the level of American farming worldwide, that the earth can support a population of 28 billion people."

It was not until October that Reagan assembled a task force on the environment. Headed by Dan W. Lufkin, chairman of the finance committee of Columbia Pictures and member of the executive committee of the National Audubon Society, the task force contains a number of well-respected figures including two former heads of EPA. But it is not clear how much influence the task force will have on future policy, given Reagan's stated priorities. . . .

Environmentalists are not necessarily hostile to the Republican creed of fiscal restraint or to the notion that the federal government has overextended itself. But if the Administration sets about to dismantle the regulatory structure that has been built up over the past decade, environmentalists predict a fierce backlash from the public. "They're going to have a firestorm," predicts John Grandy of Defenders of Wildlife. "If he tries to fight, he will have one of the bloodiest fights he's ever seen," says another environmentalist. . . .

Some in the environmental movement believe that its future now lies in action at the village green level, not with federal policies framed in Washington. Others hope that the Reagan Administration, like its predecessors, can be brought around. But the general prognosis among environmentalists is that a period of federal neglect, be it benign or otherwise, is the likely lot of their cause during the next 4 years.

[Reprinted from *Science*, Vol. 210, pp. 988-991. Copyright © 1980 AAAS.]

JAMES RIDGEWAY
Pollution Is Our Most Important Product
[*Nation*, November 7, 1981]

If it were guided by history, the Reagan Administration, with its concern for a more productive economy, would embrace the goals of the environmental movement.

The environmental movement originated in the sanitation reforms proposed by business during the Industrial Revolution. . . . At the turn of the century, President Theodore Roosevelt argued that conservation resulted in greater economic efficiency. . . . In short, environmentalism has never been a socialist or "radical" concept. It was an invention of business, and its aim was increased productivity. . . . A recent study by Data Resources Inc., a private research organization, concluded that pollution control legislation would create 524,000 jobs between 1980 and 1987; it would also stimulate investment and cause an average annual consumer price increase of only 0.4 percent.

Nonetheless, the Reagan Administration remains opposed to environmental regulations and to the environmentalists. It believes that the "free market," not the government, should allocate capital resources. Conservative politicians are out to defeat the dwindling band of moderate Republicans whose ideas and policies probably best embody the spirit of modern environmentalism.

The Administration has joined battle on several fronts. First, there is a move to eviscerate the Environmental Protection Agency. The President has proposed a 60 percent reduction in the E.P.A.'s real spending (that is, budgetary cuts of 42 percent plus the losses from a 15 percent to 20 percent inflation rate during the 1982 and 1983 fiscal years), and that 40 percent of the agency's staff be fired. These cuts and staff reductions come at a time when the agency's workload has doubled. During the next two years, the E.P.A. must enforce standards on toxic chemicals that Congress mandated in 1979.

The budget reductions also mean that funding for research to develop standards on permissible exposure to toxic chemicals will be eliminated. The projected cuts in Federal grants to states will curtail environmental programs at the state and local level.

According to William Drayton, Assistant Administrator for Planning at the E.P.A under Jimmy Carter: "Right now, the E.P.A. should be hiring the soil hydrologists, toxicologists and other skilled technicians it needs to determine whether or not the hazardous waste disposal sites it must certify are safe or not. If the E.P.A. can't hire the staff it needs to do the job, who will? Few towns or states could afford such people even before Proposition 13 and Reagan cuts in Federal aid. Consequently, this country and the E.P.A. will mistakenly certify unsafe sites—hurting affected citizens and communities, running down the E.P.A.'s technical credibility and eventually making it less and less likely that communities will accept any disposal operations."

In addition to gutting the E.P.A., the government has moved in Federal District Court in Washington, D.C., to delay the implementation of water-quality standards. The action is directed against a plan setting standards for the discharge of effluent containing sixty-five known toxic chemicals, many of them carcinogens. Industry wants the Federal District judge to throw out the standard-setting procedure and has already managed to delay its enforcement. Now the government is asking for a further delay, until 1983. At the same time, it is seeking to transfer the responsibility for setting standards to the states and industry. This represents a regression to the states' rights approach to water-pollution control of the late 1950s, which was notoriously ineffective. The government offers budgetary hardship as the reason for delay and points to projected cuts of 20 percent to 25 percent in funding and personnel at the E.P.A. division charged with setting effluent guidelines. But the cuts, of course, are the Administration's own doing. And beyond all this, the E.P.A. insists that even if standards are set, compliance will not be expected until well into the 1990s.

Since mid-June, the government has drafted five sets of "improvement" amendments to the Clean Air Act, which expires this year, and each successive draft is more crippling. The Administration proposes to weaken virtually every control in the act. The draft legislation would repeal the duty of the Federal government to designate the air pollutants for which standards must be set. The government would be given considerable "discretion" in setting ambient air standards, and the use of cost-benefit analysis would be permitted. The draft law would eliminate existing regulations in places where the air is now clean and increase the dangers posed by acid rain by permitting higher amounts of pollution from automobiles and electrical generating plants. It would reduce public participation in the standard-setting procedure and make enforcement difficult. For example, the requirement that air-quality monitoring data be made available to the E.P.A. and to the public would be eliminated, and the Federal and state governments would be given complete discretion to set deadlines for complying with standards. In sum, the Administration's draft amendments to the Clean Air Act would render the law meaningless. . . .

Thus, the Reagan Administration proceeds on several fronts, deliberately dismantling the environmental control apparatus built up since the 1950s. The result will be a rise in diseases related to environmental pollution; there will be more Love Canals and increased danger from acid rain. More than a century and a half after the height of the Industrial Revolution, the economic and human costs of pollution have not changed. In the nineteenth century, however, business advocated improving public health through environmental controls as a step toward widening markets and productivity. That vision apparently has been lost. Instead, industry and government are now joined in a belief that the American economy can prosper through a growing epidemic of environmentally-related diseases. That is the bottom line of the attack on the environmentalists.

As Governor Jerry Brown of California pointed out during the 1980 Presidential campaign, if you make $10,000 a year, you will contribute $30,000 to the Gross National Product in three years. But if environmental pollution gives you cancer, the cost of your medical treatment will add $100,000 to the G.N.P. in just one year. Shorn of rhetoric, that is precisely the kind of economic growth Reagan seeks and will probably get as a result of his attack on regulations intended to clean up the environment.

CARL POPE
The Politics of Plunder

[*Sierra*, November/December 1988]

At half past four on election day, 1980, Sierra Club volunteers and staff gather around a borrowed television set at the Club's San Francisco headquarters to watch the returns.

For the first time the Club has conducted a major voter-education drive. It's been a discouraging effort. Republican presidential candidate Ronald Reagan has barnstormed the country, attacking the Carter administration and even its Republican predecessors for turning environmental agencies over to "extremists." He has made some outlandish statements, ranging from a promise to invite the steel and oil industries to rewrite the EPA's regulations to a charge that 80 percent of the nation's air pollution problems are caused by chemicals released by trees. Despite growing controversy over Reagan's reactionary environmental stands, polls indicate that he is likely to defeat the incumbent, Jimmy Carter.

Groans fill the room as soon as the television is turned on. Even though the polls will remain open for several hours in the far West, the networks are already proclaiming Reagan the winner.

Spirits slump further as the Senate and House results pour in. In state after state, senators who have fought for the environment are being upset by their opponents. . . . Frank Church of Idaho, one of the Senate's leading proponents of wilderness, is narrowly defeated by Steve Symms, a virulent advocate of public-land exploitation. By seven o'clock only a scattering of sorrowful Sierra Clubbers remain at the election-night party.

The next morning it is clear that very few pro-environment candidates have managed to claw their way to the top of the Reagan avalanche. Representative Morris Udall, chair of the House Interior Committee, is reelected, as are most of the other key environmental players in the House. Of the environmental leaders in the Senate facing strong 1980 challenges, only Alan Cranston of California wins a decisive victory. Senator Gary Hart of Colorado wins, but barely.

Reagan's coattails are so long that the Republicans finally wrest control of the Senate from the Democrats. The new chair of the Senate Energy

Committee, with jurisdiction over the nation's public-land and energy resources, is Symms' ideological soulmate and fellow Idahoan, James McClure. The new head of the Senate Agriculture Committee is archconservative and wilderness foe Jesse Helms of North Carolina.

"The end of the environmental movement" is proclaimed by NBC News (along with the demise of feminism and civil rights). Mainstream Republicans who served on the staffs of environmental agencies under presidents Nixon and Ford, some of whom worked for Reagan when he was governor of California in the late 1960s and early '70s, are passed over for jobs. By Inauguration Day environmental policy is firmly in the hands of the "sagebrush rebels"—abrasive, conservative ideologues from the West. The rebels' antigovernment bias is strongly supported by Office of Management and Budget (OMB) Director David Stockman, a former Republican congressman from Michigan who only months earlier told Congress that toxic waste dumps are not a proper federal concern.

The Reagan Era has begun.

Today environmentalists are breathing slightly easier, and counting the few days left in Reagan's reign. The Sierra Club has moved to larger headquarters, a necessary response to a membership that soared from 180,000 during the Carter years to 480,000 in September of 1988. Ironically, Ronald Reagan has motivated far more people to join the Club and other environmental organizations than all of his predecessors combined.

Reagan, in effect, has reinvented the national environmental movement. He has done so with appointments and policy initiatives that have offended and alarmed the American people—efforts consistent with the President's general hostility toward activist government and his unlimited faith in private economic institutions. But it is one thing to promise to get the government off the taxpayers' backs. It is an altogether different proposition—and an unacceptable one to most Americans—to relieve polluting industries of the burden of complying with environmental laws. It's one thing to extol the virtues of free markets; it's another to extend that principle *ad absurdum,* offering to sell national parks to geothermal companies or amusement-park operators.

For nearly eight years the American people have been confronted with a difficult choice. In the White House a charismatic political leader has made taxpayers an appealing promise of limited government. A majority of voters have felt that Reagan and his economic programs fit well with their values of personal freedom and achievement. At the same time, in the EPA, in the Department of the Interior, in the OMB, and elsewhere in the federal bureaucracy, Reagan's zealous and often hard-edged political appointees have openly displayed their contempt for the environmental values and programs that have long since become an accepted part of American life.

The public's reaction has been to support Reagan as a person, but to make sure that his anti-environmental ethic is not translated into concrete policy. Citizens demanded and got the ouster of Interior Secretary James Watt, EPA

Administrator Anne Burford, and EPA Assistant Administrator Rita Lavelle—the first generation of Reagan's hard-line appointees. They joined environmental groups and told pollsters that their commitment to those issues was stronger than ever before. In 1984 they elected a Congress that stopped virtually all of Reagan's anti-environmental initiatives.

Faced with this formidable resistance, the Reagan administration gradually abandoned the environmental front. By the middle of Reagan's second term his administration's new initiatives were far closer to the mainstream than to the privatized, deregulated world the President's pre-inauguration team had laid out. The administration came in adamantly opposed to federal cleanup of abandoned hazardous waste dumps, for instance, yet eventually agreed to a strong Superfund bill that would provide for just that.

Now, at the end of Reagan's second term, it's clear that the past eight years have not turned out to be as disastrous as the environmentalists who watched the 1980 election returns feared; nor have U.S. businesses reaped the rich harvest they anticipated in the early months of 1981. The most disappointed of all must be the ideologues, the Watts, Burfords, and Stockmans. They had their best shot ever at the American environmental ethos. Yet they strengthened, rather than weakened, the public's determination to protect the environment—and that is one of the more surprising legacies of Ronald Reagan. . . .

There can be no question that Reagan's appointees tried on numerous fronts to weaken America's commitment to the environment.

—They talked loosely of selling some units of the National Park System, and for eight years regularly proposed eliminating federal funding for park acquisition.

—A dentist from South Carolina, James Edwards, began dismantling conservation and renewable-energy programs soon after he was named Secretary of Energy.

—Through Reagan's Task Force on Regulatory Reform, headed by Vice President George Bush, the OMB's Stockman targeted scores of environmental regulations that were later weakened, delayed, or eliminated.

—Administration officials offered mineral leases at bargain-basement prices on millions of acres of public land. They recommended putting the entire outer continental shelf (OCS) on the auction block, under lease procedures that ranged from honest giveaways to outright corruption. In its first ten OCS lease sales, the administration managed to transfer titles to prime oil tracts for $7 billion less than would have been realized using the leasing methods of previous administrations.

—Reagan appointees rebuffed repeated pleas from Canada for a reduction of the acid rain that is destroying its forests, its economy, and life in its lakes. Instead of solutions, some Reaganites talked of "more studies" while Stockman made scornful references to "billion-dollar fish."

—Appointees at the EPA crippled the Superfund toxic-waste-cleanup program, and the program's key administrator, Rita Lavelle, went to jail.

—Morale at the EPA, the National Park Service, the Fish and Wildlife Service, and the Bureau of Land Management collapsed in the face of inadequate budgets, the administration's repeated refusals to enforce the laws, and its political interference in regulatory decisions. . . .

[But] hundreds of thousands of Americans stood up to Reagan, Bush, Watt, and Burford and preserved and strengthened the country's environmental ethic. Good laws were passed and harmful ones blocked; lawsuits argued and won on their merits; scoundrels evicted from office. More people signed the Sierra Club's petition to remove Watt from Interior than had ever simultaneously petitioned Congress on any other issue. Thousands of dedicated civil servants in public agencies resisted the efforts of political appointees to disrupt the execution and enforcement of the nation's environmental statutes. The media covered environmental issues with more intensity than ever before. State and local governments assumed much of the burden that the Reaganites refused to shoulder.

Thanks in large part to environmentalist campaigns, more acreage was added to the National Wilderness Preservation System in the lower 48 states under Reagan than under any other president. Twenty-nine new wildlife refuges were established, encompassing a total of 500,000 acres; 200 new plants and animals were added to the nation's list of endangered species. The Clean Water Act, the Resources Conservation and Recovery Act, and the Comprehensive Environmental Response, Compensation, and Liability Act (the Superfund) have all been reauthorized and greatly strengthened. Lead is finally being phased out of gasoline after two generations of use. An international agreement to reduce the production of chlorofluorocarbons (CFCs), chemicals that destroy the protective stratospheric ozone layer, has been ratified. Oil leasing along the California coast has been stalled, and the Arctic National Wildlife Refuge is still closed to oil drilling.

Just this summer, the Senate renewed the Endangered Species Act by the largest margin ever—92 to 2. A majority of the House of Representatives, including 64 Republicans, went on record as favoring a massive strengthening and renewal of the Clean Air Act. The Senate declined to confirm Robert Bork and Bernard Siegan, viewed by environmentalists as Reagan's two worst judicial nominees.

In the end, even the delegates to the Republican National Convention in August demonstrated surprising disagreement with Reagan's environmental policies. In a survey conducted for the Sierra Club and other conservation groups, the delegates showed strong support for federal leadership in protecting the country's natural resources.

But . . . we should not forget that on mountaintops and beaches, in small woodlands and majestic rainforests, in cities and playgrounds, in the oceans and the atmosphere itself, reminders of the Reagan Era will linger for decades. . . .

Eight precious years have been lost. The patterns set by Reagan's policies could have irreversible consequences in ten, or twenty, or thirty years—very brief times to change the direction of cumbersome national and international economies and polities. . . .

We now need a global environmental Reconstruction. We need to ask of ourselves and our leaders more self-discipline than ever before, in part to compensate for the callousness of the last eight years. We need greater fidelity to facts, in part because our most recent leaders tried to wish them away. We need above all to remember that time matters, that events have consequences, and that the world is a wondrous and intermingled web that, when torn in one place, may unravel a thousand miles or a hundred years away.

[Reprinted by permission.]

The National Defense

1. THE MILITARY BUILD-UP AND THE NUCLEAR ARMS RACE

Long before his election as President, Ronald Reagan had called for increased military spending to strengthen America's hand in the Cold War struggle with the Soviets. His 1980 campaign warned of the weakening of U.S. defenses in the Carter years. True to his word, Reagan in the early eighties presided over an unprecedented peacetime increase in military spending. The 1983 address excerpted below is typical of his repeated calls for ever-greater military appropriations to "preserve our free way of life in a sometimes dangerous world." Defense Secretary Caspar Weinberger oversaw the flow of dollars to the Pentagon. As President Nixon's tightfisted budget director, Weinberger had won the nickname "Cap the Knife," but as Defense secretary he frustrated legislators of both parties by his refusal even to discuss spending cuts. The excerpts from Weinberger's 1985 report to Congress was one of a long series of warnings about America's "dangerous slide" in military preparedness and assurances that his gargantuan annual budget requests were "prudent and responsible." The Orlando Sentinel *editorial "Whatever Happened to 'Cap the Knife'?" represents the exasperation with Weinberger that grew steadily in the Reagan years. By 1987 even such a staunchly pro-Reagan magazine as* Business Week *was warning that "the United States can't afford everything the Pentagon wants . . ." ("Defense Spending: The Wild Blue Yonder,"* Business Week, *May 11, 1987).*

Writing in the Bulletin of the Atomic Scientists *early in 1989, Ann Markusen, professor of urban affairs and social policy at Northwestern University, looked at the domestic economic and social impact of the Reagan military spending program and found it overwhelmingly negative. In the same issue of the* Bulletin, *however, diplomatic historian John Lewis Gaddis examined Reagan's record on arms control, including the 1988 INF Treaty*

*eliminating U.S. and Soviet medium-range nuclear weapons from Europe,
and concluded that, contrary to all expectations, the old Cold Warrior had
achieved a notable breakthrough on this important front.*

RONALD REAGAN
Peace and National Security
[Address to the American People, March 23, 1983]

... At the beginning of this year, I submitted to the Congress a defense
budget which reflects my best judgment, and the best understanding of the
experts and specialists who advise me, about what we and our allies must do
to protect our people in the years ahead.

That budget is much more than a long list of numbers, for behind all the
numbers lies America's ability to prevent the greatest of human tragedies and
preserve our free way of life in a sometimes dangerous world. It is part of a
careful, long-term plan to make America strong again after too many years of
neglect and mistakes. Our efforts to rebuild America's defenses and strength-
en the peace began two years ago when we requested a major increase in the
defense program. Since then the amount of those increases we first proposed
has been reduced by half through improvements in management and procurement and other savings. The budget request that is now before the Congress
has been trimmed to the limits of safety. Further deep cuts cannot be made
without seriously endangering the security of the nation. The choice is up to
the men and women you have elected to the Congress—and that means the
choice is up to you.

Tonight I want to explain to you what this defense debate is all about, and
why I am convinced that the budget now before the Congress is necessary,
responsible and deserving of your support. And I want to offer hope for the
future.

But first let me say what the defense debate is not about. It is not about
spending arithmetic. I know that in the last few weeks you've been bombarded
with numbers and percentages....

What seems to have been lost in all this debate is the simple truth of how
a defense budget is arrived at. It isn't done by deciding to spend a certain
number of dollars. Those loud voices that are occasionally heard charging
that the Government is trying to solve a security problem by throwing money
at it are nothing more than noise based on ignorance.

We start by considering what must be done to maintain peace and review
all the possible threats against our security. Then a strategy for strengthening
peace and defending against those threats must be agreed upon. And finally
our defense establishment must be evaluated to see what is necessary to

protect against any or all of the potential threats. The cost of achieving these ends is totaled up and the result is the budget for national defense.

There is no logical way you can say let's spend X billion dollars less. You can only say, which part of our defense measures do we believe we can do without and still have security against all contingencies? Anyone in the Congress who advocates a percentage or specific dollar cut in defense spending should be made to say what part of our defenses he would eliminate, and he should be candid enough to acknowledge that his cuts mean cutting our commitments to allies or inviting greater risk or both.

The defense policy of the United States is based on a simple premise: The United States does not start fights. We will never be an aggressor. We maintain our strength in order to deter and defend against aggression—to preserve freedom and peace. . . .

This strategy of deterrence has not changed. It still works. But what it takes to maintain deterrence has changed. It took one kind of military force to deter an attack when we had far more nuclear weapons than any other power; it takes another kind now that the Soviets, for example, have enough accurate and powerful nuclear weapons to destroy virtually all of our missiles on the ground. Now this is not to say the Soviet Union is planning to make war on us. Nor do I believe a war is inevitable—quite the contrary. But what must be recognized is that our security is based on being prepared to meet all threats. . . .

We can't afford to believe we will never be threatened. There have been two world wars in my lifetime. We didn't start them and, indeed, did everything we could to avoid being drawn into them. But we were ill-prepared for both—had we been better prepared, peace might have been preserved.

For 20 years, the Soviet Union has been accumulating enormous military might. They didn't stop when their forces exceeded all requirements of a legitimate defensive capability. And they haven't stopped now.

During the past decade and a half, the Soviets have built up a massive arsenal of new strategic nuclear weapons—weapons that can strike directly at the United States.

As an example, the United States introduced its last new intercontinental ballistic missile, the Minuteman III, in 1969, and we are now dismantling our even older Titan missiles. But what has the Soviet Union done in these intervening years? Well, since 1969, the Soviet Union has built five new classes of ICBM's, and upgraded these eight times. As a result, their missiles are much more powerful and accurate than they were several years ago and they continue to develop more, while ours are increasingly obsolete. . . .

Another example of what's happened: In 1978, the Soviets had 600 intermediate-range nuclear missiles based on land and were beginning to add the SS-20—a new, highly accurate mobile missile, with three warheads. We had none. Since then the Soviets have strengthened their lead. By the end of

1979, when Soviet leader Brezhnev declared "a balance now exists," the Soviets had over 800 warheads. We still had none. A year ago this month, Mr. Brezhnev pledged a moratorium, or freeze, on SS-20 deployment. But by last August, their 800 warheads had become more than 1,200. We still had none. Some freeze. At this time Soviet Defense Minister Ustinov announced "approximate parity of forces continues to exist." But the Soviets are still adding an average of three new warheads a week, and now have 1,300. These warheads can reach their targets in a matter of a few minutes. We still have none. So far, it seems that the Soviet definition of parity is a box score of 1,300 to nothing, in their favor.

So, together with our NATO allies, we decided in 1979 to deploy new weapons, beginning this year, as a deterrent to their SS-20's and as an incentive to the Soviet Union to meet us in serious arms control negotiations. We will begin that deployment late this year. At the same time, however, we are willing to cancel our program if the Soviets will dismantle theirs. This is what we have called a zero-zero plan. The Soviets are now at the negotiating table—and I think it's fair to say that without our planned deployments, they wouldn't be there.

Now let's consider conventional forces. Since 1974, the United States has produced 3,050 tactical combat aircraft. By contrast, the Soviet Union has produced twice as many. When we look at attack submarines, the United States has produced 27, while the Soviet Union has produced 61. For armored vehicles including tanks, we have produced 11,200. The Soviet Union has produced 54,000, a nearly 5-to-1 ratio in their favor. Finally, with artillery, we have produced 950 artillery and rocket launchers while the Soviets have produced more than 13,000, a staggering 14-to-1 ratio.

There was a time when we were able to offset superior Soviet numbers with higher quality. But today they are building weapons as sophisticated and modern as our own.

As the Soviets have increased their military power, they have been emboldened to extend that power. They are spreading their military influence in ways that can directly challenge our vital interests and those of our allies. . . .

The final fact is that the Soviet Union is acquiring what can only be considered an offensive military force. They have continued to build far more intercontinental ballistic missiles than they could possibly need simply to deter an attack. Their conventional forces are trained and equipped not so much to defend against an attack as they are to permit sudden, surprise offensives of their own.

Our NATO allies have assumed a great defense burden, including the military draft in most countries. We are working with them and our other friends around the world to do more. Our defensive strategy means we need military forces that can move very quickly—forces that are trained and ready to respond to any emergency.

Every item in our defense program—our ships, our tanks, our planes, our funds for training and spare parts—is intended for one all-important purpose—to keep the peace. Unfortunately, a decade of neglecting our military forces had called into question our ability to do that.

When I took office in January 1981, I was appalled by what I found: American planes that could not fly and American ships that could not sail for lack of spare parts and trained personnel and insufficient fuel and ammunition for essential training. The inevitable result of all this was poor morale in our armed forces, difficulty in recruiting the brightest young Americans to wear the uniform and difficulty in convincing our most experienced military personnel to stay on.

There was a real question, then, about how well we could meet a crisis. And it was obvious that we had to begin a major modernization program to insure we could deter aggression and preserve the peace in the years ahead.

We had to move immediately to improve the basic readiness and staying power of our conventional forces, so they could meet—and therefore help deter—a crisis. We had to make up for lost years of investment by moving forward with a long-term plan to prepare our forces to counter the military capabilities our adversaries were developing for the future.

I know that all of you want peace and so do I. I know too that many of you seriously believe that a nuclear freeze would further the cause of peace. But a freeze now would make us less, not more, secure and would raise, not reduce, the risks of war. It would be largely unverifiable and would seriously undercut our negotiations on arms reduction. It would reward the Soviets for their massive military buildup while preventing us from modernizing our aging and increasingly vulnerable forces. With their present margin of superiority, why should they agree to arms reductions knowing that we were prohibited from catching up?

Believe me, it wasn't pleasant for someone who had come to Washington determined to reduce Government spending, but we had to move forward with the task of repairing our defenses or we would lose our ability to deter conflict now and in the future. We had to demonstrate to any adversary that aggression could not succeed and that the only real solution was substantial, equitable and effectively verifiable arms reduction—the kind we're working for right now in Geneva. . . .

It will take us longer to build the kind of equipment we need to keep peace in the future, but we've made a good start.

We have not built a new long-range bomber for 21 years. Now we're building the B-1. We had not launched one new strategic submarine for 17 years. Now, we're building one Trident submarine a year. Our land-based missiles are increasingly threatened by the many huge, new Soviet ICBM's. We are determining how to solve that problem. At the same time, we are working in the Start and I.N.F. negotiations, with the goal of achieving deep reductions in the strategic and intermediate nuclear arsenals of both sides.

We have also begun the long-needed modernization of our conventional forces. The Army is getting its first new tank in 20 years. The Air Force is modernizing. We are rebuilding our Navy, which shrank from about 1,000 in the late 1960's to 453 ships during the 1970's. Our nation needs a superior Navy to support our military forces and vital interests overseas. We are now on the road to achieving a 600-ship Navy and increasing the amphibious capabilities of our marines, who are now serving the cause of peace in Lebanon. And we are building a real capability to assist our friends in the vitally important Indian Ocean and Persian Gulf region.

This adds up to a major effort, and it is not cheap. It comes at a time when there are many other pressures on our budget and when the American people have already had to make major sacrifices during the recession. But we must not be misled by those who would make defense once again the scapegoat of the Federal budget....

If we stop in midstream, we will not only jeopardize the progress we have made to date—we will mortgage our ability to deter war and achieve genuine arms reductions. And we will send a signal of decline, of lessened will, to friends and adversaries alike.

One of the tragic ironies of history—and we've seen it happen more than once in this century—is the way that tyrannical systems, whose military strength is based on oppressing their people, grow strong while, through wishful thinking, free societies allow themselves to be lulled into a false sense of security.

Free people must voluntarily, through open debate and democratic means, meet the challenge that totalitarians pose by compulsion.

It is up to us, in our time, to choose, and choose wisely, between the hard but necessary task of preserving peace and freedom and the temptation to ignore our duty and blindly hope for the best while the enemies of freedom grow stronger day by day.

The solution is well within our grasp. But to reach it, there is simply no alternative but to continue this year, in this budget, to provide the resources we need to preserve the peace and guarantee our freedom.

CASPAR W. WEINBERGER
Annual Report to the Congress, Fiscal Year 1985

Three years ago, a newly inaugurated President Ronald Reagan stood at the West Front of the Capitol and promised that "when action is required to preserve our national security, we will act." Recognizing that the preservation of peace required more than just rhetoric or good intentions, he committed his Administration to take the steps necessary to deter aggression and promote stability and freedom in a complex and changing world.

For a President taking office in January 1981, this was not a pledge to be given lightly. By the beginning of this decade, a majority of Americans were expressing their concern, indeed their fear, that the world had become a more dangerous place. They recognized that we faced a crisis of leadership, as the impression grew both at home and abroad that the United States was a superpower on the decline, unable to protect its citizens or its interests against a growing threat.

The 1980 election sent a clear signal that the American people wanted to reverse this dangerous slide and to restore America's position in the world. They recognized that we must regain the strength of our armed forces and restore the military balance so essential for preserving deterrence. They recognized that we must begin again the quest for genuine arms reductions, not settling for negotiations that resulted in merely codifying the growth in nuclear arsenals. We seek agreements that will *reduce* armaments of all kinds to lower, equal, and verifiable levels. Finally, they recognized that the United States, while it could not and should not be the world's policeman, nevertheless needed to reassume a leadership role recognized by our allies and friends, and our foes and potential enemies.

The American people entrusted responsibility for fulfilling this mandate to Ronald Reagan, and he and his Administration accepted that responsibility. Today, we have firm leadership to keep us steady on our course—leadership that combines a realistic understanding of the dangers and complexities of our world with a firm commitment to do what is necessary to preserve peace.

In this year's *Annual Report to the Congress*, we present our defense program for preserving peace in a dangerous world. We also assess this Administration's three-year stewardship of our nation's defenses, and the progress we have made toward fulfilling the mandate entrusted by the American people to Ronald Reagan in 1980....

In 1984, we will continue our long-term defense program, all the wiser for the lessons we have learned in the past three years, and confident that we are on the right course. But let us have no illusions: the next few years will be as crucial for America's defense program as they will be difficult.

In weighing the investments we must make, we cannot forget that the costs of maintaining a strong defense are easily measured. But the benefits are not. When we spend our savings on a new car, or a new home, we have acquired a tangible good. When we spend tax dollars on food stamps or federal highways, we have created a tangible result for all to see. But although we can count our missiles, or our tanks, or our men in arms, we can never really measure how much aggression we have deterred, or how much peace we have preserved. These are intangibles—until they are lost.

Indeed, it is a paradox of deterrence that the longer it succeeds, the less necessary it appears. As time passes, the maintenance of peace is attributed not to a strong defense, but to a host of more facile assumptions: some imagined newfound "peaceful intent" of the opponent, or the spirit of détente, or growing economic interdependency.

As the bills that we as a nation put off too long continue to come due, it will be tempting to search for excuses to avoid the reckoning once more. We must not yield to that temptation. Already the Congress has cut back on our operations and maintenance budgets, threatening our improvements in readiness, and slowed down several programs, increasing the cost of what all agree we will need—and counting the dangers inherent in taking too long to secure an effective deterrent. Already critics of the defense budget are discovering a new enthusiasm for weapons that are—conveniently—still on the drawing boards, even as they oppose procurement of hardware available now to strengthen our forces.

Unfortunately, we cannot make up for a decade of neglect in only three years of higher defense budgets. Restoring—and then maintaining—the military balance requires a determined and sustained effort. If we stop in midcourse, we will only endanger the progress we have made in recent years, and invite speculation by friends and adversaries alike that the United States can sustain neither its will nor its leadership.

By the same token, if we are allowed to continue on the path we have set, we can look forward to a time, only two fiscal years from now, when defense increases can begin to slow dramatically.

The Fiscal Year 1985 *Annual Report to the Congress* presents a prudent and responsible defense budget, and provides a thorough rationale for that budget. It shows that we arrived at this budget not by picking a budget number arbitrarily, but by weighing the threats and challenges to our interests, by refining our strategy for meeting those threats, and by identifying the capabilities we need to fulfill that strategy. The report also analyzes the resources available for acquiring those capabilities, and describes in detail the specific programs for which we are requesting funds.

Most importantly, the report is a document to help members of Congress in this coming year as they confront important—and difficult—budgetary decisions that will shape America's security through the end of this century. Over the past three years, the Congress and this Administration have worked together to rebuild America's defenses and restore our leadership in the world. We have made great progress. This year, let us again work together to preserve our gains and move closer to our goal of a stronger and more secure America, which is the best guarantee of a lasting peace.

ORLANDO SENTINEL
Whatever Happened to "Cap the Knife"?
[February 10, 1982]

Whatever happened to "Cap the Knife," who sliced his way through the Nixon administration Department of Health, Education and Welfare, paring waste wherever he found it? What mystical, Arthurian process turned his razor-sharp blade into a broad, dull shovel?

When President Reagan appointed Caspar Weinberger secretary of defense, there were quick nods of approval from both ends of the political spectrum. Even those adamantly opposed to the Reagan goal of spending $1.6 trillion on defense in the next five years felt that as long as Mr. Weinberger was minding the store, at least the money would be well managed.

But this week's disclosure of the 1983 Reagan budget fuels the growing suspicion that Mr. Weinberger has become the Pentagon's chief cheerleader and may be losing a great deal of credibility as a result. The budget proposal released Saturday shows an 18.1-percent increase in defense outlays. Military expenditures would jump from $182.8 billion this year to $215.9 billion in 1983. Spending for every category of arms will increase but with the biggest increases going to the Navy for shipbuilding.

Mr. Weinberger insists that fully $7.4 billion has been trimmed from the 1983 budget by streamlining programs already on line. That streamlining includes such things as multiyear contracting and buying larger quantities of goods on single contracts. He predicts that those types of initiatives will produce savings of $41 billion through 1986. But is that enough?

Mr. Weinberger argues that military waste is under control, but within the last week it was learned that the Army is experiencing 50 percent cost overruns on its AH-64 attack helicopter and that each M-1 tank will cost $1 million more than was projected.

There will always be waste in the military and Mr. Weinberger certainly must know that. He knows numerous bases are kept open solely to placate political interests. He must know of his own generals' arguments against spending $40 billion on an "interim" program like the B-1 bomber and in favor of using genuinely interim aircraft like stretched FB-111s.

And where is the fabled fiscal discipline when applied to that $2 million-a-copy M-1 tank that still doesn't perform to specifications?

Mr. Weinberger has refused to contemplate any cuts in defense spending on the grounds that it would send the "wrong signals to the Soviets," but that contention misses the point.

When Mr. Reagan came to office, he did so with a clear mandate to improve the national defenses. A vital part of that effort involves maintaining that national consensus at a time when the administration is pushing for deeper cuts in social programs. If Mr. Weinberger had moved into his Pentagon office and started making the judicious management decisions that won him his "knife" epithet, there is a good chance the national consensus would survive.

The American public is too savvy to believe the nation's defenses are being substantially improved by the "goose liver method" of force-feeding dollar bills down the military gullet. And when that awareness turns to cynicism, the national consensus on defense will be lost.

During the first six months in office, top officials of the Reagan administration, including Mr. Weinberger, insisted that all else was secondary to revitalizing the economy. If it was true then, why is it not still true today?

Would not the national interests best be served if the "Cap the Knife" of old broke free of the siren song of the generals and, along with the other members of the president's Cabinet, sharpened his knife for the job ahead?

[Reprinted courtesy *The Orlando Sentinel*.]

ANN R. MARKUSEN
Cold War Economics
[*Bulletin of the Atomic Scientists*, January/February 1989]

During the Reagan years, the U.S. government went on the biggest peacetime spending splurge in its history. Most of it went for a whopping increase in military budgets, which escalated to an estimated $283 billion in 1988, up from $178.4 billion (in current dollars) in fiscal 1981, the last Carter year. . . .

This bold commitment of public moneys has been made in the name of national security. But after a decade, are U.S. citizens really more secure? In part, the answer to that question depends upon the degree to which such expenditures have lessened the prospects for damaging military engagements. In part, it depends on the degree to which the economy has been debilitated by the drainage of resources to the military. Military security is only one of several pressing national goals, which include the alleviation of deadly diseases and the development of safe energy sources. A comprehensive assessment of the buildup must determine whether the sacrifices on these fronts and the potential threat to the economy are worth the gains in security claimed by its proponents.

While many of the deformities introduced into the U.S. economy by the military burden have evolved over the post–World War II period, and have their roots in the rise of the Cold War, the Reagan buildup has been unique in two respects. Previous buildups, associated with Korea and Vietnam, took place amid strong commercial booms and propelled the economy toward full employment. They were accompanied by an improving income distribution, manageable deficits, and positive trade balances. The Reagan buildup has been accompanied by a severe recession in nonmilitary manufacturing, prolonged unemployment and underemployment, a worsening trade balance, alarming growth in the deficit, and deteriorating income distribution.

Second, the administration explicitly claimed that the buildup was a program for economic revitalization. The economy was to become more competitive because military research and development would have a salutary effect on economic performance. The "strategic computing initiative," for instance, purported to be a program "for national security and economic strength." The idea was to help advance the artificial intelligence required for complex battle management planning, while helping the United States best the Japanese in supercomputing.

Most of the $2.13 trillion in military spending was a public investment in research projects, new weapons procurement, facilities construction, and human capital improvements. The nation borrowed heavily to make this investment: the current deficit is now twice what it was in 1980, and by 1988 outstanding debt totaled $2.6 trillion, almost three times more than in 1980. Under Reagan, the balanced budget advocate, the United States became a net debtor nation for the first time in over a century.

The deficit itself is not necessarily a bad thing. Like a home mortgage, federal debt can be an effective way to invest in the future. One can argue that earlier Defense Department investments in programs such as the inter-state highway system and the National Defense Education Act improved the performance of the economy, although these expenditures could have been even more effective detached from their military rationales.

But the infrastructure bought with federal defense dollars in the 1980s has done little to improve the productive base of the economy through education, public works, and innovations. Investments in B-1 and Stealth bombers, MX missiles, nuclear submarines, and test beds for the Strategic Defense Initiative (SDI) do not resemble expenditures on roads, bridges, mass transit, and waterways. The latter improve efficiency in the economy and stimulate private-sector activity while providing services to consumers and taxpayers. Few payoffs of this sort can be expected from the current military buildup.

While not a particularly good investment from the point of view of productivity and long-term growth, recent military spending has been an investment nevertheless. It would be impossible to spend $2 trillion in such a concentrated way without nurturing some industries at the expense of others, some occupational groups at the expense of others, some communities at the expense of others. The militarization of the economy has created a new set of problems.

• *The gulf is growing between commercially oriented durables industries and government-dependent industries bred by the Cold War.* Aircraft, missiles, shipbuilding, communications equipment, ordnance, and instruments have benefited disproportionately from the devotion of R&D funds and the guaranteed markets that Defense Department patronage offers, while steel, autos, and machinery have lost in the competition for resources—engineers, capital, research dollars. The steel industry, for instance, was turned down in its bid for $15 million for breakthrough technology research while the Reagan administration showered more than $15 *billion* on the aerospace, electronics, and computer industries for SDI research alone. . . .

Not surprisingly, the industries that have flourished during the decade are those whose competitiveness has been heavily subsidized by taxpayers. Once broadly diversified, the U.S. economy is now heavily specialized in high technology, arms, and business services. In an era when expanded international trade has rendered the economy more dependent upon foreign markets and factories than ever before, U.S. arms exports have grown faster than any other commodity group, while net exports of machinery and high-tech products have dropped precipitously. Reversing Carter's policy, the Reagan administration encouraged arms exports, permitted sales of first-generation technologies, and allowed contractors to use government research funds to develop arms for specific areas in the Third World.

• *A second deformity of the Cold War buildup is the accelerated restructuring of the skilled workforce.* Certain scientific occupations, such as physicists and mathematicians, are favored over others, such as biologists and chemists. In math and physics, faculty and graduate students who choose to specialize in research areas of interest to the Pentagon have many more resources and opportunities available to them than those who do not. Similarly, the ranks of the engineering profession have been swollen by defense dollars, and among engineers, those specializing in aeronautical and electrical fields are favored over those in civil and mechanical ones. . . .

On the other hand, the number of blue collar jobs has been shrinking. Automation of commercial production, through the use of computers, sensors, and robots, was a major byproduct of military spending over the recent postwar period and accelerated during the Reagan years. Roboticization is a logical counterpart of military emphasis on "removing the soldier from the hazards of duty" and eliminating the human factor from high-tech warfare. As a result, the rate of blue collar worker displacement in basic manufacturing has quickened without appreciably improving those sectors' international competitiveness, because automating technologies can be installed almost anywhere on the globe that cheap, willing labor exists. Ironically, American machinery firms are not making the robots that replace the workers, partly because these firms' access to industrial engineers and capital is preempted by the military. For this reason, and because of defense-pioneered automation of manufacturing production processes generally, blue collar workers are losing jobs at historically unprecedented rates and face poor employment prospects.

The 1980s buildup has also counteracted labor trends toward greater parity for women and minority workers. Defense workers are disproportionately young, white, and male, especially in the defense-dependent segments of the science and engineering professions. With the concomitant decline in federal social spending, human services, and education, women and minorities who have made job and wage gains in these areas find their real incomes declining.

• *A costly population redistribution is another economic burden of the buildup.* Unlike any other industrialized country, the United States has experienced a massive shift of its population in the postwar period, from the older industrial belt to a new "defense perimeter," stretching from Boston, Connecticut, and Long Island down through Florida and Huntsville, Alabama, across the Plains and Texas to the Intermountain West, and reaching to Los Angeles, Orange County, San Diego, Silicon Valley, and Seattle. Taxpayer-financed moves of military personnel and defense industry scientists and engineers are a major component of this population redistribution. New communities, largely suburban, white, and sunbelt in character, have been spawned by the Cold War effort. The construction of new housing, infrastructure, and utilities for these communities taxes the economy in yet another way, especially when similar facilities are increasingly underused in older industrial cities.

The political consequences of these skewed development patterns are troubling. Whole industries (aerospace, communications), selected Fortune 500 firms (Rockwell, Lockheed, Hughes, General Dynamics), particular occupations, and an emerging set of cities are increasingly and uniquely dependent upon military spending and form a powerful lobby for a hardline foreign policy and continued large military budgets. A city like Colorado Springs, Colorado, for instance, which has flourished on defense facilities and contracts in the 1980s, votes 70 percent Republican and sends outspoken hawks to Congress. By and large, regions favored by political redistricting throughout the postwar period have been those with larger-than-average shares of defense contracts.

The 1980s buildup has accelerated this trend. Substantial and unprecedented net population losses in market-oriented industrial states like Michigan, Illinois, and Ohio are mirrored by large increases in places like central Florida, northern Virginia, and southern California, all beneficiaries of the Reagan buildup. As the B-1 congressional battles reveal, a thinly disguised political patronage operation is now being run out of the Pentagon. In some cases, weapons programs that even the military does not want are preserved through political maneuverings.

In this decade, then, the U.S. economy has undergone wrenching structural changes. In large part, these are products of the Reagan military buildup and the debt the nation incurred to pay for it. Many will be hard to reverse. Defense electronics plants might be convertible to consumer electronics, but steel mills sold for scrap will not be reopened, high-tech firms bankrupted by Japanese competition will not be revived, and machinery plants exported to Mexico will not be repatriated. Many communities, small businesses, and workers will bear the losses for many years to come. . . .

If the public and elected officials continue to buy the argument that the economy's health and competitiveness rest on military-led innovation, then undoubtedly the flow of public money into Star Wars and other high-tech programs will continue. This despite considerable evidence, including the recent Pentagon procurement scandals, that this is neither an efficient nor promising way to achieve economic competitiveness. Moreover, this military-oriented approach ignores the fact that the real goals of the economy should be to improve the public's wellbeing and standard of living. While George Bush is unlikely to break from his predecessor's military-economic policy, there may be hope that Congress will do so.

[Reprinted by permission of the *Bulletin of the Atomic Scientists*. Copyright © 1989 by the Educational Foundation for Nuclear Science.]

JOHN LEWIS GADDIS
Arms Control: Hanging Tough Paid Off
[*Bulletin of the Atomic Scientists*, January/February 1989]

The time has come to acknowledge an astonishing development: during his eight years as president, Ronald Reagan has presided over the most dramatic improvement in U.S.-Soviet relations—and the most solid progress in arms control—since the Cold War began. History has often produced unexpected results, but this one surely sets some kind of record.

Reagan was not an enthusiast for arms control before entering the White House: indeed his 1976 and 1980 campaigns appeared to reject that enterprise altogether in favor of a simpler search for national security through military superiority over the Soviet Union. . . .

[In a section of the article omitted here, Professor Gaddis reviews the widespread criticism of the arms-control process in the 1960s and 1970s for its mood of pessimism about U.S. military inferiority, its complexity, its isolation from other world realities, and its illogical focus on mere arms *control* rather than arms *reduction*. As President, Gaddis argues, Reagan incorporated these criticisms "into a new approach to arms control that would in time, and against conventional wisdom, produce impressive results."]

The principal means by which he accomplished this were as follows:

• *Rebuilding self-confidence.* There are rare moments in history when public moods reverse themselves almost overnight. One occurred in March 1933, when Franklin Roosevelt replaced Herbert Hoover in the White House; another took place in Great Britain in May 1940, when Winston Churchill became prime minister; still another occurred in Western Europe in June 1947, when Secretary of State George C. Marshall announced the economic recovery plan that came to bear his name. The mood reversal that followed Reagan's January 1981 inauguration was by no means as dramatic as these, but it occurred: long before the new administration had completed its military buildup, before Paul Volcker and the Federal Reserve Board had checked inflation, and before OPEC's disarray had turned the energy crisis into an oil glut, the *perception* had become widespread that events were beginning to break Washington's way. And that made a big difference.

It has since become commonplace to criticize Reagan for having placed greater emphasis on imagery than on substance during his years as president. But leadership begins with the creation of self-confidence, and that—as Roosevelt, Churchill, and Marshall all knew—is a psychological process depending less upon the rational calculation of tangible gains than upon the ability to convince people that however bad things may be at the moment, time is on their side. Reagan managed during his first months in office to project—and therefore to instill—a degree of self-confidence that went well beyond anything his predecessor had achieved. Without that shift from pessimism to optimism, much of what followed could hardly have taken place.

• *Spooking the Soviets.* The second element in the Reagan strategy proceeded logically from the first—to persuade the Kremlin that time was working against it. Nor was it so difficult to do, because events were beginning to demonstrate precisely this: Afghanistan was revealing the costs of what Paul Kennedy has called "strategic overstretch"; "Solidarity" had brought Poland to the edge of open rebellion; economic stagnation was becoming a serious problem inside the Soviet Union; and an increasingly sclerotic Kremlin leadership was responding to these difficulties with near catatonic immobility. In one sense, Reagan was lucky to have come into office at a trough in American fortunes and a peak in those of the Soviets. Things could not get much worse, and were likely to get better. But more than luck is involved in the ability to recognize that such trends are under way, and to capitalize upon them. Reagan's leadership proved decidedly superior to Carter's in that respect.

Several subsequent Reagan administration actions sought to reinforce the idea that time no longer favored Moscow. The U.S. military buildup was launched with the intention of so straining an already inefficient economy that the Soviet leadership would have little choice but to make substantial concessions on arms control. Similar intentions lay behind the Strategic Defense Initiative. The vision of a shift from deterrence to a defense based on

American technological superiority would, it was thought, shock the Soviets into contemplating for the first time significant reductions in their own long-range strategic forces.

At the same time, the administration was skillfully defusing both the U.S. nuclear freeze movement and opposition to the deployment of Pershing II and cruise missiles in Western Europe by calling for actual *reductions* in nuclear weapons, and by holding out, through SDI, the prospect of ultimately making them obsolete altogether. To the extent that the Soviets had counted on such groups to constrain administration freedom of action—and they almost certainly had—the effect again was to demonstrate that time was no longer on Moscow's side.

• *Negotiation from strength.* A third element in the Reagan strategy was the principle that negotiations should take place only from a position of strength. The idea dates from the Truman administration's military buildup following the outbreak of the Korean War. Over the years it had come to be understood as a way of evading negotiations altogether, since "strength" was so relative a concept that one might never actually attain it and since adversaries would presumably never negotiate from "weakness." There was reason to believe, at the outset of the Reagan years, that this devious approach was alive and well. Presidential subordinates gleefully put forward "killer" proposals for arms control talks, while the Pentagon swallowed huge military appropriations without any indication that "strength" was about to be achieved.

An important characteristic of Reagan's leadership, however, was that he was *not* devious; when he spoke of the possibility that a military buildup might actually lead to reductions in strategic weapons, he appears to have meant precisely what he said. He also understood, perhaps instinctively, a point George Kennan had been arguing: that the arms control process had become too complex while producing too little, and that the only way to rebuild a domestic consensus in support of it was to hold out clear, simple, and sweeping objectives, such as a 50 percent cut in strategic weapons on both sides.

With the 1984 elections coming up and with indications that Congress would resist further defense budget increases, it could be argued that the administration had little choice but to appear to seek negotiations with the Soviets. Certainly some Reagan advisers felt that negotiations so protracted as to produce no results were almost as desirable as having no negotiations at all. But what many of Reagan's subordinates did not understand—and what those who seek to explain what subsequently happened will have to comprehend—is that while the president may have shared their conservatism, he did not share their cynicism. For him the only question was with whom to negotiate.

• *Responding to Gorbachev.* It is difficult to see that much could have been accomplished in this respect until a functional Soviet leadership had been established. That happened in March 1985, and a fourth element in the

Reagan strategy soon emerged, which was to acknowledge Mikhail Gorbachev as a new kind of Soviet leader whose chief priority was internal reform, and with whom one could, in the realm of external affairs, find common interests. The White House was therefore ready to respond when Gorbachev began modifying long-standing Soviet positions on arms control in a way quite consistent with what the Reagan strategy had anticipated. Neither critics on the left, who had favored negotiations for their own sake, nor those on the right, who had sought negotiation from strength, were in any position to object. The long-stalemated arms control process suddenly accelerated, producing by the final year of the Reagan administration not only an Intermediate-range Nuclear Forces (INF) Treaty that contained unprecedented Soviet concessions on asymmetrical reductions and on-site verification, but substantial progress as well toward agreement on deep cuts in long-range strategic systems, and at least the possibility of a grand compromise that would delay if not defer altogether the deployment of SDI.

There were, to be sure, deficiencies in the Reagan strategy. Characteristically, the president found it easier to think of SDI as he had advertised it—as a first step toward abolishing nuclear weapons altogether—than as the successful bargaining chip it turned out to be. This created an opportunity for Gorbachev to endorse nuclear abolition by the year 2000 and thus to align himself with the president against Reagan's own skeptical advisers. There were few signs of progress toward conventional arms limitation, or toward restricting nuclear testing. Little thought had been given to how the United States might respond if the relaxation of controls that perestroika required were to produce actual rebellions among Soviet nationality groups, or within Eastern Europe. And almost no thought appeared to have been given to the relationship between national security and national solvency—an issue to which Gorbachev himself seemed keenly attuned.

Still, the clock on the front cover of the *Bulletin* was set back, a year ago, for the first time since 1972. That symbolic act ought to make us think critically—and without preconceptions—about how we got to that point. It was not by means of arms control as traditionally practiced: the old SALT process would never have survived the Reagan administration's insistence on asymmetrical reductions instead of symmetrical limitations, on intrusive rather than remote verification, and on the virtues of strategic defense as opposed to mutual vulnerability. Strength this time did lead to negotiations, bargaining chips did produce bargains, and "hanging tough" did eventually pay off.

The Soviets deserve much of the credit for what happened. They made most of the concessions, a pattern not likely to be repeated often in the future. It was the Reagan administration, however, that assessed correctly the potential for Soviet concessions. And because of the way it came about, this new approach to arms control has won firmer domestic support within the United States than the SALT process ever did; witness the caution both sides showed in not making it an issue during the otherwise hotly contested 1988 presidential election. How valid the approach will be in years to come remains to be seen, but as Reagan leaves office it would be uncharitable—and historically irresponsible—to begrudge the strategic vision of an adminstration once thought by many of us to have had none at all.

[Reprinted by permission of the *Bulletin of the Atomic Scientists.* Copyright © 1989 by the Educational Foundation for Nuclear Science.]

2. THE STRATEGIC DEFENSE INITIATIVE

In his March 23, 1983, speech on national defense, President Reagan unexpectedly issued a call for research on space-based strategic defense systems which could render nuclear weapons "impotent and obsolete." This so-called Strategic Defense Initiative (SDI), with its challenge to long-established concepts of nuclear deterrence through mutual vulnerability to attack, set off a fierce national debate. While supporters praised SDI as a "high frontier" strategy, critics dismissed it with the derisive nickname "Star Wars."

Some newspapers, such as the Manchester, New Hampshire, Union Lead-er, *supported SDI, but most did not. Reagan's plan to "militarize space," warned the* St. Louis Post-Dispatch, *was a "reckless new step in the arms race." By mid-April the pro-SDI* National Review *conceded that the idea had been greeted by "a chorus of instant rejection and ridicule." Nevertheless, the* National Review *shrewdly noted, Reagan was succeeding in his immedi-ate political objective: to neutralize the nuclear-freeze movement. In 1981–1983, alarmed by the Reagan military build-up, millions of Americans had en-dorsed a call for a bilateral freeze on the testing and deployment of nuclear weapons. Reagan's proposal spoke to the same fear of nuclear war that the freeze activists were exploiting, and to a considerable extent he preempted that campaign. While Americans debated the feasibility of missile-defense systems, the freeze movement collapsed. In the summer of 1983 the* Bulletin of the Atomic Scientists *published a sampling of the Star Wars debate, including statements by administration spokesmen, scientists, and editors. The* Bulletin's *summary concluded with an extract from a* New York Times

op-ed piece in which Massachusetts Institute of Technology scientists George
Rathjens and Jack Ruina challenged the assumptions underlying Reagan's
speech. The President's vision was attractive, they concluded, "just as a
fountain of youth or a universal cure for cancer is attractive—but it is cruel
and misleading to hold out such false hope."

RONALD REAGAN
The Strategic Defense Initiative
["Peace and National Security" Address, March 23, 1983]

My predecessors in the Oval Office have appeared before you on other
occasions to describe the threat posed by Soviet power and have proposed
steps to address that threat. But since the advent of nuclear weapons, those
steps have been directed toward deterrence of aggression through the promise
of retaliation—the notion that no rational nation would launch an attack that
would inevitably result in unacceptable losses to themselves. This approach
to stability through offensive threat has worked. We and our allies have
succeeded in preventing nuclear war for three decades. In recent months,
however, my advisers, including in particular the Joint Chiefs of Staff, have
underscored the bleakness of the future before us.

Over the course of these discussions, I have become more and more deeply
convinced that the human spirit must be capable of rising above dealing with
other nations and human beings by threatening their existence. Feeling this
way, I believe we must thoroughly examine every opportunity for reducing
tensions and for introducing greater stability into the strategic calculus on
both sides. One of the most important contributions we can make is, of
course, to lower the level of all arms, and particularly nuclear arms. We are
engaged right now in several negotiations with the Soviet Union to bring
about a mutual reduction of weapons. I will report to you a week from
tomorrow my thoughts on that score. But let me just say I am totally
committed to this course.

If the Soviet Union will join with us in our effort to achieve major arms
reduction we will have succeeded in stabilizing the nuclear balance. Nevertheless it will still be necessary to rely on the specter of retaliation—on
mutual threat, and that is a sad commentary on the human condition.

Would it not be better to save lives than to avenge them? Are we not
capable of demonstrating our peaceful intentions by applying all our abilities
and our ingenuity to achieving a truly lasting stability? I think we are—
indeed, we must!

After careful consultation with my advisers, including the Joint Chiefs of
Staff, I believe there is a way. Let me share with you a vision of the future

which offers hope. It is that we embark on a program to counter the awesome Soviet missile threat with measures that are defensive. Let us turn to the very strengths in technology that spawned our great industrial base and that have given us the quality of life we enjoy today.

Up until now we have increasingly based our strategy of deterrence upon the threat of retaliation. But what if free people could live secure in the knowledge that their security did not rest upon the threat of instant U.S. retaliation to deter a Soviet attack; that we could intercept and destroy strategic ballistic missiles before they reached our own soil or that of our allies?

I know this is a formidable technical task, one that may not be accomplished before the end of this century. Yet, current technology has attained a level of sophistication where it is reasonable for us to begin this effort. It will take years, probably decades, of effort on many fronts. There will be failures and setbacks just as there will be successes and breakthroughs. And as we proceed we must remain constant in preserving the nuclear deterrent and maintaining a solid capability for flexible response. But is it not worth every investment necessary to free the world from the threat of nuclear war? We know it is!

In the meantime, we will continue to pursue real reductions in nuclear arms, negotiating from a position of strength that can be insured only by modernizing our strategic forces. At the same time, we must take steps to reduce the risk of a conventional military conflict escalating to nuclear war by improving our nonnuclear capabilities. America does possess—now—the technologies to attain very significant improvements in the effectiveness of our conventional, nonnuclear forces. Proceeding boldly with these new technologies, we can significantly reduce any incentive that the Soviet Union may have to threaten attack against the United States or its allies.

As we pursue our goal of defensive technologies, we recognize that our allies rely upon our strategic offensive power to deter attacks against them. Their vital interests and ours are inextricably linked—their safety and ours are one. And no change in technology can or will alter that reality. We must and shall continue to honor our commitments.

I clearly recognize that defensive systems have limitations and raise certain problems and ambiguities. If paired with offensive systems, they can be viewed as fostering an aggressive policy and no one wants that.

But with these considerations firmly in mind, I call upon the scientific community who gave us nuclear weapons to turn their great talents to the cause of mankind and world peace; to give us the means of rendering these nuclear weapons impotent and obsolete.

Tonight, consistent with our obligations under the ABM Treaty and recognizing the need for close consultation with our allies, I am taking an important first step. I am directing a comprehensive and intensive effort to define a long-term research and development program to begin to achieve our ultimate goal of eliminating the threat posed by strategic nuclear missiles. This could pave the way for arms control measures to eliminate the weapons themselves. We seek neither military superiority nor political advantage. Our only purpose—one all people share—is to search for ways to reduce the danger of nuclear war.

My fellow Americans, tonight we are launching an effort which holds the purpose of changing the course of human history. There will be risks, and results take time. But with your support, I believe we can do it.

MANCHESTER (NEW HAMPSHIRE) UNION LEADER
Why Not Try Survival?

[March 25, 1983]

Well, it's back to the drawing board for the political, clerical and news media wings of the peacenik movement. President Reagan, it seems clear from his nationally televised address Wednesday night, has finally latched on to the concept of *Mutual Assured Survival* as the logical replacement for the current MAD doctrine of so-called *Mutual Assured Destruction*. The engineers, scientists and military men, headed by Lieutenant General Daniel O. Graham, who have been promoting the so-called "High Frontier" approach to national defense, apparently have achieved a major breakthrough at the White House.

The problem now faced by those who overtly or covertly seek unilateral disarmament by the United States was summed up succinctly in a recent column by Phyllis Schlafly. Addressing the need for the crash effort to develop a protective umbrella of satellites capable of sensing and tracking Soviet long-range missiles that can then be destroyed by on-board interceptors, Schlafly wrote: *"High Frontier can't kill a single human being, Russian or American; so there is nothing for the pacifists to be agitated about."*

But agitated they are. Long before Reagan addressed the nation on the issue, the Federation of American Scientists was complaining about the "destabilizing" effects of "High Frontier," contending that if we develop the ability to shoot down Soviet-launched ICBMs, the Russians would feel threatened and perhaps launch a preemptive nuclear strike against us. Talk about reaching for arguments to justify the Soviet Union's first-strike nuclear capabilities! (The anti-nukes have had time to marshal their forces against development of a protective umbrella that would destroy incoming Soviet missiles and end U.S. reliance on retaliation as a deterrent to nuclear war. But millions of Americans who heard the President speak Wednesday night probably were hearing about if for the first time, even though some scientists and technicians were maintaining its feasibility 20 years ago—which fact in itself constitutes a damning indictment of the news censorship policies pursued by much of the liberal news media.)

Acknowledging that development of the system, the components of which could range from missiles to laser beams based in or on the ground, constitutes a "formidable technical task, one that may not be accomplished before the end of this century," the President called on the scientists "who gave us nuclear weapons to turn their great talents to the cause of mankind and world peace; to give us the means of rendering those nuclear weapons impotent and obsolete."

The Great Communicator made a strong case for the proposed shift in U.S. policy from reliance on retaliation to prevention.... [But] if today's peace-at-any-price types have their way, the day of national security through "High Frontier" technology will never dawn. Instead, by placing our faith in the twin follies of nuclear freeze and peace-through-weakness, we will have blundered into nuclear war.

[Reprinted by permission.]

ST. LOUIS POST-DISPATCH
A Star Wars Defense

[March 23, 1983]

In his speech Wednesday night on national security, President Reagan said that his concept of an absolute defense against nuclear missiles "holds the promise of changing the course of human history." Yet behind the noble rhetoric, his address was an intensely political one, intended to sell to the American people his extravagant military buildup. Moreover, Mr. Reagan offered a plan that can only be described as one of the most dangerous, ill-considered defense propositions that any president has ever put before the nation.

Make no mistake about it: Mr. Reagan is proposing to embark on a major escalation of the arms race in the only environment that is now relatively free of military activity. We can fight wars on land, in the air, on the sea and under the sea. Space remains the only arena in which the superpowers cannot now do combat. Mr. Reagan would change that by developing and deploying an antimissile system that, through exotic technologies, would ostensibly render the nation immune from atomic attack.

It would, of course, do no such thing. The Reagan plan would cost untold billions, involve a research and development effort that would rival the scope of the Manhattan Project (and provide less assurance of success) and, in the end, leave America no more secure than it is now. Indeed, if there were any prospect that Mr. Reagan's plan might actually work, the chances of nuclear war would be dramatically increased. The plan would certainly lead the Soviets to fear that, under the cover of such a system, the U.S. might launch a first-strike, a concern that would wreck the stability of the strategic balance.

The president's proposal is predicated upon the naive assumption that nuclear missiles represent the only threat at the disposal of the Soviet Union. Yet even if a foolproof antimissile system could be deployed in space, the nation would still be susceptible to attack from enemy bombers. A star wars defense system would do nothing to deter a cruise missile strike, for these weapons fly at tree-top level with extreme accuracy. Moreover, even a workable antimissile system would be vulnerable to decoys and other countermeasures. And, at bottom, no one could be certain that it would be effective against a massive ballistic missile attack.

In any case, as Mr. Reagan conceded, such a system would not be available for many years. In the meantime, he is saying that not a penny can be cut from his plan to increase defense spending by 10 percent. He is holding out the pie-in-the-sky prospect of nuclear immunity as an excuse to spend trillions in the next few years on the Pentagon. To that end, he reiterated the familiar litany of the Soviet buildup. His presentation included photos of Soviet military activity in the Western hemisphere—including one of an airstrip in Grenada that Canada (!) is helping to build.

Neither the people nor Congress should be fooled. The Reagan military program is excessive and must be cut back. His proposal to militarize space must be seen for the reckless new step in the arms race that it is.

[Reprinted courtesy *St. Louis Post-Dispatch*.]

NATIONAL REVIEW
"Star Wars"
[April 15, 1983]

Set aside for a moment the question of feasibility. If the President were to go on TV tomorrow evening and announce that we had developed and deployed an effective defense against missile attack, would that not, self-evidently, be cause for rejoicing? We have of course been inundated with accounts of the horrors of nuclear war, the flood rising recently as we prepare to counter the Soviet deployment of SS–20s in Europe. If nuclear warfare could be apocalyptic, would not a defense against nuclear attack be good news?

It is difficult not to believe that if such a defensive effort had been proposed by, say, Kennedy or Mondale, it would have been received very respectfully—would indeed, quite probably, have been hailed as courageous, progressive, humane, pioneering.

President Reagan's proposal that we pursue a serious nuclear-defense effort met, instead, with a chorus of instant rejection and ridicule. Democrats lost no time in calling it a "Star Wars" fantasy, a scenario for "pin-ball" warfare in space. McGeorge Bundy rushed into print with denigratory remarks. Jerome Wiesner at MIT condemned it. Republican Senator Mark Hatfield, who is virtually a pacifist, professed himself appalled at the idea of extending military operations to space, perhaps preferring that they take place, if at all, in Oregon.

Now space is already the scene of extensive activity of a military character by both the U.S. and the USSR, with the USSR making several times the U.S. investment in precisely the area of research the President focused upon. The Soviets have experimented extensively with "killer" satellites designed to knock out our reconnaissance and communications satellites, vital in the event of conflict. Research into exotic weapons is much further advanced than is generally realized by non-specialists. Yesterday's exotic weapon is today's standard equipment, and to imagine that technology can somehow be made to stand still goes against all historical experience.

If Reagan's proposals were so self-evidently absurd as his critics claim, why then did Mr. Andropov react so violently to them—angrily accusing Reagan of plotting to "disarm" the Soviet Union by making its missiles useless?

One suggestion worth exploring has to do with the first-strike implications of a successful missile defense. To undercut that objection, Reagan has now suggested that we might share certain kinds of defensive technological information with the Soviets, in order that neither side would gain a sudden military advantage from an effective defense deployment.

Though no one today can guarantee the development of a viable defense against missiles, and though it would lie some years in the future in any case, a variety of approaches have been under study for some time. They include non-nuclear air/ground systems using a kind of shrapnel, as in High Frontier; nuclear-armed anti-missiles; and laser beams, perhaps bounced off mirrors orbiting in space. It would take a bold prophet to guarantee that *no* such defense is feasible.

Politically, the President scored psychologically against the freeze advocates and their apocalyptic backers, and placed himself visibly on the side of saving lives and cities. It was no doubt this political aspect that infuriated his critics, that and their instinctive suspicion of any proposal that would enhance American power and security.

BULLETIN OF THE ATOMIC SCIENTISTS
Onward and Upward with Space Defense
[June/July 1983]

[This article began with an excerpt from President Reagan's March 23, 1983, address, reprinted above.]

President Reagan's March 23 address to the nation opened to public debate an array of critical issues concerning arms control, the arms budget and defense strategies. He envisioned as a solution to the endlessly escalating, mutual balance of nuclear terror the eventual development of a space-based defense against strategic missiles. On the one hand, critics from both the military and scientific establishments quickly characterized his proposal as either an unrealistic objective or a cruel hoax and suggested that it could only raise false hopes. On the other hand, Secretary of Defense Caspar Weinberger, physicist Edward Teller, Science Adviser George Keyworth and others strongly defended the President's proposal.

The debate is only beginning, and no doubt it will become more complex and partisan. Although the outcome of that debate is of the greatest possible consequence to all of us, issues of secrecy and national security may obscure it from full public participation. Therefore, the Bulletin *is publishing the following edited excerpts from early, major positions on the issue.*

Secretary of Defense Caspar Weinberger elaborated on Reagan's proposal on "Meet the Press," March 27.

Question: How would you handle this program so that the East-West balance would remain intact and the Russians would not be scared into desperate measures?

Weinberger: Both nations are working to try to get a thoroughly reliable defense against incoming missiles. Once this is achieved, then you would have a new means of keeping the strategic balance which depends not on fear of retaliation, but on a proven ability to defend.

Question: Another criticism is that you would transfer that age-old history of warfare between offensive and defensive weapons into space and end up with the same sort of problem—you would have smarter missiles dealing with smarter defenses.

Weinberger: Well, there's no question that as you try to develop systems of this kind others who are interested in offensive capabilities will try to develop countermeasures. We are interested in defensive capabilities. And we will try to develop a system that is so reliable that it will, in effect, render impotent all of these nuclear missiles. And that, I think, would be an enormous step forward for mankind and something that would give us real hope.

Question: Why shouldn't the Soviet Union be fearful and concerned? If we succeed in the President's plan we will, some years hence, be able to knock down any of their missiles. Presuming that they will not be able to knock down our missiles, that would give us a tremendous advantage, a tremendous superiority. Why should they not be alarmed?

Weinberger: I would hope and assume that the Soviets, with all the work they have done and are doing in this field, would develop about the same time an effective defense, which would completely remove these missiles and the fears they cause.

The other reason the Soviets have no need to worry is that they know perfectly well that we will never launch a first strike. And all of their attacks, and all of their preparations—I should say, all of their acquisitions in the military field in the last few years—have been offensive in character. . . .

Question: What would [a space-based ABM system] do for cruise missiles, which hug the ground and presumably could come through that system?

Weinberger: Well, the defensive systems the President is talking about are not designed to be partial. We want to get a system which will develop a defense that is—

Question: Total? Against all incoming missiles of any kind?

Weinberger: Yes, And I don't see any reason why that can't be done. Bear in mind that in 1947, Dr. Vannevar Bush, who was one of the most noted scientists we had at that time, said the whole concept of a missile that would rise out of a silo in one continent and could be targeted and directed with accuracy to hit any kind of target in another continent was an absolute fantasy. And yet, something like eight years later, the Soviets had such a system.

There have been a lot of people who have derided our ability to reach the moon. But fortunately, we had President Kennedy at that time, who took the position that this not only could but should be done. And a very few years later, we did it. So I don't have any real doubts of the American ability to do this.

George Keyworth, science adviser to the President, was asked why so few independent scientists endorsed the President's proposal.

This is an interesting psychological phenomenon. So many scientists are steeped in the assured-destruction theory that they may be either sanguine about it or even unaware of its implications. Scientists propose such formidable works as interplanetary transport or controlled fusion and yet when the President calls for help in the defense field, they respond without the same creativity.

When asked whether the scientific community is opposed more for political

than for technical reasons, Keyworth said, "that is precisely what I am saying."
U.S. News and World Report,
April 5, 1983

General John W. Vessey, Jr., chairman of the Joint Chiefs of Staff, joined with Sam Donaldson on ABC News in the following exchange.

Donaldson: What about the suggestion that if we attempt to perfect a defense certainly the other side will attempt and probably perfect an overload capacity or an offense against that defense?

General Vessey: The other side will always try to build its war machine to carry out its own particular plans and achieve its war objectives.

Donaldson: And won't they be able to do it?

General Vessey: Well, our policy is a strategy of deterrence and that is to make it clear to the Soviets that they cannot achieve their war objectives.

Donaldson: I understand the goal and the strategy but I am asking you your expert opinion. Can the other side build an offense that is successful against any defense that we construct?

General Vessey: Well, time alone will tell.

Donaldson: Well, is that good enough to base our strategy on—time alone will tell?

General Vessey: Neither you nor I can foresee the future, but one thing we know is that governments have a tendency to follow a given track unless someone tries to change it. The track in recent years has been to rely on offensive retaliation. We have suggested that technology may lead us to a little brighter hope in terms of defense.

"This Week with David Brinkley,"
March 27, 1983 . . .

Daniel O. Graham, former head of the Defense Intelligence Agency and director of the Project High Frontier (under the auspices of the Heritage Foundation) warned that

. . . the president doesn't have time to wait for a technological consensus to form inside the regular government. It takes the U.S. 12 to 18 years to produce a major weapons system: Think of the B-1, the MX, Stealth. By the time a strategic defense could be built through regular channels, Mr. Reagan would be 92 years old and the Soviets would have bought or stolen the technology for defense from U.S. and European countries and be building their own version using IMF credits. It is urgent that the President appoint a panel of scientists and strategists to design a set of defensive systems using current technology—just as American presidents did when we built the ICBM, the Polaris and indeed the atomic bomb. Otherwise, the initiative Mr. Reagan has gained will evaporate in a matter of months.

The Wall Street Journal,
April 8, 1983

Kosta Tsipis, director of the program in science and technology for international security at MIT, wrote for the Los Angeles Times:

It is undoubtedly flattering to engineers and scientists that the President has faith in their ability to produce a technological fix to liberate the world from the specter of nuclear holocaust. But we are stuck, and will remain so, with the technical reality that inexpensive offensive nuclear weapons can eventually overwhelm any defense. Given this inescapable fact, the President's announced plan for avoiding nuclear war seems to be a grave lapse of responsibility because it offers false hopes for security.

Since the know-how to build nuclear weapons will be on earth indefinitely, the only realistic alternative to deterrence as a means of avoiding nuclear war is to begin negotiating with the Soviet Union to resolve the conflict between us. The most likely outcome of a U.S. effort to build defense systems for our cities will be an increase in the number and sophistication of Soviet offensive weapons and an intensification of the nuclear arms race.

Los Angeles Times,
March 30, 1983

William J. Perry, former undersecretary of defense for research and engineering in the Carter Administration described the technology of a space-based laser system:

A space-based laser would be designed to attack an ICBM during the period that the missile was still under powered flight. The ICBM would thus be destroyed, not only before it reached its target, but before it even had a chance to release its multiple warheads. To hit an ICBM target with enough laser energy would require having the laser on a low-altitude "battle station" that must be located over the launch area when it fires its laser beam. Because of the orbital motion of the satellite, not only one but a whole constellation of satellites—about 20—would be necessary to shoot down any particular ICBM at any given time that it might be launched.

A few seconds would be required to detect, track, lock on and dwell on the target long enough to burn a hole through it. Therefore, any given laser is tied up for several seconds in this operation, which has to occur during the few minutes the ICBM is in powered flight. The 20 satellites required for continuous coverage of the launch area could attack in sequence perhaps tens of ICBMs that were launched simultaneously, but they could not handle a mass attack of even a few hundreds of ICBMs from one geographical area. Therefore, the base number of 20 satellites would have to be multiplied by about ten to deal with a mass attack. In other words, several hundred satellites continually orbiting the earth would be needed to maintain enough laser beams to deal with a mass attack against the United States.

The necessary laser weapons in these several hundred battle stations would be immensely complex. The lasers would require an operational pointing and tracking accuracy of a few inches at a range of a few hundred miles; that is, better than one part in a million accuracy, requiring a feasible but difficult and expensive development program. Once the beam is properly pointed, it must have sufficient energy to burn a hole in the missile skin. This would require a more than tenfold increase in power over what has been demonstrated for high-energy lasers. I believe that these problems would eventually yield to a determined and expensive development program, but this new generation technology would have to be demonstrated before we could begin to build the hundreds of operational laser weapons systems and put them in space.

A laser system with these capabilities would be too large to be launched from the space shuttle. For each of the several hundred battle stations, four or five shuttle launches may be required to place its components in orbit for assembly in space. (During this assembly phase, the system would be extremely vulnerable to attack or disruption.) My most optimistic view is that such a program would cost well in excess of $100 billion in today's dollars and could not reach a beginning operation status until some time in the next century.

Washington Post, March 27, 1983

Former Secretary of Defense Harold Brown was skeptical that technology could create a Fortress America.

If a single weapon can destroy a city of hundreds of thousands, only a perfect defense (which, moreover, works perfectly the first time) will suffice. The extreme destructiveness of nuclear weapons is magnified by the concentration and fragility of urban society. To this must be added the availability to the attacker of the tactic of concentrating its forces to saturate and overwhelm any possible defense, even if an individual defensive weapon can destroy an individual attacking weapon.

In these circumstances, the prospects for a technical solution to the problem of preserving modern society in the face of an actual thermonuclear war—whether that solution calls for laser antiballistic missile systems in space, elaborate civil defense schemes or combinations of these with counterforce capability (that is, ways of destroying enemy weapons before they are launched) seems to me very poor. The effort to attain such technical solutions could itself be quite dangerous if it created an illusion that such a solution has been achieved or is likely to be.

Washington Post, March 27, 1983

Wolfgang K.H. Panofsky is director of the Stanford Linear Accelerator at Stanford University. He doubts that the President's vision could be realized.

The problem is that you cannot coerce technology by a policy decision. It will not do to invoke the analogy of going to the moon, or building a nuclear weapon, where Presidents Kennedy and Roosevelt, respectively, undertook those great initiatives. In both of these cases the decisions were preceded by exhaustive and careful studies indicating these projects to be feasible, albeit at large effort. No study has indicated the feasibility of a massive, impenetrable defense to protect the population of the United States against the combined nuclear threat of missiles, both ballistic and air-breathing, airplanes and other means of delivery.

There is no foreseeable technical means to eliminate the mutual hostage relationship that now exists between the people of the United States and those of the Soviet Union. The large arsenals of nuclear weapons have brought this situation upon us. If a nuclear war starts, under any doctrine, in any theater of war, through the first use of nuclear weapons by either the United States or the Soviet Union, then a grave risk to the future of civilization as we know it will exist. This risk will not be ameliorated but will only be increased if we add yet another layer of weaponry, rather than reducing what we already have. . . .

There is one additional grave risk inherent in the President's announcement. If the concept of a secure defense umbrella proposed by the President were to receive wide credence, then the question of sustained nuclear war fighting could be viewed in a different manner. Specifically, should a secure defense umbrella against nuclear weapons over the entire country be accepted as a realistic concept, then this could support the view that nuclear war fighting under the cover of that umbrella might become acceptable. For all these reasons, I consider the presidential initiative to be ill-advised.

San José Mercury News,
April 7, 1983

Kurt Gottfried, physicist at Cornell University, considered the implications of a program to develop a defensive system in space upon existing arms control proposals.

The uproar that greeted President Reagan's call for "means of rendering nuclear weapons impotent and obsolete" has demonstrated that his vision is largely based on science fiction. Everyone also has noted that such a missile defense would be incompatible with the ABM Treaty. But one crucial question remains to be raised: In order to protect its ability to pursue these far-out weapons programs, has the Administration purposely refrained from negotiating arms-control agreements that address imminent threats to our national security?

One may ask why we should care about a comprehensive test ban if we can have a perfect defense against missiles. The ban is essential because any nation that wants to develop nuclear weapons will be severely hampered if it cannot carry out tests. Hence, we are neglecting the imminent and real threat of nuclear proliferation to chase after an unattainable defense in the unforeseeable future.

The schemes for "laser battle stations" in space require a whole new arsenal to defend these stations. If we intend to deploy such ABMs, it is logical to oppose restrictions on the development of anti-satellite weapons, because such weapons will be needed to defend the ABMS. This must be one reason why the Administration has ignored the promising 1981 Soviet draft treaty for controlling weapons in space.

Los Angeles Times,
April 13, 1983

In concluding this brief summary of responses to President Reagan's proposal, we quote George Rathjens and Jack Ruina's essay published in the New York Times, March 27, 1983.

These technologies pose intriguing scientific challenges, but developing such weapons would hardly achieve the president's goal of "eliminating the threat posed by strategic nuclear missiles." Much more would be needed: means for coping with the adversary's countermeasures, including other objects, means for protecting the antiballistic defense system itself and means for aiming beams, rays or projectiles. Most important, it would require coordinating all the components in a complex system that could defend not just a few isolated points but the whole country against attacks that might come at any time from any direction and that might include bombers, cruise missiles and ballistic missiles.

What troubles us is less the expenditure of a billion dollars a year on research than holding out a vision of hope—the hope of an infallible defense—that is virtually impossible to achieve. It is not hard to understand why the Administration found this vision attractive—but it is cruel and misleading to hold out such false hope.

Reagan and the World

1. THE IRAN-CONTRA SCANDAL

The worst crisis of the Reagan presidency broke late in 1986 with the revelation that a National Security Council aide, Oliver North, with the approval of National Security Adviser John Poindexter and others, had secretly supplied arms to Iran in an effort to free U.S. hostages held by pro-Iranian terrorists, and had illegally diverted funds from these arms sales to U.S.-supported contras *fighting the leftist government of Nicaragua. Through much of 1987 the Iran-Contra scandal, or Iranamok, as some called it, dominated the media.*

Reagan first denied any wrongdoing and called North "a national hero." But when a presidentially appointed investigative panel headed by former Senator John Tower issued a scathing report in March 1987, the President went on TV to acknowledge that serious mistakes had been made. Yet he denied knowledge of the illegal diversion of funds and announced changes in White House personnel and National Security Council procedures. Praised by some commentators, Reagan's speech left others unimpressed. The Baltimore Sun *found it a web of "omissions," "circumlocutions," and "Reaganesque fantasies" showing little evidence of change in a presidency characterized by "aloofness and inattention to detail." Writing in the* New Republic, *Gail Sheehy saw in Reagan's handling of the Iran-Contra affair a deep-seated psychological pattern of denying unpleasant realities that had served Reagan well over a long life.*

The report of a congressional investigation in August 1987 sent Reagan back on TV. Again he conceded that his preoccupation with the hostages' plight had led to serious mistakes, but he disclaimed awareness of any illegalities. The Washington Post *was unimpressed. Despite months of revelations, it declared, Reagan still had "not come fully to terms with the most convulsive events his administration has known so far." This potpourri of comment on the Iran-Contra affair concludes with an essay by Roger*

Rosenblatt published in Time *late in 1986 when the story first broke. Reagan's well-known propensity for personalizing complex social and political issues sometimes worked to his advantage, Rosenblatt reflected, but in this instance it had caused things to go horrendously awry.*

RONALD REAGAN
Address on the Tower Commission Report
[March 4, 1987]

For the past three months, I've been silent on the revelations about Iran. You must have been thinking, "Well, why doesn't he tell us what's happening? Why doesn't he just speak to us as he has in the past when we've faced troubles or tragedies?" Others of you, I guess, were thinking, "What's he doing hiding out in the White House?"

The reason I haven't spoken to you before now is this: You deserved the truth. And, as frustrating as the waiting has been, I felt it was improper to come to you with sketchy reports, or possibly even erroneous statements, which would then have to be corrected, creating even more doubt and confusion. There's been enough of that.

I've paid a price for my silence in terms of your trust and confidence. But I have had to wait, as have you, for the complete story.

That's why I appointed . . . a special review board, the Tower board, which took on the chore of pulling the truth together for me and getting to the bottom of things. It has now issued its findings. . . .

I've studied the board's report. Its findings are honest, convincing and highly critical, and I accept them. Tonight I want to share with you my thoughts on these findings and report to you on the actions I'm taking to implement the board's recommendations.

First, let me say I take full responsibility for my own actions and for those of my Administration. As angry as I may be about activities undertaken without my knowledge, I am still accountable for those activities. As disappointed as I may be in some who served me, I am still the one who must answer to the American people for this behavior. And as personally distasteful as I find secret bank accounts and diverted funds, as the Navy would say, this happened on my watch.

Let's start with the part that is the most controversial. A few months ago I told the American people I did not trade arms for hostages. My heart and my best intentions still tell me that is true, but the facts and the evidence tell me it is not.

As the Tower board reported, what began as a strategic opening to Iran deteriorated in its implementation into trading arms for hostages. This runs counter to my own beliefs, to Administration policy and to the original strategy we had in mind. There are reasons why it happened but no excuses. It was a mistake.

I undertook the original Iran initiative in order to develop relations with those who might assume leadership in a post-Khomeini Government. It's clear from the board's report, however, that I let my personal concern for the hostages spill over into the geopolitical strategy of reaching out to Iran. I asked so many questions about the hostages' welfare that I didn't ask enough about the specifics of the total Iran plan. . . .

Now, another major aspect of the Board's findings regards the transfer of funds to the Nicaraguan contras. The Tower board wasn't able to find out what happened to this money, so the facts here will be left to the continuing investigations of the court-appointed independent counsel and the two Congressional investigating committees. I'm confident the truth will come out about this matter as well.

As I told the Tower board, I didn't know about any diversion of funds to the contras. But as President, I cannot escape responsibility.

Much has been said about my management style, a style that's worked successfully for me during eight years as governor of California and for most of my presidency. The way I work is to identify the problem, find the right individuals to do the job and then let them go to it. I've found this invariably brings out the best in people. They seem to rise to their full capability, and in the long run you get more done.

When it came to managing the N.S.C. staff, let's face it, my style didn't match its previous track record. I've already begun correcting this. As a start, yesterday I met with the entire professional staff of the National Security Council. I defined for them the values I want to guide the national security policies of this country. I told them that I wanted a policy that was as justifiable and understandable in public as it was in secret. I wanted a policy that reflected the will of the Congress as well as the White House. And I told them that there'll be no more freelancing by individuals when it comes to our national security.

You've heard a lot about the staff of the National Security Council in recent months. I can tell you, they are good and dedicated Government employees, who put in long hours for the nation's benefit. They are eager and anxious to serve their country.

One thing still upsetting me, however, is that no one kept proper records of meetings or decisions. This led to my failure to recollect whether I approved an arms shipment before or after the fact. I did approve it; I just can't say specifically when. Rest assured, there's plenty of record-keeping now going on at 1600 Pennsylvania Avenue. . . .

I'm taking action in three basic areas—personnel, national security policy and the process for making sure that the system works.

First, personnel. I've brought in an accomplished and highly respected new team here at the White House. They bring new blood, new energy, and new credibility and experience.

Former Senator Howard Baker, my new chief of staff, possesses a breadth of legislative and foreign affairs skills that's impossible to match. I'm hopeful that his experience as minority and majority leader of the Senate can help us forge a new partnership with the Congress, especially on foreign and national security policies. I'm genuinely honored that he's given up his own Presidential aspirations to serve the country as my chief of staff.

Frank Carlucci, my new national security adviser, is respected for his experience in government and trusted for his judgment and counsel. Under him, the N.S.C. staff is being rebuilt with proper management discipline. Already, almost half the N.S.C. professional staff is comprised of new people.

Yesterday I nominated William Webster, a man of sterling reputation, to be Director of the Central Intelligence Agency. Mr. Webster has served as Director of the F.B.I. and as a U.S. District Court judge. He understands the meaning of "Rule of Law." . . .

I have also directed that any covert activity be in support of clear policy objectives and in compliance with American values. I expect a covert policy that if Americans saw it on the front page of their newspaper, they'd say, "That makes sense."

I have had issued a directive prohibiting the N.S.C. staff itself from undertaking covert operations—no if's, and's or but's.

I have asked Vice President Bush to reconvene his task force on terrorism to review our terrorist policy in light of the events that have occurred.

Third, in terms of the process of reaching national security decisions, I am adopting in total the Tower report's model of how the N.S.C. process and staff should work. I am directing Mr. Carlucci to take the necessary steps to make that happen. He will report back to me on further reforms that might be needed.

I've created the post of N.S.C. legal adviser to assure a greater sensitivity to matters of law.

I am also determined to make the Congressional oversight process work. Proper procedures for consultation with the Congress will be followed, not only in letter but in spirit.

Before the end of March I will report to the Congress on all the steps I've taken in line with the Tower board's conclusions.

Now what should happen when you make a mistake is this: You take your knocks, you learn your lessons and then you move on. That's the healthiest way to deal with a problem. This in no way diminishes the importance of the other continuing investigations, but the business of our country and our people must proceed. I've gotten this message from Republicans and Democrats in Congress, from allies around the world—and if we're reading the signals right, even from the Soviets. And, of course, I've heard the message from you, the American people.

You know, by the time you reach my age, you've made plenty of mistakes if you've lived your life properly. So you learn. You put things in perspective. You pull your energies together. You change. You go forward.

My fellow Americans, I have a great deal that I want to accomplish with you and for you over the next two years, and, the Lord willing, that's exactly what I intend to do. Goodnight and God bless you.

BALTIMORE SUN
Reagan's Limited Hang-Out
[March 6, 1987]

Ronald Reagan is now well-launched on a campaign to put the Iran-contra debacle behind him, to turn the nation's attention from what he described yesterday as "inside-Washington politics" to the fun things of the presidency—speeches to adoring audiences, trips to Venice and Berlin, maybe even an arms-agreement summit with Soviet leader Mikhail S. Gorbachev.

Though presidential events may proceed on schedule, inside-Washington will be marching to its own drummer. Two congressional committees and a special prosecutor selected by Mr. Reagan will be following up all those tantalizing leads in the Tower Commission report. Congress will be fighting, perhaps as early as next week, over aid to the Nicaraguan rebels while the money trail from Iran to the contras is still uncharted.

Just why Washington reality won't conform any longer to Reaganesque fantasies lies embedded in the artful formulations of the president's Wednesday night speech. On the surface it was good stuff—a mixture of contrition, folksiness and firm resolution to do better. "By the time you reach my age (76)," said the Communicator, "... you learn, you put things in perspective, you pull your energies together, you *change.*"

Alas, there was little internal evidence of change. Not once did he admit that the very idea of sending arms to terrorist Iran was wrong. He talked about poor record-keeping at the White House but not the shredding of some of those records or the drafting of false chronologies. His explanation for *three* months of presidential silence was bizarre. "I felt it was improper to come to you with sketchy reports or possibly even erroneous statements," the president told his fellow Americans, neglecting to remind them that he had done precisely that *four* months ago.

As for aid to the contras, in possible violation of laws prohibiting government assistance, Mr. Reagan merely repeated that he didn't know about any diversion of Iranian arms sale profits to the rebels. He made no mention of the private-aid network set up by former National Security

Council aide Oliver North, or of Colonel North's memo alleging that "the president obviously knows why he has been meeting" with network contributors.

In defending his detached "management style," the president said it had "worked successfully" before, only to go off track in the arms deals because of mistakes in "execution" by "free-lancing" aides. But had Mr. Reagan's aloofness, his inattention to detail really worked in the past? Former budget director David Stockman has written that Mr. Reagan simply didn't know—or want to know—that his huge 1981 tax cuts would create mountainous deficits. At the Reykjavik summit, an unprepared Mr. Reagan was "snookered" (in the word of the House Armed Services Committee) by the Russians.

Despite the omissions and circumlocutions that abounded in the president's Wednesday night speech, his acceptance of responsibility for what happened on his watch was assuring. We are heartened by his pledge to put the recommendations of the Tower Commission into practice and his appointment of Howard Baker as White House chief of staff. Iran-contra has changed everything, much of it for the better, and Mr. Reagan's task is to prove he can really change with it.

[Reprinted courtesy *The Sun.*]

GAIL SHEEHY

Reality? Just Say No

[*New Republic*, March 30, 1987]

Several days before Ronald Reagan made his March 4 speech on Iranamok, the word from his friends and advisers was that he was still unwilling to admit his mistake. And despite the expressions of sorrow and regret that ultimately were written into the speech, those predictions were right. He has yet to explain adequately his own responsibility in the arms deal, and it is still not clear whether he will be able to recover from four months of dissembling, dithering, and silence.

In answer to the question that began as a joke and grew to be the focal point of the Tower Commission's questions—What did the president forget and when did he forget it?—Reagan finally claimed, "I don't remember—period." How could a president forget authorizing a violation of his own oft-stated anti-terrorism policy? Coming after a yes-no-maybe answer, Reagan's disclaimer is hard to believe. Hard, that is, for the rest of us. What may really be involved here, however, is not a memory lapse, not a legal denial, but psychological denial. Reagan apparently cannot remember what he cannot admit to himself.

For months the president insisted that he didn't swap arms for hostages. It remained for Tower Commission member Brent Scowcroft to explain that President Reagan's "concept" of his Iran initiative "was not accurately reflected in the reality of the operation." Yet even in his confessional speech, Reagan was unable to extricate himself from his fantasies. "A few months ago I told the American people I did not trade arms for hostages. My heart and my best intentions still tell me that is true, but the facts and the evidence tell me it is not." In other words, throughout the crisis, and even to some extent at the moment of what was supposed to be a mea culpa, the presid'ent of the United States denied the truth to himself. . . .

This hallmark of the Reagan character has now been labeled a "management style," implying that it is a conscious choice. That style has been described as "detachment" from the details of government. This is misleading. When the president, refusing to listen to the protests of his Cabinet officers, dispatched two Marines (McFarlane and Oliver North) to pay off the government that bankrolled the Beirut barracks bombing in which 241 of their fellow Marines were killed, he had to go well beyond detachment.

We are all familiar with the defense mechanism of denial. When one is first confronted with a shocking loss or crisis, the unconscious mind may generate a temporary "I don't believe it, this can't be happening" response until the ego is ready to deal with the new reality. This is normal, and we all do it from time to time. But Ronald Reagan has always stayed on the surface of events, absorbed facts selectively, and denied the dark side of life. Denial of unpleasant realities long ago became Reagan's characteristic problem-solving style.

The distortions produced by such defense mechanisms become part of a person's view of the world. Truths too uncomfortable to admit are unconsciously altered or postponed, and the altered truth then becomes *subjectively* true. The president cannot do what the whole country is demanding—get on top of the facts and admit his own mistakes—unless his psychological defenses allow him to admit those facts to himself. Is this possible, at the age of 76?

Since he was a child, Reagan has been denying harsh realities and concocting his own, more pleasant alternatives. As Garry Wills pointed out in *Reagan's America: Innocents at Home*, Reagan's father was a salesman who played fast and loose with facts and passed himself off as a "practipedist," a highfalutin title for a man with no credentials other than a correspondence course degree and an X-ray machine in his shoe store. A shy boy in immense glasses, Reagan seized on make-believe for his self-presentation. He acted out roles created for him by his mother in church skits. And always he denied the darkest aspect of his childhood—the hard-drinking father who shamed him.

From the time Reagan entered radio, then Hollywood, then TV, his gift for pretense was rewarded again and again. He earned his reputation in radio during the Depression by concocting whole ball games from the scraps of paper that came off a telegraph relay while he sat in a studio 300 miles away. . . .

What happens when a lifelong denier comes up against a problem he can't deny? He does all the odd, disconcerting things that people who have seen Reagan over the past months have described variously as "monumental indifference," "stubbornness," "sloth," "shuffling," "drifting into oft-repeated anecdotes," wearing a necktie over Christmas that played "Jingle Bells," and in every way refusing to come to grips with the reality. Is this, as John Tower would have it, an aberration?

When the Iran-*contra* scandal first broke, the president relied on the coping strategies that had always worked for him. First, the salesman's speech. He had previously been able to make us believe that *he* believed what he read off the TelePrompTer. When his deep voice quivered with emotion, and he talked of his "visions" and the "miracle" that is America, it was as though some divine afflatus had descended upon him to point the way for all of us. That was the Reagan magic. Suddenly his dream-spinning solipsism didn't work. He tried using the Reagan charm on the media in a rare press conference on November 19. But they kept throwing facts at him, and with no script, he had nothing to fall back on but confusion, dissembling, and denial. Eleven of his answers on the Iran scandal began with the word "no."

To learn that half the country believed him to be lying, to be caught in a quagmire over the very issue that pulled down his predecessor, to be hounded week after week by leaders of his own party who told him to wake up and face reality, to undergo surgery again only to come back to the White House and be confronted with unpleasant facts about what the government did under his stewardship—all of it may have strained Reagan's mental powers to a dangerous degree. For denial is a slow poison.

The most convenient explanation for the president's mental predicament is that he is getting old. It is true that aging exaggerates any distortion in a person's problem-solving abilities. But Reagan's failure to perform his duty is part of a much deeper psychological pattern. Campaigning in 1980, Reagan defused the age issue by promising the American people that he would undergo regular tests for senility if he became president. As the popular incumbent in '84, however, Reagan retreated from that pledge and substituted a Catch-22. He would take the tests only if there was some "indication that I was drifting." He added, "Nothing like that has happened."

"Drifting" is mild compared to the judgments rendered on Ronald Reagan's mental acuity in the last few weeks. Former Senator Edmund Muskie admitted on "Face the Nation" that the three members of the Tower panel "were all appalled by the absence of the kind of alertness and vigilance to his job...that one expects of a president." Even Howard Baker, before being named White House chief of staff, questioned the president's ability to remember complex matters over a long period of time: "You found that the half-life of that memory was short." Apparently the president's need to protect himself psychologically may have prevented him from taking even routine steps to protect himself legally on Iranamok.

Yet if Ronald Reagan came to assume that he was above reality, it was in large measure because we the electorate coddled him into believing it. Voters, followed by Congress and the media, lowered their standards to accommodate this hypnotically happy president. He didn't have to work a full week or keep notes or referee policy disputes among his advisers. No amount of press reports of his misstatements of fact seemed to register. On the contrary, they became part of fond Reagan lore. It was his stock-in-trade to "forget" facts that interfere with his perception of himself as pure in motive and true to his word. The "Teflon President" sobriquet, intended by Representative Pat Schroeder as a criticism, was construed as a compliment.

Under Reagan we all developed the habit of denial. Here at last was the president who embodied our fantasy vision of America: a bullet-proof, media-proof, crisis-proof leader—the only man in the country who never seemed to age. The real question is not whether he can make it through the next two years, if half-asleep. The more sobering possibility is that we the electorate, content to partake of his self-indulgence as our own, will simply roll over and beg to finish the dream.

[Reprinted by permission of *The New Republic*. Copyright © 1987 The New Republic, Inc.]

RONALD REAGAN
Address on the Iran-Contra Affair
[August 12, 1987]

My fellow Americans, I've said on several occasions that I wouldn't comment about the recent Congressional hearings on the Iran-Contra matter until the hearings were over. Well, that time has come, so tonight I want to talk about some of the lessons we've learned. . . .

These past nine months have been confusing and painful ones for the country. I know you have doubts in your own minds about what happened in this whole episode. What I hope is not in doubt, however, is my commitment to the investigations themselves.

So far, we've had our investigations—by the Justice Department, the Tower board, the independent counsel and the Congress. I requested three of those investigations, and I endorsed and cooperated fully with the fourth—the Congressional hearings—supplying over 250,000 pages of White House documents, including parts of my own private diaries. Once I realized I hadn't been fully informed, I sought to find the answers.

Some of the answers I don't like. As the Tower board reported, and as I said last March, our original initiative rapidly got all tangled up in the sale of arms, and the sale of arms got tangled up with the hostages. Secretary Schultz and Secretary Weinberger both predicted that the American people would immediately assume this whole plan was an arms-for-hostages deal and nothing more. Unfortunately, their predictions were right.

As I said to you in March, I let my preoccupation with the hostages intrude into areas where it didn't belong. The image—the reality—of Americans in chains, deprived of tł eir freedom and families so far from home, burdened my thoughts. This was a mistake.

My fellow Americans, I have thought long and often about how to explain to you what I intended to accomplish, but I respect you too much to make excuses. The fact of the matter is that there's nothing I can say that will make the situation right. I was stubborn in my pursuit of a policy that went astray.

The other major issue of the hearings, of course, was the diversion of funds to the Nicaraguan contras.

Colonel North and Admiral Poindexter believed they were doing what I would've wanted done—keeping the democratic resistance alive in Nicaragua. I believed then and I believe now in preventing the Soviets from establishing a beachhead in Central America.

Since I have been so closely associated with the cause of the contras, the big question during the hearings was whether I knew of the diversion. I was aware the resistance was receiving funds directly from third countries and from private efforts, and I endorsed those endeavors wholeheartedly; but, let me put this in capital letters, I did not know about the diversion of funds. Indeed, I didn't know there were excess funds.

Yet the buck does not stop with Admiral Poindexter, as he stated in his testimony; it stops with me. I am the one who is ultimately accountable to the American people. The admiral testified he wanted to protect me; yet no President should ever be protected from the truth. No operation is so secret that it must be kept from the commander in chief. I had the right, the obligation, to make my own decision.

I heard someone the other day ask why I wasn't outraged. Well, at times, I've been mad as a hornet. Anyone would be—just look at the damage that's been done and the time that's been lost. But I've always found that the best therapy for outrage and anger is action.

I've tried to take steps so that what we've been through can't happen again, either in this Administration or future ones. . . . I am also adopting new, tighter procedures on consulting with and notifying the Congress on future covert-action findings. We will still pursue covert operations when appropriate, but each operation must be legal, and it must meet a specific policy objective.

The problem goes deeper, however, than policies and personnel. Probably the biggest lesson we can draw from the hearings is that the executive and legislative branches of Government need to regain trust in each other. We've seen the results of that mistrust in the form of lies, leaks, divisions and mistakes. We need to find a way to cooperate while realizing foreign policy can't be run by committee. And I believe there is now the growing sense that we can accomplish more by cooperating.

And in the end, this may be the eventual blessing in disguise to come out of the Iran-contra mess. . . .

WASHINGTON POST
Mr. Reagan's Speech
[August 13, 1987]

It was a bit odd to hear President Reagan stating last night that there was nothing he could say to make right the situation that grew out of his sale of arms to Iran. There *is* something presidents can say when things go wrong—and he certainly said some part of it. No one wants the sort of groveling that abases the man or the office. Mr. Reagan did not do that, and should not have. But almost everyone expects to hear conveyed a sense that the president truly understands what went wrong, has absorbed the implications of it, has absorbed as well the shock and dismay caused by it, and is then prepared to move on.

In his speech on the Iran-contra affair, Mr. Reagan fairly gave himself high marks for cooperating with the various inquiries. He acknowledged that events had been "confusing and painful" and had left "doubts" in the country. It took some courage to acknowledge that "I was stubborn in my pursuit of a policy that went astray." In that sense it was the right speech. He didn't have to address everything and he could be expected to be more understanding of his own administration's failings than outsiders would be.

Yet it was evident once again that Mr. Reagan's thermostat measuring political outrage, including political outrage that has cost his administration dear, is set low. It is not simply that he did not address some of the more important matters raised in the congressional hearings and that in some he did address—the origin of the arms sales, for instance—his presentation went past much that the testimony had revealed.

In saying that his secretaries of defense and state had "predicted that the American people would immediately assume this whole plan was an arms-for-hostages deal and nothing more," he passed over all the sad testimony about their exclusion from the policy circle. In declaring that "the buck does not stop with Adm. Poindexter," he failed to explain or even ask how it was that he too was kept in the dark. He called "the biggest lesson" of the hearings the need for executive-legislative trust, as though the two branches were equally at fault for the "lies, leaks, divisions and mistakes." You don't have to believe the congressional record on funding the contras has been constant or a model of legislative precision to know that the main burden of fault clearly falls on the administration. Meanwhile, he ignored that parts of the American government had run operations and made plans that skirted or broke the law.

It was a brisk and brief speech. Mr. Reagan was appearing while he and Congress are on vacation and before Congress issues its own recommendations. He was at pains to cite the steps he has taken to clean up the debris and the broader agenda he still intends to pursue. Still, for all that he tried to put this affair behind him, the main impression he left was that he has not come fully to terms with the most convulsive events his administration has so far known.

[Copyright © 1987 *The Washington Post.*]

ROGER ROSENBLATT
The Too Personal Presidency
[*Time*, November 24, 1986]

Last Thursday night the President attempted to persuade the nation that his decision to deal arms to Iran was merely a gesture of rapprochement, but logic suggests that those arms were meant to secure the release of U.S. hostages in Lebanon. What shocks Americans about this transaction is that it seems so uncharacteristic of a President who has railed against trading with terrorists, and who appears to sense that the public agrees with his position. In fact, the effort to free individuals in Lebanon at a possible extreme cost is perfectly consistent with the way Reagan has always conducted the presidency's business. In forests of complex issues, Reagan likes to point to the trees, to individuals. The suggestion is that individuals embody policies, that if one appreciates the situation or nature of a particular person, he will also understand general actions taken in that person's behalf.

Think back to all you know of Ronald Reagan, and there is almost always some other person in the picture. Originally that person was you, the individual tree he addressed with startling success when he posed the question in the 1980 presidential debates, "Are you better off than you were four years ago?" In the six years since, you have remained pre-eminent in the President's view. It still is you he addresses in weekly radio broadcasts and in television appearances, establishing an intimacy by look and voice that television, for all its domestic directness, usually denies.

Britain is America's ally, but that abstract agreement is brought to life by personification, by the friendship and ideological comradeship of Reagan and Margaret Thatcher. Libya is America's enemy, but that enmity glowers as a private hostility between Reagan and Muammar Gaddafi. If the values of American initiative need commending, Reagan will shed his spotlight on a Mother Hale of Harlem, as he did in the 1985 State of the Union message, and elevate one woman to emblemize an entire economic and social theory. If heroism in war is to be honored, a single veteran will stand beside the President on the White House steps, creating a tableau that speaks, if imprecisely, for itself.

To see the world in terms of individuals may succeed occasionally as a political tactic, but the tactic would never be consistently effective if such a view were not part of a deep and sincerely held vision. Reagan wholeheartedly seems to believe that individuals and stories about individuals are the keys to general truths. That vision can go crazily awry; Reagan is known for responding to general questions with irrelevant, albeit funny or touching, anecdotes. But the vision itself can be valid and clarifying. When John Donne wrote, "I am a little world made cunningly," it was a comfort to believe that the overwhelming complexities of the cosmos could be reduced to the size of a man.

Whatever sense one can make of the secret dealings that led to arms transfers to Iran in exchange for the hostages' freedom may be traced to Reagan's microcosmic vision, yet Reagan's reductions seem far more emotional than rational. In the Iran transaction he apparently felt the plight of the hostages as one would feel the plight of one's family in danger, and his emotional response took precedence over his country's stated policy against trading with terrorists, its neutrality in the Iran-Iraq war, its fair-and-square relations with other countries—over every major issue to which the hostage situation potentially was tied.

He may also have assumed that most of his countrymen would share his view. A certain reasoning was on his side. For one thing, it makes more sense to try and coax Iran back into the world than to watch it burn and smolder further out of reach. The Ayatollah, at age 86, cannot live forever, though it must be noted that his mother, age 105, is rumored to be still with us. For another thing, individuals do count. Israel's Shimon Peres, who has spoken obliquely of his country's role in the arms negotiations, defended the Reagan Administration's action as an exception that proves the rule. No one can doubt the rigidity of America's normal position on trading with terrorists, Peres argued, yet a democracy's central obligation must always tilt toward its individual citizens.

So the question is of gains and losses, just as it was most recently in Reagan's handling of the Daniloff incident and the summit meeting with Gorbachev in Iceland. In each of those instances, the President once again focused on individuals. So moved was Reagan at a newsman's imprisonment, he was determined to solve that problem alone, at the possible expense of creating others. So sure was Reagan that he could charm Gorbachev in Reykjavik, he overlooked the fact that he was meeting with both a man and a system. Fortunately for Reagan, the uproar over his trading a spy for a journalist rose and vanished rapidly, and even more fortunately, he did not fly home from Iceland having agreed thoughtlessly to a total ban of nuclear weapons. In both situations his luck, not his philosophy, prevailed.

In the Iran affair, however, both his luck and his philosophy may have run dry, for there basic understandings between the public and the presidency were broken that are considerably more serious than the White House reckoned. To a point, the people will tolerate, even applaud, a President's leapfrogging of rules and restrictions, as long as the people perceive a worthwhile goal achieved. But their tolerance will go quickly if they feel that presidential self-assurance is giving way to recklessness. One feels fervently for the men imperiled by the kidnapers, and for their anxious families, but from the standpoint of national honor and practical sense, it is difficult to argue that their release is worth destroying the long-term trust of our allies or creating perpetual incentives for terror.

In a way, the American people asked for what they got in this incident by having always treated Reagan exactly as Reagan has treated the people. If Reagan has zeroed in on individual members of the Republic to score his points, the Republic has also zeroed in on, and favored, Reagan as a man. Not the office but the individual has garnered an attitude of such all-embracing faith these past six years—an attractive individual indeed, when one considers some of the discrepancies between Reagan's promises and his deliveries. But the people never wholly lost sight of the presidential office, even if they are dazzled by a most engaging occupant. They know the value of a principle as well as the value of a life. In the case of Iran, too many principles were seized, too many killed.

2. CENTRAL AMERICA

Oliver North's scheme for funneling illegal aid to the Nicaraguan contras was wholly in tune with President Reagan's fierce determination to combat communism in Latin America—the theme of his speech to a joint session of Congress in April 1983. Beginning with a geography lesson—"El Salvador is nearer to Texas than Texas is to Massachusetts"—the President went on to argue that America's vital strategic interests required U.S. opposition to the

*guerrillas who were fighting El Salvador's pro-U.S. government, and contin-
ued U.S. support for the CIA-financed* contra *army fighting the Sandinistas of
Nicaragua. He urged congressional funding for a four-point military, economic, and diplomatic program to bolster America's friends and undermine
America's enemies south of the border.*

*The nation's newspapers responded predictably: Democratic papers echoed
the* Boston Globe's *dismissal of Reagan's speech as "political theatrics"
and "Red Scare oratory"; Republican papers shared the* Richmond Times-
Dispatch's *view that the President had spoken wisely and that his opponents'
assessment of the communist threat in Latin America was "dangerously
unrealistic." One of the strongest critical voices, again predictably, was the
vehemently anti-Reagan periodical* The Nation, *which denounced his address
as "ferocious, distorted, and inflammatory."*

Suiting action to words, Reagan not only continued the campaign for
contra *aid, but in October 1983 authorized a U.S. invasion of the tiny
Caribbean island of Grenada to overthrow a radical government allied with
Fidel Castro's communist regime in Cuba.*

The debate over contra *aid and related issues continued through Reagan's
two terms, in the halls of Congress and in the nation's press. Writing in*
Commentary *in 1986, conservative political consultant Max Singer argued
that America's unwillingness to give clear-cut support to "a popular, nationalist democratic group" fighting a "Communist tyranny" in Nicaragua
would discourage democratic forces throughout the region and lead to the
further spread of communism and its "juggernaut of lies, deceit, and
brutality."*

RONALD REAGAN
Central America: Defending Our Vital Interests
[Address Before a Joint Session of Congress, April 27, 1983]

It would be hard to find many Americans who are not aware of our stake in
the Middle East, the Persian Gulf, or the NATO line dividing the free world
from the communist bloc. And the same could be said for Asia.

But in spite of, or maybe because of, a flurry of stories about places like
Nicaragua and El Salvador, and, yes, some concerted propaganda, many of
us find it hard to believe we have a stake in problems involving those
countries. Too many have thought of Central America as just that place way
down below Mexico that can't possibly constitute a threat to our well-being.

And that's why I have asked for this session. Central America's problems
do directly affect the security and the well-being of our own people. And
Central America is much closer to the United States than many of the world

trouble spots that concern us. So as we work to restore our own economy, we cannot afford to lose sight of our neighbors to the south.

El Salvador is nearer to Texas than Texas is to Massachusetts. Nicaragua is just as close to Miami, San Antonio, San Diego, and Tucson as those cities are to Washington where we're gathered tonight. But nearness on the map doesn't even begin to tell the strategic importance of Central America, bordering as it does on the Caribbean—our lifeline to the outside world. Two-thirds of all our foreign trade and petroleum pass through the Panama Canal and the Caribbean. In a European crisis, at least half of our supplies for NATO would go through these areas by sea. It's well to remember that in early 1942 a handful of Hitler's submarines sank more tonnage there than in all of the Atlantic Ocean. And they did this without a single naval base anywhere in the area.

Today, the situation is different. Cuba is host to a Soviet combat brigade, a submarine base capable of servicing Soviet submarines, and military air bases visited regularly by Soviet military aircraft. . . .

If the Nazis during World War II and the Soviets today could recognize the Caribbean and Central America as vital to our interests, shouldn't we also?

For several years now, under two administrations, the United States has been increasing its defense of freedom in the Caribbean Basin. And I can tell you tonight, democracy is beginning to take root in El Salvador which, until a short time ago, knew only dictatorship. The new government is now delivering on its promises of democracy, reforms, and free elections. It wasn't easy, and there was resistance to many of the attempted reforms with assassinations of some of the reformers. Guerrilla bands and urban terrorists were portrayed in a worldwide propaganda campaign as freedom fighters representative of the people. Ten days before I came into office, the guerrillas launched what they called a "final offensive" to overthrow the government. And their radio boasted that our new Administration would be too late to prevent their victory.

They learned democracy cannot be so easily defeated. President Carter did not hesitate. He authorized arms and ammunition to El Salvador. The guerrilla offensive failed but not America's will. Every president since this country assumed global responsibilities has known that those responsibilities could only be met if we pursued a bipartisan foreign policy.

As I said a moment ago, the Government of El Salvador has been keeping its promises, like the land reform program which is making thousands of farm tenants, farm owners. In a little over 3 years, 20% of the arable land in El Salvador has been redistributed to more than 450,000 people. That's 1 in 10 Salvadorans who have benefited directly from this program.

El Salvador has continued to strive toward an orderly and democratic society. The government promised free elections. On March 28th, little more than a year ago, after months of campaigning by a variety of candidates, the suffering people of El Salvador were offered a chance to vote—to choose the kind of government they wanted. And suddenly the so-called freedom fighters in the hills were exposed for what they really are—a small minority who want power for themselves and their backers, not democracy for the people. The guerrillas threatened death to anyone who voted. They destroyed hundreds of buses and trucks to keep the people from getting to the polling places. Their slogan was brutal: "Vote today, die tonight." But on election day, an unprecedented 80% of the electorate braved ambush and gunfire and trudged for miles, many of them, to vote for freedom. And that's truly fighting for freedom. We can never turn our backs on that. . . .

Yes, there are still major problems regarding human rights, the criminal justice system, and violence against non-combatants. And, like the rest of Central America, El Salvador also faces severe economic problems. But in addition to recession-depressed prices for major agricultural exports, El Salvador's economy is being deliberately sabotaged. Tonight in El Salvador—because of ruthless guerrilla attacks—much of the fertile land cannot be cultivated; less than half the rolling stock of the railways remains operational; bridges, water facilities, telephone and electric systems have been destroyed and damaged. In one 22-month period, there were 5,000 interruptions of electrical power; one region was without electricity for a third of a year. . . .

They don't want elections because they know they would be defeated. But, as the previous election showed, the Salvadoran people's desire for democracy will not be defeated. The guerrillas are not embattled peasants armed with muskets. They are professionals, sometimes with better training and weaponry than the government's soldiers. The Salvadoran battalions that have received U.S. training have been conducting themselves well on the battlefield and with the civilian population. But, so far, we've only provided enough money to train 1 Salvadoran soldier out of 10, fewer than the number of guerrillas that are trained by Nicaragua and Cuba.

And let me set the record straight on Nicaragua, a country next to El Salvador. In 1979, when the new government took over in Nicaragua, after a revolution which overthrew the authoritarian rule of Somoza, everyone hoped for the growth of democracy. We in the United States did too. By January of 1981, our emergency relief and recovery aid to Nicaragua totaled $118 million—more than provided by any other developed country. In fact, in the first 2 years of Sandinista rule, the United States directly or indirectly sent five times more aid to Nicaragua than it had in the 2 years prior to the revolution. Can anyone doubt the generosity and good faith of the American people? . . .

No sooner was victory achieved than a small clique ousted others who had been part of the revolution from having any voice in government. Humberto Ortega, the Minister of Defense, declared Marxism-Leninism would be their guide, and so it is. The Government of Nicaragua has imposed a new dictatorship; it has refused to hold the elections it promised; it has seized control of most media and subjects all media to heavy prior censorship; it denied the bishops and priests of the Roman Catholic Church the right to say mass on radio during holy week; it insulted and mocked the Pope; it has driven the Miskito Indians from their homelands—burning their villages, destroying their crops, and forcing them into involuntary internment camps far from home; it has moved against the private sector and free labor unions; it condoned mob action against Nicaragua's independent human rights commission and drove the director of that commission into exile.

In short, after all these acts of repression by the government, is it any wonder that opposition has formed? Contrary to propaganda, the opponents of the Sandinistas are not die-hard supporters of the previous Somoza regime. In fact, many are anti-Somoza heroes who fought beside the Sandinistas to bring down the Somoza government. Now they've been denied any part in the new government because they truly wanted democracy for Nicaragua, and they still do. Others are Miskito Indians fighting for their homes, their lands, and their lives.

The Sandinista revolution in Nicaragua turned out to be just an exchange of one set of autocratic rulers for another, and the people still have no freedom, no democratic rights, and more poverty. Even worse than its predecessor, it is helping Cuba and the Soviets to destabilize our hemisphere.

Meanwhile, the Government of El Salvador, making every effort to guarantee democracy, free labor unions, freedom of religion, and a free press, is under attack by guerrillas dedicated to the same philosophy that prevails in Nicaragua, Cuba, and, yes, the Soviet Union. Violence has been Nicaragua's most important export to the world. It is the ultimate in hypocrisy for the unelected Nicaraguan Government to charge that we seek their overthrow when they're doing everything they can to bring down the elected Government of El Salvador. The guerrilla attacks are directed from a headquarters in Managua, the capital of Nicaragua.

But let us be clear as to the American attitude toward the Government of Nicaragua. We do not seek its overthrow. Our interest is to ensure that it does not infect its neighbors through the export of subversion and violence. Our purpose, in conformity with American and international law, is to prevent the flow of arms to El Salvador, Honduras, Guatemala, and Costa Rica. We have attempted to have a dialogue with the Government of Nicaragua, but it persists in its efforts to spread violence....

Nicaragua's neighbors know that Sandinista promises of peace, nonalliance, and nonintervention have not been kept. Some 36 new military bases have been built; there were only 13 during the Somoza years. Nicaragua's new army numbers 25,000 men supported by a militia of 50,000. It is the largest army in Central America supplemented by 2,000 Cuban military and security advisers. It is equipped with the most modern weapons, dozens of Soviet-made tanks, 800 Soviet-bloc trucks, Soviet 152-MM howitzers, 100 antiaircraft guns, plus planes and helicopters. There are additional thousands of civilian advisers from Cuba, the Soviet Union, East Germany, Libya, and the

PLO [Palestine Liberation Organization]. And we are attacked because we have 55 military trainers in El Salvador.

The goal of the professional guerrilla movements in Central America is as simple as it is sinister—to destabilize the entire region from the Panama Canal to Mexico. If you doubt me on this point, just consider what Cayetano Carpio, the now-deceased Salvadoran guerrilla leader, said earlier this month. Carpio said that after El Salvador falls, El Salvador and Nicaragua would be "arm-in-arm and struggling for the total liberation of Central America." . . .

Now, before I go any further, let me say to those who invoke the memory of Vietnam: There is no thought of sending American combat troops to Central America; they are not needed—indeed, they have not been requested there. All our neighbors ask of us is assistance in training and arms to protect themselves while they build a better, freer life.

We must continue to encourage peace among the nations of Central America. We must support the regional efforts now underway to promote solutions to regional problems. We cannot be certain that the Marxist-Leninist bands who believe war is an instrument of politics will be readily discouraged. It's crucial that we not become discouraged before they do. Otherwise the region's freedom will be lost and our security damaged in ways that can hardly be calculated.

If Central America were to fall, what would the consequences be for our position in Asia, Europe, and for alliances such as NATO? If the United States cannot respond to a threat near our own borders, why should Europeans or Asians believe that we are seriously concerned about threats to them? If the Soviets can assume that nothing short of an actual attack on the United States will provoke an American response, which ally, which friend will trust us then? . . .

[The President concluded by listing his Administration's four basic goals in Central America: (1) vigorous efforts to further democracy, human rights, and free elections in the region; (2) economic aid programs to enhance health care, agriculture, and industry; (3) "security assistance" to nations threatened militarily by Cuba and Nicaragua; and (4) support for "dialogue and negotiations—both among the countries of the region and within each country."]

BOSTON GLOBE
Reagan's Central America Speech
[April 29, 1983]

President Reagan's extraordinary speech appealing for support for his Central America policy tests both the political maturity and moral compass of the American people.

Can Americans in the 1980s still be dazzled by patriotic theatrics, fooled by misleading recitations of events and historical analogies, impressed by superficial calls for "bipartisan" unity and jerked into line by Red Scare oratory? Or after nearly four decades of experience, have Americans developed some sophistication about the post-colonial world?

Can we recognize the imperative for change in unjust political systems and understand that evolution becomes revolution if it has to? Do we sense the limitations of our Communist adversaries, certainly in their grasp and perhaps even in their reach? Have we grown enough through experiences as different as losing the Vietnam War and seeing the Third World anew through Peace Corps eyes to understand that it *is* possible for the United States to get ahead of the curve of history if we want to?

Before the joint session of Congress, Reagan was trying to leapfrog the legislators and get to the voters. He was trying to drum up popular support for an unpopular Central American policy that is heavily oriented to military suppression of political problems, and that is by degrees failing. Of equal political importance, he was also trying to pin the blame for that impending failure on Congress.

The President was not bellicose in tone, but he was stony on issues of substance. The civil war in El Salvador rooted in a brutal history of oppression was falsely blamed on the Nicaraguans, Cubans and Soviets. Assertions were made but, as usual, no evidence of substantial aid to the Salvadoran rebels was produced. The existence of democrats in the Salvadoran left was obscured by his references to "professional" guerrillas. The President promised support for "democracy, reform and human freedom," then incongruously listed Guatemala among countries "pledged" to that course.

The leftist Nicaraguan regime was maligned, but the CIA's "covert" war to topple it went unmentioned. The supposed threat to the hemisphere was artfully linked to Hitler's submarines. The 1947 Truman Doctrine for the postwar defense of Europe was quoted at length and misapplied. The canard about Soviet intervention to place missiles in Central America—a threat that has been traced to Administration sources but no further—was voiced again.

In the Democratic response to the President's speech, Sen. Dodd (D-Conn.) gave an alternate view of the deepening regional crisis in Central America against which Reagan's message can be measured. Dodd pledged opposition to the establishment of Marxist states in the hemisphere and to defend the real security interests of the hemisphere by military means. But, he said, "the painful truth is that many of our highest officials seem to know as little about Central America in 1983 as we knew about Indochina in 1963."

As Dodd pointed out, the Salvadoran rebels have offered to negotiate unconditionally. The Pope has endorsed such a dialogue. Important U.S. allies in the region—Mexico, Panama, Venezuela and Colombia—all favor it. Virtually all sectors of El Salvador, including important elements in the military, have come to see this as the only solution, but none dare say so openly because of the threat of the murderous right wing.

President Reagan adopted the term "political solution" as his goal, but does not accept its meaning. It cannot be confined, as Reagan wants, to narrow procedural issues surrounding an election aimed at maintaining the status quo. A political solution will require negotiations between the rebels and the Salvadoran government over the whole range of issues that divide them—negotiations founded on a far greater understanding of Central American history and realities than Reagan's speech exhibited.

[Reprinted courtesy *Boston Globe.*]

RICHMOND (VIRGINIA) TIMES-DISPATCH
Fighting the Plague
[April 29, 1983]

One sentence in President Reagan's speech to Congress Wednesday night cogently capsuled the justification for the United States' efforts to save El Salvador from communism. "If the Nazis during World War II and the Soviets today could recognize the Caribbean and Central America as vital to our interests," he asked, "should not we also?"

Of course we should. The propinquity of Central America and the high military and commercial value of the sea lanes in that area make it profoundly important to the welfare of the United States. Hitler knew this when he sent his submarines into the area; the Soviet Union knows this, too, which is why it is aiding the Marxists in El Salvador and elsewhere in the region. Having swallowed Cuba and embraced Nicaragua, the Soviets lust for all of Latin America.

It is this stark truth that President Reagan presented to Congress and the American people in his appeal for their support of his policies in El Salvador. It was an eloquent and reasonable exhortation to Congress to join in a bipartisan attempt to block communism in El Salvador lest it spread, like a plague, throughout the region and to the very borders of the United States.

The president recognizes the need for a two-pronged approach to the problems in El Salvador. That country's welfare is threatened militarily by the guerrillas and economically by the region's natural deficiencies and by socio-political traditions that have limited the opportunities of the masses. Those threats must be met militarily and economically, and Mr. Reagan would do this by offering military aid and advice—though not, as he emphasized Wednesday night, American troops—and economic assistance to

El Salvador. But Congress, so far, has failed to give his program the support it must have to work.

Opposition to the president is being led, of course, by the Democrats, whose dangerously unrealistic views were summarized by Connecticut Sen. Christopher J. Dodd, the party's official respondent to Mr. Reagan's speech. The senator argued, in essence, that the United States should forget about military aid, promote a negotiated settlement to the strife in El Salvador and offer economic assistance. Piously, he declared that Democrats, like Mr. Reagan, "will oppose the establishment of Marxist states in Central America."

Have Sen. Dodd and his Democratic colleagues learned nothing about communism from the chronicle it has so clearly written? Given the communists' record of seizing total power once they have negotiated their way into a government, how can the Democrats in good conscience advocate a negotiated settlement? They should instead urge the guerrillas to participate in free elections and accept whatever verdict the voters render. And it is foolish to suggest that the United States could save El Salvador by economic assistance. The military forces of the abandoned Salvadoran government would be no match, in the long run, for the guerrilla forces that would continue to receive strong assistance from the Soviet Union and its proxies.

As for Sen. Dodd's solemn declaration that the Democrats will oppose the establishment of Marxist states in Central America, it is fair to ask: When? After they have become firmly established? When Marxism is spreading along the banks of the Rio Grande?

The time to oppose Marxism in Central America is now, before it has engulfed any more countries. And the way to oppose it is through the combined use of economic, social and military assistance—the approach that President Reagan advocates.

[Reprinted courtesy *Richmond Times-Dispatch*.]

NATION
Reagan Draws the Line
[May 7, 1983]

President Reagan delivered a ferocious, distorted and inflammatory address on Central America to a joint session of Congress, and then forgot to add the punch line. His vision of the Soviet threat south of the border was as apocalyptic as any proposed in this new cold war: "The national security of all the Americas is at stake. . . . If we cannot defend ourselves there, we cannot expect to prevail elsewhere . . . and the safety of our homeland would be put at jeopardy." To meet this terminal menace the Administration will appoint a roving ambassador and seek a supplemental aid appropriation. The big bang ended in one small whimper.

Reagan's speech was full of false historical analogies, willful fabrications of fact and fatuous name-calling. But its most egregious error was the assumption that America's national security required imperial control of Central America. Such a notion inevitably means support for tyrannical client regimes, which in turn generate rebellions whose leaders are forced to seek ideological and military aid outside the U.S. orbit. Thus, the predictions of global threat become self-fulfilling.

That is the lesson of Vietnam, and of Cuba and Nicaragua. Reagan acknowledges part of it: that American troops cannot be sent abroad to impose an American solution. He may come to understand another part: that military means cannot be employed to resolve what is essentially a political crisis.

But he has yet to see that it is his definition of "America's vital interests" that must be changed before the threat he envisions will dissolve. If those interests mean total control and widespread repression, then he—and we— have already lost. But if they involve even the possibility of freedom and independence for the people of "all the Americas," then real peace will be at hand.

MAX SINGER
Losing Central America
[*Commentary*, July 1986]

A civil war... is taking place in Nicaragua. On one side are the Sandinista party (FSLN) and the Nicaraguan government, which the FSLN acquired by fraud and holds by force. The FSLN is a Marxist-Leninist party closely allied with the Soviet Union and Cuba. It receives large amounts of Soviet aid which it is using to build the biggest armed forces in Central America. Since it seized power after the overthrow of Somoza in 1979, between five and ten thousand operatives have come from the Communist bloc and other states involved in international terrorism to help the Sandinistas set up their military and internal-security programs (about one foreigner for every 50 people in Nicaragua's non-farm labor force).

Externally, the Sandinistas have committed aggression by means of armed subversion against their three neighbors (El Salvador, Honduras, and Costa Rica). At home, they have attacked the free trade unions and all other independent institutions; they are trying to replace the Catholic Church with an atheistic "church of the poor"; they have persecuted the black and Indian minority population; and they have undermined the economy. They have also established an elaborate secret-police apparatus which makes extensive use of torture and murder, and now holds 6,500 political prisoners in inhuman conditions (in addition to 2,500 of Somoza's National Guardsmen who have been held for more than seven years already).

The other side in the Nicaraguan civil war—usually called the *"contras"**—includes virtually the whole spectrum of Nicaraguan political life from Left to Right, all sectors of society, and the largest volunteer (unpaid) peasant army raised in Latin America in fifty years. The aim of this popular-resistance movement, whose leadership had been part of the fight against Somoza, are democracy, independence, and freedom of religion, plus some vague economic and social reforms.

Ranged on the side of the Sandinistas are Mexico, the major Latin American democracies, Canada, the European democracies (except Germany), and the Socialist International. Some of their support—including hundreds of millions of dollars—goes directly to the Sandinistas. Some of it takes the form of backing the so-called Contadora process, the diplomatic effort organized by Mexico and aimed at a settlement which would destroy the *contras* in exchange for promises by the Sandinistas to refrain from external aggression and perhaps also to move toward internal pluralism.†

In the U.S. almost the entire Democratic party and most of the mainstream church organizations are also lined up behind the Sandinistas. On the other hand, the U.S. government, some private American citizens, and other countries acting in secret (probably including Israel and Taiwan) are on the side of the *contras*. A majority of the members of the Organization of American States (OAS), representing the whole of Latin America, also favors the *contras*, but the issue has not been brought up in the OAS and so this group has not played a prominent role in the debate over Nicaragua.

This description of the Nicaraguan conflict must sound like madness to anyone unfamiliar with the facts. In a civil war pitting a Communist tyranny supported by the Soviet Union and the terrorist powers against a popular, nationalist democratic group supported by the United States, why should most of the democracies side with the Communists? Why should the victims and potential victims of Sandinista aggression oppose the Sandinistas' enemies? Why should Christian organizations side with the party that persecutes the Christian faithful? Obviously most of the people in the democratic world

---

* Often the name *"contras"* is used by their enemies as shorthand for "counterrevolutionary." But here it is used the way Jeane J. Kirkpatrick uses it, to stand for "counter-tyranny."

† Originally the Contadora countries were Mexico, Panama, Colombia, and Venezuela. Recently Argentina, Brazil, Peru, and Uruguay have been added as the "Contadora support group." Five Central American countries (Nicaragua, El Salvador, Honduras, Costa Rica, and Guatemala) have also been associated with the process.

who are lined up with the Communists must see the facts differently from the way they are summarized above.

Some, of course, do. But many of the key participants in the debate recognize, at least privately, the truth of some such description as I have just given. Others simply regard the truth about Nicaragua as irrelevant—their position is determined by other concerns. . . .

[In a section of the article omitted here, Max Singer offers his explanation for the failure of Europe or Latin America to rally behind Reagan's anti-Sandinista position. These reasons include deep-seated anti-U.S. prejudices in Europe and long-standing patterns of dependency on the United States which prevent Costa Rica and other Central American countries from taking decisive foreign-policy initiatives, even on issues of vital concern to the region.]

This failure of the democracies, both in Europe and in Latin America, to speak clearly against the Sandinistas and for the *contras* is bound to have a profound impact on the people of Nicaragua themselves.

There are several different "audiences" in Nicaragua, each of which has to try to figure out who is likely to end up in control of the country. The first audience is the general population who can in small ways help either the *contras* or the Sandinistas or can stay strictly neutral. Second is the part of the urban population that might try to start a clandestine resistance movement against the Sandinistas—despite the horror of such warfare and the difficulty of clandestine operations against the brutal, state-of-the-art security apparatus that East Germans and others have provided to the FSLN. Third are those who might in a crisis participate in a "general uprising." Fourth are the troops of the Sandinista army who will fight either well or poorly when they get into heavy combat with the *contras*, depending to some extent on how they see the legitimacy and future of the Sandinista regime. (So far these Sandinista troops have mostly fought poorly.) Finally there are the Sandinistas themselves.

Most discussion of what will influence the actions of Nicaraguans has emphasized factors like Sandinista repression, living conditions, perceptions about *contra* leadership and policy, etc. But Nicaraguans would be superhuman if their actions were not also strongly influenced by who looks to them like the winner. Most people are reluctant to risk torture, death, or even loss of income, when there seems little chance of success.

How do prospects look today to those in Nicaragua who are deciding how to bet their lives and who know all too well that the *contras* will be defeated unless they get a continuous supply of military assistance from the U.S.?

Probably they can prudently bet that President Reagan will continue to believe in the *contra* cause. But from a distance the struggles in Congress over *contra* aid must have produced some doubt as to whether the President would have enough political capital to win a series of such battles. And the

Nicaraguan trying to judge the reliability of U.S. aid cannot take much comfort from the tides of the debate in Congress or the country so far.

It is true that by 1985 congressional and much other influential opinion in the U.S. had clearly begun to recognize the truth about the Sandinista regime, and ' ɔ turn away from supporting it. But this must be a very limited source of reassurance to someone who is wondering about the reliability of the U.S. First he must be concerned about the five-year period that elapsed before the U.S. policy debate caught up with the facts of the Nicaraguan conflict: safety requires a faster response. Second, it must worry him that many of those in the U.S. who have recently lost their illusions about the Sandinistas now have nearly equally false information about the *contras*—much of it from the same sources that propagated their former views.

Any Nicaraguan trying to judge the reliability of the U.S. commitment to the *contras* must be struck by how few of the Congressmen who have recently become disillusioned with the Sandinistas seem to have drawn any conclusions from their experience. They are not acting as if they were angry at having been deceived for years, or as if they were concerned about the continuing power and consequences of the system responsible for the long success of the Sandinista deception. And those who have been anxiously following our political struggle over *contra* aid must be frustrated by how much more the outcome is influenced by extraneous elements in U.S. politics than by the reality in Nicaragua.

As for the Sandinistas themselves, so far they have been able to have it both ways. They speak and act like Communists, brutally suppressing democratic organizations, but they are treated with great respect by most of the democratic world. They do not need to feel at all isolated, and they have not been forced to choose between Communism and the West. They must be greatly reassured by the steady stream of encouragement from all the democracies. . . .

There is . . . little hope any longer that the democracies can be turned away from their support of the Communist side in the Nicaraguan civil war. The case is too hard to make without the Central Americans, especially Costa Rica.

Given this problem, and given all the opposition in Congress to the *contras*, President Reagan will find it hard, if not impossible, to dissuade those in Honduras who feel that their most prudent course is to limit *contra* use of Honduran territory. If the Hondurans were to take steps in this direction, the smell of defeat might begin to hang over the *contras*, and the resulting downward momentum could destroy them faster than we could act to save them.

With this accomplished, the Sandinistas would be able to consolidate their power at home and would be ready to move in one of two directions abroad. They might decide to step up the guerrilla war in El Salvador and Guatemala, perhaps maneuvering so that the armies of those countries felt forced to take power again. The guerrillas, heavily supported from Nicaragua, including "disguised" Nicaraguan personnel, would be in a good position to defeat such politically isolated post-coup governments, in the kind of long drawn-out political-military struggle we have seen before.

Alternatively, the Sandinistas could first go after Costa Rica and Honduras. There the technique would probably be to use groups that were not themselves Communist but were sympathetic and vulnerable to Communist control, and which with Sandinista, Mexican, and Cuban help could obtain power without Nicaragua's army crossing the border. The majority of the people would want to resist, but they would be divided and sapped by doubt of their chances, and any cry to Washington would be drowned out by strong local voices telling us that our "help" was unwanted and unneeded.

Unless we were lucky, there would be no point in this process at which the U.S. could turn the tide, for we too would be divided and sapped by doubt—not so much of our chances as of whether the Sandinistas had "really" broken their agreement. Either way, thanks to a combination of European apathy, Mexican cynicism, Central American dependency, Communist skill and energy, and U.S. disunity, Central America would within five or ten years be as Communist as Eastern Europe. Not only would additional millions of poor souls be doomed to live under totalitarian tyranny, but a great opportunity would also have been lost to demonstrate that people willing to fight for their freedom can successfully resist the Communist coalition and the juggernaut of lies, deceit, and brutality it always sets in motion.

[Reprinted by permission of Max Singer, from *Commentary*, July 1986, by permission; all rights reserved.]

3. THE SOVIET UNION

On no issue did President Reagan reverse himself more spectacularly than in his view of the Soviet Union. True to his reputation as an unbending anticommunist, Reagan early in his term, as we have seen, denounced Russia as "an evil empire" and "the focus of evil in the modern world." But as Mikhail Gorbachev nudged the Soviet Union toward greater openness at home and a more conciliatory stance abroad, Reagan's tone moderated accordingly. The veteran Cold Warrior ended his public career with a mission to Moscow marked by cordial tête-à-tète with Gorbachev, the signing of the Intermediate-range Nuclear Forces (INF) Treaty, and apparent progress on a still more comprehensive nuclear-weapons-reduction agreement in the so-called START talks.

The selections below convey the range of responses to the remarkable process that brought Reagan to Red Square in that hopeful spring of 1988. Angry rumblings emanated from right-wing publications shocked by their hero's defection from the ranks of Cold War true believers. While the Manchester Union Leader *labeled Reagan's Moscow trip "a sad week for the free world," William F. Buckley's* National Review *proclaimed the President's newfound cordiality toward the regime he had labeled an "evil empire" only five years earlier an exercise in Orwellian doublethink.*

But Newsweek *columnist Meg Greenfield saw in Reagan's embrace of Gorbachev dramatic evidence of the way personal relationships could dissolve his ideological rigidities—a trait she found appealing. Veteran political writer Murray Kempton gave Reagan's Moscow performance a far cooler review, but he did conclude that the President's hatred of "government bureaucrats" had struck a resonant chord with ordinary Soviet citizens. This section ends with an assessment by Gail Lapidus and Alexander Dallin, international affairs specialists at Berkeley and Stanford respectively, of the sources, limits, and long-term implications of Reagan's amazing rapprochement with the Soviets.*

MANCHESTER (NEW HAMPSHIRE) UNION LEADER
No More Evil
[June 5, 1988]

Aides are blaming either fatigue or a wish to be polite to his host for President Reagan's appalling remark that mere bureaucracy is responsible for the plight of Soviet dissidents and refuseniks.

Whatever the reason, we think the President's words and Soviet boss Gorbachev's response to them sum up forcefully what was wrong with this summit and what ails the fading Reagan administration.

The President told Moscow and the world last week that any problem Soviet Jews and other dissidents have in getting out of the Soviet slave state is probably one of bureaucratic red tape and certainly not because of Communist government policy.

"I'm not blaming you," Reagan told a Communist newsman who had asked about the President's earlier criticism of the Soviet Union's human rights violations.

"I'm blaming bureaucracy. We have the same type of thing happen in our country."

With that one incredible response, the President severely damaged what had been the only saving grace of this deplorable summit love-in with the Communists.

Until then, on the matter of human rights, Mr. Reagan had been forthright, candid, and eloquent in speaking out against Soviet repression of religion, of free speech, of free thought and movement.

But in return for his "bureaucracy apology" and his glowing remarks about Gorbachev's hard work on reform, what did Mr. Reagan get from his new friend?

Gorbachev figuratively spit in the President's face, chastising him at their joint appearance for failing to do more on East-West relations. Later, as the President's plane was leaving the USSR, the chief thug was telling so-called "peace activists" that he didn't need lectures by others on human rights and that he had no intention of changing his government's repressive policies.

President Reagan has convinced himself that the man who heads the evil empire has ended its treachery and is trying to be one of the good guys, and facts to the contrary will not sway him.

It was a sad week for the free world, indeed.

[Reprinted by permission of *The Union Leader.*]

WILLIAM F. BUCKLEY, JR.
So Long, Evil Empire
[*National Review*, July 8, 1988]

At 27, he was an agricultural economist with Moscow's Institute of Economics and a university lecturer. But Stalin looked kindly on him during the Great Purge and, instead of shooting or exiling him, made him chief of the U.S. division of the People's Commissariat of Foreign Affairs. From there he went as counselor to the Soviet Embassy in Washington, becoming ambassador in 1943 as well as the USSR's representative to the UN Security Council, where he established the Soviet tradition of vetoing any moves designed to promote peace with freedom. In 1946 he became deputy foreign minister. And Stalin's approval of him made him a candidate for the Central Committee of the Communist Party. He became first deputy foreign minister in 1949 and foreign minister in 1957. He was directly involved in the diplomatic and military action against the students in Budapest, serving under Khrushchev. Under Brezhnev, he presided over the purge of the Prague Spring in Czechoslovakia in 1968. Andrei Andreyevich Gromyko is now the President of the Soviet Union, and the first person to greet President Ronald Reagan as he descended from Air Force One at Vnukovo Airport on Sunday.

The itinerary of Mr. Reagan might have been conceived by the Brothers Grimm. No fairy tale could have made the trip more regally satisfying. The rich decor was courtesy of dead czars, the last one executed by someone in honor of whom a Russian city is named. The grand paintings and decorations were done by European and Russian masters of the eighteenth and nineteenth centuries. The children were trained to sing American folk songs in English. And, beginning with Gorbachev himself, the Russian Court had learned to sing, if every now and then with a touch of diffidence, the praises of peace and co-existence. Ronald Reagan lectured to the intellectuals about an obscure episode in an obscure Russian novel and received a standing ovation. It was a dream, it was nirvana, it was—mind-blowing.

There was that one terribly sour note, sounded day after day. Every time Mr. Reagan looked especially pleased, especially satisfied, especially carried away by the *Gemütlichkeit* of it all, you would hear a voice. Not a Russian voice, but a good, twangy American voice, and always that voice would ask the same question:

"Is this what you called the evil empire, Mr. President?"

"What was that about the evil empire, Mr. President?"

"Tell us about the evil empire, Mr. President."

Finally, worn down by this hectoring over his melodramatic excess of years gone by, Mr. Reagan said: "I was talking about another empire."

We sinners believe, because we were taught to believe and do give internal assent to the mandate, that we must forgive, seventy times seven times. But Mr. Reagan is engaged now not in forgiveness, but in what Orwell called vaporization. Big Brother decides to change a historical or a present fact, and evidence inconvenient to the new thesis is simply made to—disappear.

Run the fingers lightly over the globe, pausing at outposts of the Soviet Empire. In Nicaragua, using Soviet arms, they are promoting war and aggression and drafting 17-year-olds while suffering a 60 per cent cut in their standard of living.

In Cuba, where people continue to die in the effort to flee from it, there is dire poverty and the most aggressive conventional armed force in the Western Hemisphere, paid for by the Soviet Union.

In Bulgaria, the dictator Zhivkov still reigns. Several years ago he sent a secret agent to inject poison into the veins of a Bulgarian refugee poet, as he was promenading over Waterloo Bridge in London.

In Poland, General Jaruzelski, proconsul for Gorbachev, hacks down those who fight for a free labor-union movement.

In Ethiopia, starvation is imminent for two million people at the hands of the dictator Mengistu, shored up by the Soviet Union.

In Southeast Asia, dire poverty and huge supplies of weapons keep the North Vietnamese in charge of the human misery brought on by Soviet-backed aggression.

Mr. Reagan does well to encourage changes in the Soviet system. Something wildly exciting is indeed going on in the Soviet Union. But to greet it as if it were no longer evil is on the order of changing our entire position toward Adolf Hitler on receiving the news that he has abolished one extermination camp. The Soviet Union has a very long way to go before it brings reasonable freedom to those who live under it. We sow only confusion when we retract the statement that it is evil to support the systematic suppression of human rights everywhere your empire reaches. Mikhail Gorbachev may be the spokesman for what is being attempted within the Soviet Union, but Andrei Gromyko continues as president of what continues to be an evil empire.

MEG GREENFIELD

The Great Personifier

[*Newsweek*, June 13, 1988]

I knew this would happen—Reagan's going all sentimental and "soft on communism" in the view of his devout followers, I mean. The visit to Moscow guaranteed it. Riding through Leningrad one afternoon, a few days before he reached the Soviet Union, I spied a couple of lads, very Huck Finn in appearance, scrambling down a riverside bank to join yet another who was fishing with a crudely crafted pole. "Wait till the president sees this," I found myself thinking, not meaning these particular boys in a city he wasn't even going to visit, but rather the individual Russian child—not to mention the individual Russian mama and papa and *babushka* and the rest. Reagan's mellow reactions in Moscow tell us more about him than they do about the state of relations between the two superpowers; they confirm much of what we have learned about the man's political imagination and his political sympathies. Our supposed right-wing ideologue has no gift at all for ideology, theory or abstraction. He is the Great Personifier.

As Reagan's term nears its end, more people are trying to rationalize its central contradiction: the affable, sublimely tolerant nature of the man versus the unforgiving nature of so many of his policy pronouncements. Some very interesting analysis explains him in the context of a lifelong career as a performer, with its concentration on character rather than ideas and its essential simulation. The only caution I would raise would be against going too far in the simulation part of the reading, in effect reducing the theory to a charge of hypocrisy and double-dealing. For, however the Reagan mechanism actually works, it is plain to me that the man is not simply pretending in his responses to the army of individuals who cross his path or playacting as politicians do when they "drop in" on average citizens to show how human they are or otherwise faking his susceptibility to the human encounter. True, he is utterly inaccessible to some people who see him. But he is an absolute sucker, a goner for most.

Consider how Reagan has countenanced disloyal behavior among his employees and friends. It seems that once he knows you he can almost never find it in his heart to really clop you, no matter what the provocation. Donald Regan, taking out after the president's wife, finally established where the outer limits of this magnanimity lie. But by and large Reagan is a hopeless empathizer; all you need to do is get into his presence with a hard-luck story or the mere fact of your existence as a normal, vulnerable person; his ferocious political positions of a lifetime may collapse. Recall Reagan associates explaining how it was meeting with the hostages' desolate families that brought him to his ill-conceived arms deal with the Iranians. Remember the innumerable episodes in which Reagan the hardhearted on questions of social welfare would positively *melt* in the presence of an individual who had been victimized by precisely the forces he had refused to acknowledge or combat—Reagan trying to get a newly laid-off black man a job, etc. He wants to oblige, to ingratiate, to help. He understands—but only if you are there.

In an odd way, the opposite of all this for Reagan—his excursions in theorizing—isn't really so different after all. For in the absence of real-life, flesh-and-blood people on which to base an opinion or perception, Reagan isn't so much given to abstraction as he is to allegory. He personifies his ideas in images and anecdotes that invariably have a human shape: the cheating, lying bosses of the "evil empire"; the Cadillac-driving welfare queen and other emblems of villainy are matched by the sentimentalized, fairy-tale figures of virtue... invariably nice moms, selfless soldiers and innocent, flaxen-haired little girls. This is the scheme of things according to Reagan, and whether it's vice or virtue he is talking about, it always has a human face. But those consigned to the bad-guy ranks in the allegory can generally escape by turning up in actual life and exploding Reagan's stereotype of who and what they are. I figure that it would take no more than one or two personal meetings with a hard-working, heart-rending GS-7 (preferably patriotic, God-fearing and the mother of three) to upend Reagan's lifetime prejudice against bureaucrats. If he has found a place in his heart for

Gorbachev, can workers at the Department of Housing and Urban Development be far behind?

I find myself at the edge of making fun of all this, but never quite willing to go all the way. That is because the political world I inhabit is populated by so many people who are the exact reverse of Reagan in these matters. I mean people who can see and deal only in percentages, trends, abstractions, theories, principles and demographic readouts, who base all their social and political sympathies on such things, but who frankly can't stand people. Well, that overdoes it—but not by much. We do live in a world where compassion is granted much more freely to demographic entities than to the guy standing next to you on the bus or the not-our-type family that wants to move in the neighborhood. Reagan loves you only if you are there. That's not exactly adequate in a president. But too many of his political antagonists love you only if you are not, which is worse. He has to see you as a person. They have to see you as a number—a socially damning, guilt-inducing number.

These latter people I see as the Cosmics. They deal in geopolitics, geostrategy, global trends, statistical probabilities and other assorted whooshing forces and crashing chords on the great international pipe organ, and they could certainly tell you (and over the past few days already have) what was homely and small-town and wrong with Reagan's performance in Moscow. Some of it I buy. But, despite myself, I rather *liked* the fact that our president was moved by his human encounters, and I liked unconditionally the fact that he went out of his way to meet and encourage individual human-rights victims, a practice disparaged as mere "casework" by some of those Cosmics who despair that the president doesn't see the big picture. Yes, Reagan made some fatuous remarks in Moscow, and, yes, it is dangerous to generalize from anecdotes and atypical encounters. But I think he came home better off and wiser than he left.

MURRAY KEMPTON
At the Summit
[*Newsday*, June 2, 1988]

President Reagan goes home freighted with honors from the revolution. And, if we are to believe the Soviet Foreign Office as much as he seems to for the moment, one of these honors is godfatherdom-in-absentia to two newborn children, a boy named Ron and a girl named Reagana.

The Politburo is not famous for overmuch trust in the spontaneity of the masses, and we cannot be sure that these babes were not delivered to the christening bowl by command decision. Even so, this announcement has its tones of the artistically credible, because such evidence as can be said to exist seems to suggest that the Reagan persona was an object of continual pleasure and even occasional delight to ordinary Russians.

It has before now been remarked that the diplomatic genius of America resides in our talent for making peace with countries with which we do not happen to be at war. We have seldom had a president whose execution of these historically irrelevant functions is as adroit as this one's, and those who groan at the flaccidity of his grip upon issues great and small underestimate his true mastery of the requisite style.

Saint Jerome once expressed his discontent with the early Christians by saying that they were capable of as many roles as there are sins to commit. Our president is, of course, so without sin as to seem unaware of its existence, except as an abstraction, and we could more properly describe him as capable of as many roles as there are charms to dispense.

Cast his part for formal address, and he serves you up Reagan the Renaissance man tripping the green valleys and leaping the treacherous crags of the whole culture of man, contemplating his portfolio of the drawings of the young Kandinsky, sleigh-riding with Gogol, sorrowing over the memoirs of Anna Akhmatova, thrilling with the discovery of the Uzbek poets, and then, still unwearied, sitting up with the late show to check before correcting the misjudgment of the Motion Picture Academy of Arts and Sciences when it withheld its Oscar from *Friendly Persuasion* and *Butch Cassidy and the Sundance Kid*.

But conscript him to the colloquies of give-and-take and he will deliver the Reagan of simple nonsense, a wonderfully worked counterfeit of a dumbness equal to our own. The time comes for questions at the University of Moscow, and one student asks whether he will meet with a delegation of American Indians who have traveled here to submit their century-old complaints. The President replies that, when he gets home, he will be "very pleased to meet them and see what their grievances are or what they feel they might be. . . . And you'd be surprised—some of them became very wealthy because some of [their] reservations were overlaying great pools of oil, and you can get very rich pumping oil. And so—I don't know what their grievances might be."

The windfall profits tax on oil, perhaps? A student asks why he had seen fit to present Mikhail Gorbachev with a list of three hundred Soviet citizens asserting deprivations of their human rights.

"Now I'm not blaming you—I'm blaming bureaucracy," the President answers. "We have the same type of thing happen in our own country. And every once in a while, somebody has to get the bureaucracy by the neck and shake it loose and say, 'Stop doing what you're doing.' And this is the type of thing and the names that we have brought."

If he had known what he was doing, he could not have found a key better tuned to the Russian soul. He hates bureaucrats and so do the Russians, from experiences of longer standing and more painful intimacy. One of the oldest traditions in this nation's history is the voice of some victim of an administrative injustice, vast or little, saying that such things could not be "if the czar only knew."

Czars come and go, but life keeps to its dreary and inequitable round. And if it is human to think of one's czar as a man with a heart too warm to permit the excesses of petty officialdom, it is just as human to draw comfort in cherishing the image of the czar who does not know. We might wonder, indeed, whether Reagan's manner may not appeal to Gorbachev's constituents more profoundly than to his own.

When Gorbachev and Reagan held their final press conferences, there may have been Americans possessed of a modicum of patriotism who shuddered at the pitiable figure their president cut in contrast with a general secretary who ran the whole range of his piano with impeccable touch on every key. Here was Gorbachev carrying the impression that no sparrow that falls escapes his notice, and, half an hour later, there came Reagan cloaked with every assurance that he lives where no sparrow ever falls anyway.

There was an inquiry about the homeless in America. The President replied that he had heard of people who sleep in the street because they apparently have no place to live, but he has been solaced in that gloomy thought by learning of a "young woman" the police tried to drag from her pavement, who had gone to court to establish her constitutional liberty to freeze all night on the sidewalk of her choice.

Perhaps the Russians do not find this sort of stuff as absurd as some of the rest of us who have less reason than they to think of the state as a universally oppressive nuisance. The President talks their language; he salutes them as the God-fearing people they very probably are in the main; and he blames all their troubles on bureaucrats. And we ought not to be surprised at how cunningly he may have touched the tenderness of their memory of the all-kind czar who did not know.

GAIL W. LAPIDUS AND ALEXANDER DALLIN
The Pacification of Ronald Reagan
[*Bulletin of the Atomic Scientists*, January/February 1989]

The contradictory legacy of the Reagan era is nowhere more evident than in the administration's dealings with the Soviet Union.

Admirers credit Ronald Reagan with historic achievements. His unswerving commitment to building up U.S. military power and confronting the Soviets politically, militarily, and economically, they argue, compelled the Soviet leadership to acknowledge the bankruptcy of its past policies. . . . The lessons that many Reagan admirers draw from this experience is that a combination of military power and political determination is the essential ingredient for dealing successfully with the Soviet Union.

Critics on the political right disagree. They maintain that in its final years the Reagan administration deviated from the principled course on which it embarked in 1981. Succumbing to domestic pressures as well as to the blandishments of a clever new leader—a "refined Stalinist" in Gucci garb, as one congressman put it—the administration launched on a risky new path of rapprochement with the Soviets, a policy which, they fear, could revive the delusions of détente, erode public support for adequate military spending, and jeopardize the long-term security interests of the Western alliance.

Both these assessments are misleading and invite us to learn the wrong lessons from the experience of the 1980s. In reality, the improvement since 1985 in U.S.-Soviet relations owes less to specific policies of the Reagan administration than it does, first, to longer-term changes in the international environment and inside the Soviet Union, which began well before Reagan took office; and, second, to changes in leadership and outlook in Moscow which were neither produced nor controlled by Washington. Signs of an impending crisis were discernible before 1981. And although the demonstration of U.S. military resolve and massive spending for a military buildup in the 1980s probably sharpened Moscow's dilemmas, Soviet policies and outlook would not have changed as dramatically without the passing of the Brezhnev coalition. Had Leonid Brezhnev or Konstantin Chernenko remained in office, the original Reagan policy might have proved counterproductive.

Actually, the improvement in relations forced the Reagan administration to abandon some of its initial assumptions and stances and to return to a more traditional, moderate approach to the Soviets, based on bipartisan support from Congress.

Ronald Reagan came to office committed to a far-reaching change in domestic and foreign priorities. Accusing previous administrations of underestimating the Soviet threat, permitting the erosion of U.S. military strength, and acquiescing in a dangerous expansion of Soviet power, he pledged to give highest priority to challenging "Soviet imperialism" on all fronts. The point of departure was a two-camp image of the world which saw the communists as dangerous and evil. Initially the new administration dismissed differences between Soviet officials or among communist parties and states as insignificant. . . .

An alarmist assessment of Soviet military capabilities was used to justify sharp increases in U.S. military spending, sustained by curtailing domestic social programs and incurring huge budget deficits. Unprecedented requests for defense appropriations amounted to an open-ended wish list rather than reflecting any criteria for assessing the effectiveness of defense outlays.

During his first term, Reagan similarly sought to use economic policy, political warfare, the human rights issue, and intervention by proxy in Third World conflicts to confront, embarrass, and delegitimize the Soviet system and to destabilize the Soviet empire.

But the blunt confrontational rhetoric proved difficult to translate into policy; in a number of areas the new objectives were substantially scaled down and the impulse to conduct an anti-Soviet crusade was moderated:

• Reagan learned that the unratified SALT II Treaty, which he had initially denounced as "fatally flawed," actually served U.S. interests, as the Joint Chiefs saw it, and the United States continued to observe its terms.

• The administration was obliged to renew arms control negotiations with the Soviets, under pressure from U.S. public opinion as well as from Europeans who insisted that the 1979 allied decision to deploy intermediate-range missiles in Europe was contingent on arms control progress.

• The effort to conduct economic warfare was vitiated by the administration's eagerness to lift the grain embargo imposed by President Jimmy Carter in 1979; and the NATO allies bitterly opposed administration efforts in the early 1980s to prevent their participation in building the Siberian natural gas pipeline.

• The Reagan administration backed down from the "tough" approach initially envisaged for Eastern Europe once it understood the consequences that would follow from declaring a default on the Polish debt.

• On human rights, the administration shifted from its initial grandstanding intended to embarrass the Soviet authorities to quiet diplomacy which began to achieve results.

Although the trend toward greater pragmatism was clear, administration policy was marked to the end by numerous zigzags and reversals, bureaucratic conflicts, and incoherence. As the new policymakers encountered the reality of the world abroad, they frequently found that their prior beliefs did not fit. . . . And when Mikhail Gorbachev became general secretary in March 1985, the changes introduced by the new Soviet leadership reinforced the growing pragmatism in Washington. . . .

Gorbachev's accession to power brought dramatic changes in both substance and style of Soviet policy. Without challenging the basic institutions of an authoritarian one-party state, he began promoting economic decentralization, individual initiative, political liberalization, greater openness and freedom of expression, and a more truthful approach to the Soviet past and present. His departures in foreign policy were equally far-reaching, most notably a changing conception of security, a new calculus of the costs and benefits of foreign commitments, and a desire for greater participation in the international community.

The complex of new policies regarding arms control, regional conflicts, human rights, information policy, and international contacts is the product of these changed assumptions rather than a response to particular U.S. policies. The new approach—dubbed the "new political thinking"—is the indirect result of a long-term process that includes both U.S. containment policy after World War II and the détente of the 1970s, which exposed an influential part of the Soviet elite to Western achievement and values.

Ronald Reagan met with Mikhail Gorbachev five times, beginning in late 1985. On his visit to Moscow in mid-1989 he declared the days when he called the Soviet Union an "evil empire" part of a bygone era. He has helped give arms control a new legitimacy in the eyes of the American public. More broadly, the change in U.S.-Soviet relations was mirrored in a significant mellowing of Western opinion about the Soviet Union.

Less apparent have been the limits of progress. The Reagan administration failed to conclude a momentous arms control agreement that would have reduced strategic stockpiles on each side by 50 percent, largely because it lacked the political will to see it through, and because it was unable to come up with a coherent defense policy within which to fit the cutbacks. The United States has been similarly indecisive in framing its approach to the reduction of conventional forces, let alone negotiating a common stand with its NATO partners.

More fundamentally, the Reagan administration began a transition to a new Soviet-American relationship without identifying just what that new relationship could realistically be. Nor did it set out any benchmarks by which the United States could gauge its progress, or lack thereof, in dealing with the Soviets.

What was being said about the Soviet Union when the Reagan administration came into office—that it was impervious to change, for example, reads today like a catalog of the ludicrous. This should stand as a lesson about the danger of acting upon ideological preconceptions.

A second lesson concerns the limits on U.S. power. The Bush administration faces the challenge of redefining America's global role at a time when economic constraints, the nature of nuclear weapons, changes in the structure of international power, and domestic needs all circumscribe its freedom of action.

While its future is uncertain, Gorbachev's revolution holds out enormous promise of a fundamental change in domestic and foreign policies alike, which calls for imagination as well as prudence by the United States. . . . There are significant, perhaps unprecedented opportunities ahead in Soviet-American relations that need to be explored with expert knowledge, will and skill.

[Reprinted by permission of the *Bulletin of the Atomic Scientists*. Copyright © 1989 by the Educational Foundation for Nuclear Science.]

End of an Era

CONCLUDING ASSESSMENTS

The effort to decipher Reaganism and to understand Reagan's enduring popularity continued to his last day in office and beyond. Reagan's farewell address, delivered on January 11, 1989, offered observers a final occasion to assess his remarkable mastery of TV. The speech was vintage Reagan, highlighting his achievements, gliding over the setbacks and failures, and ending with a paean to America, the shining "city on a hill," and a call for a rebirth of patriotism, including the Hollywood variety. (The "thirty seconds over Tokyo" mentioned by Reagan as a memorable moment of American history was an allusion to the movie of that title.)

The farewell address offered a litmus test of observers' political ideology. While the Indianapolis Star *hailed it as an admirable antidote to "pessimistic intellectuals [who] wallow on the dismal side of American life," and the* Denver Post *compared Reagan favorably with Franklin D. Roosevelt, the* St. Louis Post-Dispatch *and* Commonweal *deplored its sentimentality, evasions, and easy nostalgia.*

More general assessments of the Reagan era differed widely as well. Nation's Business *praised "six years of economic growth" and hailed "the age of the entrepreneur," while former White House staffer David Gergen marveled in* U.S. News and World Report *at Reagan's "keen understanding of the spoken word" and argued that his unfailing insouciance reflected not superficiality but the "larger vision" of history that would prove his greatest legacy. The* New Republic's *T.R.B., by contrast, dismissed the whole idea of assessing the "legacy" of a President who was "virtually brain dead." Yet economist Robert Samuelson, writing in the same magazine, saw Reagan's "ability to stay above events" as a considerable source of strength.*

This section, and the book, ends with a selection which typically sums up the ongoing ambivalence about Reagan. The Albuquerque Journal *acknowl-*

edged his failings and the thinness of his "don't worry, be happy"
message, but concluded that when all was said and done, the bottom line in
1989 was the same as it had been in 1981: 'America really likes Ronald
Reagan.''

RONALD REAGAN
Farewell Address to the American People
[January 11, 1989]

My fellow Americans, this is the 34th time I'll speak to you from the Oval
Office, and the last. We have been together eight years now, and soon it will
be time for me to go. But before I do, I wanted to share some thoughts, some
of which I have been saving for a long time.

It has been the honor of my life to be your President. So many of
you have written the past few weeks to say thanks, but I could say as much
to you. Nancy and I are grateful for the opportunity you gave us to
serve.

One of the things about the Presidency is that you're always somewhat
apart. You spend a lot of time going by too fast in a car someone else is
driving, and seeing the people through tinted glass—the parents holding up a
child, and the wave you saw too late and couldn't return. And so many times
I wanted to stop, and reach out from behind the glass, to connect. And
maybe I can do a little of that tonight.

People ask how I feel about leaving, and the fact is parting is "such
sweet sorrow." The sweet part is California, and the ranch, and freedom.
The sorrow? The goodbyes, of course, and leaving this beautiful place.

You know, down the hall and up the stairs from this office is the part of the
White House where the President and his family live. There are a few
favorite windows I have up there that I like to stand and look out of early in
the morning. The view is over the grounds here to the Washington Monument, and then the Mall, and the Jefferson Memorial. But on mornings when
the humidity is low, you can see past the Jefferson Memorial to the river, the
Potomac, and the Virginia shore. Someone said that's the view Lincoln had
when he saw the smoke rising from the battle of Bull Run. I see more prosaic
things: the grass on the banks, the morning traffic as people make their way
to work, now and then a sailboat on the river.

I have been thinking a bit at that window. I've been reflecting on what the
past eight years have meant, and mean. And the image that comes to mind
like a refrain is a nautical one—a small story about a big ship, and a refugee,
and a sailor.

It was back in the early Eighties, at the height of the boat people, and the sailor was hard at work on the carrier Midway, which was patrolling the South China Sea. The sailor, like most American servicemen, was young, smart and fiercely observant. The crew spied on the horizon a leaky little boat—and crammed inside were refugees from Indochina hoping to get to America. The Midway sent a small launch to bring them to the ship, and safety. As the refugees made their way through the choppy seas, one spied the sailor on deck, and stood up and called out to him. He yelled, "Hello American sailor—Hello Freedom Man."

A small moment with a big meaning, a moment the sailor, who wrote it in a letter, couldn't get out of his mind. And, when I saw it, neither could I.

Because that's what it was to be an American in the 1980's: We stood, again, for freedom. I know we always have, but in the past few years the world—again, in a way, we ourselves—rediscovered it.

It has been quite a journey this decade, and we held together through some stormy seas. And at the end, together, we are reaching our destination.

The fact is, from Grenada to the Washington and Moscow Summits, from the recession of '81 to '82 to the expansion that began in late '82 and continues to this day, we've made a difference.

The way I see it, there were two great triumphs, two things that I'm proudest of. One is the economic recovery, in which the people of America created—and filled—19 million new jobs. The other is the recovery of our morale: America is respected again in the world, and looked to for leadership. . . .

Back in 1980, when I was running for President, it was all so different. Some pundits said our programs would result in catastrophe. Our views on foreign affairs would cause war, our plans for the economy would cause inflation to soar and bring about economic collapse. I even remember one highly respected economist saying, back in 1982, that "The engines of economic growth have shut down here and across the globe and they are likely to stay that way for years to come."

Well, he—and the other "opinion leaders"—were wrong. The fact is, what they called "radical" was really "right"; what they called "dangerous" was just "desperately needed."

And in all that time I won a nickname—"The Great Communicator." But I never thought it was my style or the words I used that made a difference—it was the content. I wasn't the great communicator, but I communicated great things, and they didn't spring full blown from my brow, they came from the heart of a great nation—from our experience, our wisdom, and our belief in the principles that have guided us for two centuries.

They called it The Reagan Revolution, and I'll accept that, but for me it always seemed more like The Great Rediscovery: a rediscovery of our values and our common sense.

Common sense told us that when you put a big tax on something, the people will produce less of it. So we cut the people's tax rates, and the people produced more than ever before. The economy bloomed like a plant that had been cut back and could now grow quicker and stronger. Our economic program brought about the longest peacetime expansion in our history: real family income up, the poverty rate down, entrepreneurship booming and an explosion in research and new technology. We are exporting more than ever because American industry became more competitive, and at the same time we summoned the national will to knock down protectionist walls abroad instead of erecting them at home.

Common sense also told us that to preserve the peace we'd have to become strong again after years of weakness and confusion. So we rebuilt our defenses—and this New Year we toasted the new peacefulness around the globe. Not only have the superpowers actually begun to reduce their stockpiles of nuclear weapons—and hope for even more progress is bright—but the regional conflicts that rock the globe are also beginning to cease. The Persian Gulf is no longer a war zone, the Soviets are leaving Afghanistan, the Vietnamese are preparing to pull out of Cambodia and an American-mediated accord will soon send 50,000 Cuban troops home from Angola. . . .

And something else we learned: once you begin a great movement, there's no telling where it will end. We meant to change a nation, and instead, we changed a world.

Countries across the globe are turning to free markets and free speech—and turning away from the ideologies of the past. For them, the Great Rediscovery of the 1980's has been that, lo and behold, the moral way of government is the practical way of government. Democracy, the profoundly good, is also the profoundly productive. . . .

"We the people" tell the Government what to do, it doesn't tell us. "We the people" are the driver—the Government is the car. And we decide where it should go, and by what route, and how fast. Almost all the world's constitutions are documents in which governments tell the people what their privileges are. Our Constitution is a document in which "We the People" tell the Government what it is allowed to do. "We the people" are free.

This belief has been the underlying basis for everything I have tried to do these past eight years.

But back in the 1960's when I began, it seemed to me that we had begun reversing the order of things—that through more and more rules and regulations and confiscatory taxes, the Government was taking more of our money, more of our options, and more of our freedom. I went into politics in part to put up my hand and say, "Stop!" I was a citizen-politician, and it seemed the right thing for a citizen to do.

I think we have stopped a lot of what needed stopping. And I hope we have once again reminded people that man is not free unless government is limited. There's a clear cause and effect here that is as neat and predictable as a law of physics: as government expands, liberty contracts.

Nothing is less free than pure communism, and yet we have, the past few years, forged a satisfying new closeness with the Soviet Union. I've been asked if this isn't a gamble, and my answer is no, because we're basing our actions not on words but deeds.

The détente of the 1970's was based not on actions but promises. They'd promise to treat their own people and the people of the world better, but the gulag was still the gulag, and the state was still expansionist, and they still waged proxy wars in Africa, Asia, and Latin America.

This time, so far, it's different: President Gorbachev has brought about some internal democratic reforms and begun the withdrawal from Afghanistan. He has also freed prisoners whose names I've given him every time we've met. . . .

We must keep up our guard—but we must also continue to work together to lessen and eliminate tension and mistrust.

My view is that President Gorbachev is different from previous Soviet leaders. I think he knows some of the things wrong with his society and is trying to fix them. We wish him well. And we'll continue to work to make sure that the Soviet Union that eventually emerges from this process is a less threatening one. . . .

I've been asked if I have any regrets. I do.

The deficit is one. I've been talking a great deal about that lately, but tonight isn't for arguments, and I'm going to hold my tongue.

But an observation: I've had my share of victories in the Congress, but what few people noticed is that I never won anything you didn't win for me. They never saw my troops; they never saw Reagan's Regiments, the American people. You won every battle with every call you made and letter you wrote demanding action.

Well, action is still needed. If we're to finish the job, Reagan's Regiments will have to become the Bush Brigades. Soon he'll be the chief, and he'll need you every bit as much as I did.

Finally, there is a great tradition of warnings in Presidential farewells, and I've got one that's been on my mind for some time.

But oddly enough it starts with one of the things I'm proudest of the past eight years: the resurgence of national pride that I called "the new patriotism." This national feeling is good, but it won't count for much, and it won't last unless it's grounded in thoughtfulness and knowledge.

An informed patriotism is what we want. And are we doing a good enough job teaching our children what America is and what she represents in the long history of the world?

Those of us who are over 35 or so years of age grew up in a different America. We were taught, very directly, what it means to be an American, and we absorbed almost in the air a love of country and an appreciation of its institutions. If you didn't get these things from your family you got them from the neighborhood, from the father down the street who fought in Korea or the family who lost someone at Anzio. Or you could get a sense of patriotism from school. And if all else failed, you could get a sense of patriotism from the popular culture. The movies celebrated democratic values and implicitly reinforced the idea that America was special. TV was like that, too, through the mid Sixties.

But now we're about to enter the Nineties, and some things have changed. Younger parents aren't sure that an unambivalent appreciation of America is the right thing to teach modern children. And as for those who create the popular culture, well-grounded patriotism is no longer the style.

Our spirit is back, but we haven't reinstitutionalized it. We've got to do a better job of getting across that America is freedom—freedom of speech, freedom of religion, freedom of enterprise—and freedom is special and rare. It's fragile; it needs protection.

We've got to teach history based not on what's in fashion but what's important: Why the pilgrims came here, who Jimmy Doolittle was, and what those 30 seconds over Tokyo meant. You know, four years ago on the 40th anniversary of D-Day, I read a letter from a young woman writing to her late father, who'd fought on Omaha Beach. Her name was Lisa Zanatta Henn, and she said, we will always remember, we will never forget what the boys of Normandy did. Well, let's help her keep her word.

If we forget what we did, we won't know who we are. I am warning of an eradication of the American memory that could result, ultimately, in an erosion of the American spirit.

Let's start with some basics—more attention to American history and a greater emphasis on civic ritual. And let me offer lesson No. 1 about America: All great change in America begins at the dinner table. So tomorrow night in the kitchen I hope the talking begins. And children, if your parents haven't been teaching you what it means to be an American—let 'em know and nail 'em on it. That would be a very American thing to do.

And that's about all I have to say tonight. Except for one thing.

The past few days when I've been at the window upstairs, I've thought a bit of the shining "city upon a hill." The phrase comes from John Winthrop, who wrote it to describe the America he imagined. What he imagined was important, because he was an early Pilgrim—an early "Freedom Man." He journeyed here on what today we'd call a little wooden boat; and, like the other Pilgrims, he was looking for a home that would be free.

I've spoken of the shining city all my political life, but I don't know if I ever quite communicated what I saw when I said it. But in my mind, it was a tall proud city built on rocks stronger than oceans, wind swept, God blessed, and teeming with people of all kinds living in harmony and peace—a city with free ports that hummed with commerce and creativity, and if there had to be city walls, the walls had doors, and the doors were open to anyone with the will and the heart to get here.

That's how I saw it, and see it still.

And how stands the city on this winter night? More prosperous, more secure and happier than it was eight years ago. But more than that: after 200 years, two centuries, she still stands strong and true on the granite ridge, and her glow has held steady no matter what storm.

And she's still a beacon, still a magnet for all who must have freedom, for all the Pilgrims from all the lost places who are hurtling through the darkness, toward home.

We've done our part. And as I "walk off into the city streets," a final word to the men and women of the Reagan Revolution—the men and women across America who for eight years did the work that brought America back:

My friends, we did it. We weren't just marking time, we made a difference. We made the city stronger—we made the city freer—and we left her in good hands.

All in all, not bad. Not bad at all.

And so, goodbye.

God bless you. And God bless the United States of America.

INDIANAPOLIS STAR
America Is Standing Tall Again

[January 8, 1989]

America is standing tall again after the eight years of the Ronald Reagan presidency.

Confidence is healthy and health-giving. It is like fresh air, a strong heartbeat, the spring in the walk of a healthy individual. It is the spark of daring and the catalyst of action. It assures poise in time of challenge, test and trouble.

Detractors have sneered at the president's Hollywood background. But his roots go as deep in Middle Western life and the realities of hard knocks as those of Sinclair Lewis, Theodore Dreiser, Sherwood Anderson, Willa Cather and other honest recorders of the American experience. Ronald Reagan is no elitist. Unlike his effete scorners, he is a man of the people.

His critics have jeered him for drawing inspiration from the nation's myths of pioneers, wildcatters, cowboys and adventurers.

But the nation's myths are interwoven with important and enduring truths. The revolutionary patriots, the Founding Fathers, Andy Jackson, Molly Pitcher, Daniel Boone, Anthony Wayne, Betsy Ross, Davey Crockett, Stonewall Jackson, U.S. Grant, Chief Crazy Horse, Booker T. Washington, P.T. Barnum and Thomas A. Edison were all real people.

So many more great ones, colorful and seemingly bigger than life, and millions of "ordinary people" who were heroic but unsung crowd the pageant of America over the generations that the truth is beyond the capacity of anyone to see, grasp and digest, and much is distilled into myth.

The heroes that John Wayne played, the film frontiersmen, and Scarlett O'Hara and Rhett Butler are all mythic, and the myth reflects an immense, significant reality, and so do many other myths, as most people know.

Both the truth and myth of America are full of heroism, courage and achievement, as were the truth and myth of ancient Greece and Rome and Israel and America's Asian, African and American Indian ancestors. They have their tragic side too, their crimes and failures. All civilizations do.

It has been the habit too much, too long for obsessed, pessimistic intellectuals to wallow on the dismal side of American life, to try to drag everyone else into it, to hold the nation and everything about it up to scorn and to spray the population with a penetrating poison of sickly guilt.

Ronald Reagan during the past eight years has rallied Americans who reject that obsession with malaise and who believe the sound ideals and ideas that have had such a powerfully creative part in the building of America are valid for the present and the future.

He never said this society was perfect. He acknowledged its defects.

But he restored the strong faith of millions in the soundness of values that made America strong and free, and—yes—kind and gentle too.

That is some legacy.

[Reprinted courtesy the *Indianapolis Star*.]

DENVER POST
Roosevelt and Reagan
[January 15, 1989]

Ronald Reagan did more to shift American attitudes toward government than any president since Franklin D. Roosevelt.

Roosevelt moved America into a more liberal direction by showing that government could do more for its citizens. Reagan shifted the spectrum back by arguing eloquently that citizens could do more for themselves.

Yet both men preserved far more than they dismantled. Most historians credit Roosevelt with actually saving the capitalist system—by smoothing out the harsh edges and erratic cycles that threatened to destroy it. Similarly, Reagan halted the trend toward an expanded welfare state, but he left the fundamentals of Roosevelt's "social safety net" largely intact.

Roosevelt and Reagan also built their popularity on the same two basic tools—a mastery of electronic media and liberal use of Keynesian economics. Roosevelt's radio "fireside chats" gave him an intimate relationship with the American public that no president had enjoyed before him. Reagan used both television and radio to build the same bond with the voters.

Economically, the irony is that Roosevelt used deficit spending, in peacetime, with a reluctance that made America's recovery from the Great Depression a slow and unsteady affair. Reagan denounced deficit spending in his speeches, but embraced it in his budget with a fervor that tripled the national debt in eight years.

That vast debt is the greatest liability the president will leave to posterity. It also must be said that the progress of minority Americans slowed under his administration, while such signs of social disintegration as homelessness and drug abuse festered.

But he also rebuilt America's confidence and pride. He strengthened the military—and helped restore respect for America's fighting men and women. In foreign affairs, he sensed when to parlay that strong bargaining position into meaningful arms control agreements and warmer relations with a Soviet Union that now is undergoing its own sweeping internal reforms.

It will take historians years to balance the successes and failures of Reagan's administration. But as Americans bid him a fond farewell, few citizens would dispute the fact that he made a difference in our lives.

[Reprinted courtesy the *Denver Post*.]

ST. LOUIS POST-DISPATCH
Ronald Reagan's America
[January 13, 1989]

President Ronald Reagan's farewell address served to remind the nation of one of the reasons for his immense popularity. He made no demands. Much of his 20-minute speech Wednesday night—like so much of his rhetoric throughout his presidency—was devoted to making Americans feel good about themselves.

In Mr. Reagan's America there are no structural problems. All difficulties are seen as merely temporary obstacles that people can solve by rolling up their sleeves and pitching in. Hence, in Ronald Reagan's America, there is no need for a minimum wage or housing assistance, and the growing disparity between rich and poor is a reflection of hard work by the former and lack of initiative on the part of the latter.

As his valedictory reminded us, his was a presidency of nostalgia. He painted a picture of an America that can be found only in a Norman Rockwell illustration or a Jimmy Stewart movie. The odd thing was that Mr. Reagan himself believed in this fanciful portrait, which may explain why he was so successful in communicating it.

There's nothing wrong with getting Americans to take pride in their country, of course, unless that is all there is to the message. The shame is that Mr. Reagan never used his considerable communication skills to rally the people to noble causes or to remind them of their obligations to others. He was not willing to challenge his fellow citizens or lead them up new Everests.

[Reprinted courtesy *St. Louis Post-Dispatch.*]

COMMONWEAL
Gone with the Wind
[February 10, 1989]

If proof of Ronald Reagan's lack of self-comprehension is wanted, we need go no further than his farewell address. He ought to be remembered for it. Who else could have offered so much self-praise, so many half-truths, and so much sentimentality so effectively? "They call it the Reagan revolution," he brimmed. "We meant to change a nation, and instead, we changed a world." "We've done our part." "All in all, not bad. Not bad at all."

No warnings here. No mention of crises that face the republic. Nothing about racism. Nothing about the global environment. Nothing about national addictiveness, nuclear mismanagement, homelessness, the financial IOU's we are leaving to our children. And certainly nothing about corruption in government or the growing gap between rich and poor.

In a remarkable collection of what Oliver Sacks calls "clinical tales" (*The Man Who Mistook His Wife for a Hat*, Summit, 1985), the neurophysiologist draws special attention to the perceptual gifts of certain individuals society generally considers as neurologically impaired. In "The President's Speech," Sacks reports that he happened to walk into an aphasia ward one evening just as the president began an address over national television. This is what he observed: "There he was, the old Charmer, the Actor, with his practiced rhetoric, his histrionisms, his emotional appeal—and all the patients were convulsed with laughter. . . . The president was, as always, moving—but he was moving them, apparently, mainly to laughter. What could they be thinking?''

Sacks then discusses the ability of aphasiacs to understand the "tone-color" of language—that quality of speech which communicates the inner meaning of words rather than just the assemblage of words themselves—and to know unerringly the verisimilitude of a speaker's voice. "Thus it was the grimaces, the histrionisms, the false gestures and, above all, the false tones and cadences of the voice which rang false for these immensely sensitive patients. . . . That is why they laughed at the president's speech." While we normals were fooled, "only the brain-damaged remained intact, undeceived." . . .

What is needed after eight years of Ronald Reagan and the Reagan inversion is not a gentle breeze, but a fierce and cleansing wind.

[Copyright © 1989 the Commonweal Foundation.]

NATION'S BUSINESS
As the Reagan Era Ends—An Appraisal and an Appreciation
[December 1988]

President Reagan certainly wasn't smiling when he made his first economic-policy statement to the nation nearly eight years ago. "I regret to say," the newly inaugurated Chief Executive told the American people, "that we are in the worst economic mess since the Great Depression."

And a mess it was. Back-to-back inflation rates of 13.3 percent in 1979 and 12.4 percent in 1980 represented the highest peak since World War I. Living standards eroded as higher costs outstripped pay raises. Interest rates that soared past 20 percent had crippled the housing, auto and related industries. The high cost of American goods abroad was a major barrier to full U.S. participation in the rapidly expanding global marketplace.

Shortly thereafter, the President submitted to Congress a revolutionary plan that called for reliance on the enterprise system, not on government, as the basis of a healthy economy. "Reaganomics" had four principal initiatives: tax reductions that would stimulate investment and production; spending restraint that would shrink the size of government; elimination of federal regulations that were choking business growth; and a stable monetary policy to hold inflation in check.

The President was proposing nothing less than the reversal of the philosophy, entrenched for a half-century, that the government should have a major role in the marketplace.

He was challenged from the outset. His tax policies would favor only the wealthy, his opponents said, while spending restraints would penalize the poor. They defended as essential even those federal regulations that resulted in higher consumer costs without achieving the purposes envisioned when the controls were adopted. And they saw nothing wrong with running the money-printing presses faster when a little economic stimulus was needed.

President Reagan prevailed, however. The verdict on his economic program is written in the six years of steady economic growth that it has produced. In those years, the nation has seen inflation and interest rates plunge, the creation of 17 million jobs, an entrepreneurial renaissance, the recovery of manufacturing industries and a boom in exports. Taxpayers in the highest brackets have paid more, not less, to the government, while those in the lowest brackets have seen their tax liabilities eliminated or sharply reduced. Key social programs have continued to grow.

As impressive as those achievements are, they are part of a larger context in which the Reagan era should be evaluated. The past eight years will be seen historically as a transition from the governmental philosophy of the 20th century to that of the 21st century.

The Depression-spawned concept of government as the guarantor of economic health has given way to the age of the entrepreneur. While some resistance remains, protectionism is fading as a major issue. Americans recognize that the real challenge is to become more competitive in global markets.

Another important result of the Reagan era is the growing recognition throughout the world that market incentives succeed and government-controlled economies fail. Nations that had pursued policies ranging from socialism to outright Marxism now realize that meaningful jobs, resources, goods and services are not created by government edict but by individuals spurred by the hope of return on the time, money and effort they invest.

That doctrine has even gained acceptance, to an extent not yet apparent, in the Soviet Union and the People's Republic of China, which had been competing not so long ago to demonstrate which was more loyal to the economic gospel of Karl Marx. And, because economic and individual freedoms are inseparable, many people who have never known either might, not too far down the road, enjoy both.

President Reagan's legacy in terms of benefits to his own country and to much of the rest of the world is one that will endure long beyond his tenure in office, and it is one for which he deserves the thanks and appreciation of freedom-loving people everywhere.

DAVID R. GERGEN
Ronald Reagan's Most Important Legacy
[*U.S. News and World Report*, January 9, 1989]

His critics insisted that a long career in Hollywood explained Ronald Reagan's magic as a communicator, and when I first began working for him in the White House, I wondered if they might be right. Certainly no other President has felt so utterly at home before a camera. . . .

But over the three years that I was on his staff, I came to realize that Reagan had much greater strengths than mere stage presence. Far more than his critics appreciate, Reagan also possessed a keen understanding of the spoken language. He came to political maturity during the FDR era, having listened intently to the Fireside Chats on the radio. He not only memorized some of Roosevelt's best passages but he also learned that to reach people effectively in their living rooms, a leader should speak with directness, simplicity and warmth. There is little of the heroic rhetoric of a Kennedy in his speeches nor the Biblical intonations of a Lincoln. Reagan told me that he enjoyed speaking to people as neighbors and always liked to leave them with an unusual statistic or a story they might chew over when the speech was finished. And unlike most of his predecessors, he loved to write his own speeches whenever he could. Words flowed smoothly from his pen. He drafted his first inaugural address on an airplane from Washington to California, and when we examined his note pad afterward, we found that he had written it straightaway, crossing out only a handful of words. That draft survived as a near final text, and it was a great hit.

But there is another strength to Reagan that is more important than all the rest. Most of today's politicians grew up after the second World War and are afflicted by the doubts and anxieties of the postmodern age. Their speeches, no matter how finely honed, rarely inspire public confidence because the men themselves have no apparent core.

Reagan is clearly different. Having grown up in an earlier age, he came honestly to his beliefs in America because he saw the country overcome the Great Depression and turn back tyranny. He lived through the days when America rose to the status of a great power; most of our other leaders have been there only for its glide down. To Reagan, the old verities of freedom, hope and progress are not dusty relics but living truths. Voters see that in him, and they see that his words relate to the way he lives, whether in taking John Hinckley's bullet or in fighting off cancer. In White House meetings, it was striking how often we on the staff would become highly agitated by the latest news bulletins, thinking his Presidency was about to descend into a deep valley. Reagan saw the same events as nothing more than a bump in the road; things would get better tomorrow. His horizons were just not the same as ours.

Well, snapped critics, that simply proves that Reagan didn't understand what was going on. I, for one, left the White House thinking that the critics were wrong about Reagan. Sure, he made plenty of mistakes along the way, but the man did have a larger vision about America and the central importance of individuals taking responsibility for their own lives. Over time, he converted much of the country to his own views and values. Indeed, his beliefs in free markets and personal freedoms are spreading across other continents, too. It is tempting to measure Ronald Reagan's performance by how much he changed our national-income statistics or our defenses. His more important legacy is in how much he changed our minds.

T.R.B. [ROBERT WRIGHT]
Legacy? What Legacy?

[*New Republic*, January 9 and 16, 1989]

The term "Reagan legacy" implies that the consequences of this administration's actions can meaningfully be attributed to Reagan; that within his brain have resided coherent policy strategies that have succeeded (or failed) by virtue of their correspondence to (or inconsistency with) the real world. Well, even many conservatives will admit these days that "coherent" and "real world" are not terms that spring immediately to mind when they think of Ronald Reagan's brain. And if you sit them down and buy them a beer, they'll often go further, and admit that Ronald Reagan is responsible for the state of the nation in roughly the sense that Mr. Magoo is responsible for the state of his environment.

Still, the next day these same conservatives will be busily defending the "Reagan legacy" with a straight face. My favorite Reagan legacy defense is the idea that his foreign policy brought the Soviets to heel. Reagan, we are told, showed in Grenada and Libya that he was willing to see tens of Americans die for American ideals, and he showed in Afghanistan and Nicaragua that he was willing to pay tens of thousands of foreigners to die for them. The Soviet Union finally realized it couldn't afford to match us man for man (or missile for missile). Gorbachev's speech at the United Nations, then, was an admission that Reagan had taught him a lesson.

For the sake of argument, let's grant the conservative case (which does have *some* merit) that American assertiveness really did reshape Soviet foreign policy. Shouldn't we then give Reagan credit for holding the line against communism, for steadfastly bringing to fruition the policy of "containment" first laid out by George Kennan nearly a half century ago?

Don't be silly. Ronald Reagan doesn't know George Kennan from George Kennedy (whom he probably gets mixed up with John Kennedy). At the beginning of his administration, Reagan knew exactly one thing about the Soviet Union: it was the "evil empire," the bad guys. And you fight bad guys at every step. What rendered Reagan suddenly conciliatory in mid-administration wasn't any dramatic change in Soviet behavior. . . . What changed Reagan's tune, rather, was the cue he's always responded to: applause. Mikhail Gorbachev had been winning global acclaim by talking peace. Reagan wanted some of the action. It's that simple.

In economic policy, the idea of a Reagan legacy is even more ridiculous. Again, let's hypothetically concede the conservative premise: that the economy is sound, that the budget deficit won't come back to haunt us. There remains one problem with any defense of "Reaganomics." The term itself implies that (*a*) the administration steered the economy to its present state with a well-thought-out policy; and (*b*) Reagan had a clue as to what that policy was. Granted, there *was* a policy, originally: supply-side economics. What's more, it was simple enough for Reagan to understand (a clear warning sign, in retrospect). Tax cuts were going to make people work so hard that incomes would grow briskly and the tax coffers would fill up. Obviously, the present deficit is a king-size refutation of this scenario. What actually happened is that Reagan's tax cuts served as a fiscal stimulus, which, when combined with tight monetary policy, yielded low inflation and high growth (though only after years of high unemployment, which lastingly exacerbated inner-city poverty). In short, as many have noted, the Reagan economic boom was due to an old-fashioned Keynesian shot in the arm. And if you think that was part of Reagan's strategy, try mentioning J. Maynard Keynes to him. Chances are he'll start reminiscing about what a great show "Dobie Gillis" was.

Conservatives have lately been dwelling on Eisenhower-Reagan comparisons. Remember, they say, the liberal intelligentsia considered Eisenhower a simpleton when he left office, but he's since been rehabilitated: turns out he was a smart guy. Like Reagan, he wasn't always on top of policy details, or eloquent at press conferences. But he got the job done. Maybe future historians will similarly uncover Reagan's genius.

Fat chance. Eisenhower's press conference transcripts read like Supreme Court rulings compared to Reagan's. And Eisenhower's personal correspondence reveals a solid grasp of the big issues and a hard, articulate intelligence. Has Reagan even written any letters that deal analytically with public policy? True, both administrations were high-delegation, but in Eisenhower's case the president did the delegating. In Reagan's case tasks are delegated *to* him—tasks like going to the Kennedy Center. . . .

The Reagan administration was, in its final years, an ongoing struggle among advisers for the soul of a man who was virtually brain dead. The fact that things worked out no worse than they did is either a tribute to the institutional sturdiness of the presidency or proof of the existence of God.

ROBERT J. SAMUELSON

The Enigma: Ronald Reagan's Goofy Competence

[*New Republic*, January 9 and 16, 1989]

A huge puzzle hangs over Ronald Reagan's presidency. By conventional measures, it's been enormously successful. Double-digit inflation is gone. The economy is in its second-longest expansion since World War II. Reagan championed the most sweeping tax reform in decades. He proposed—and Congress enacted—a program of catastrophic health insurance for the elderly and a major overhaul of welfare. Abroad, he signed the first arms control agreement (the INF treaty) that actually reduces nuclear stockpiles. All these achievements enjoy widespread bipartisan approval. If anyone else (say, Jimmy Carter) had compiled this record, he'd be leaving to loud cheers. Reagan's reputation, however, is more complex.

Everyone concedes his popularity and accomplishments. But he's also treated with casual contempt, as if his success were a fluke. James Reston of the *New York Times* recently ridiculed "Reagan's easy optimism, his amiable incompetence, his tolerance of dubs and sleaze, his cronyism, his preoccupation with stars, his indifference to facts and convenient forgetfulness." This captures the conventional wisdom. Reagan's seen as a public relations president, often ignorant of policy. The picture is more than journalistic invention. The memoirs of White House aides (David Stockman, Donald Regan) show a man aloof from everyday government. So there's a puzzle. How did someone who worked so little at being president do so well at it? The answer is that you don't have to work hard to be a good president.

It's no accident that Reagan is the first two-term president since Eisenhower.

Nor is it a coincidence that, despite high personal popularity, both these presidents have been held in low esteem by the journalistic and political elites who dominate presidential commentary. There's an unspoken idea of what a successful president should be like, and neither Eisenhower nor Reagan has conformed. This ideal president should be a forceful leader and activist. He should have a clear national vision and the political savvy to get Congress and the public to follow him. Eisenhower never fit this mold, and Reagan seemed to only at first—when the "Reagan revolution" was a popular political and media myth. Both men reacted to events. Each seemed disengaged. Ike played golf. Ron chopped wood.

The trouble with the idealized presidents is that it has little to do with the real world. Presidents do not succeed based on how well they advance a personal agenda. These agendas are usually overwhelmed by outside events. Truman is best remembered for the Marshall Plan: a program he didn't design for a problem that barely existed when he replaced Roosevelt. Presidents succeed or fail by how well they make sound judgments on a few issues— where presidential decisions count—that vitally affect the nation's future. Everyday management of government (including most congressional actions) doesn't matter much. Reagan bungled important matters, most obviously the budget deficits. But these lapses were outweighed by his good judgment on inflation, dealing with the Soviets, and tax reform. By contrast, most other recent presidents have failed the good judgment test. . . .

To explain Reagan's success, his critics are full of theories. One is "luck." Reagan had little to do with his administration's achievements and everything to do with its failures. Thus: Paul Volcker (former chairman of the Federal Reserve Board and a 1979 appointee of Carter) defeated double-digit inflation; Treasury Secretary James A. Baker III engineered tax reform; Secretary of State George Schultz (and the rise of Mikhail Gorbachev) made arms control possible; other subordinates handled catastrophic health insurance and welfare reform. But Reagan's incompetence led to the fiascos, from budget deficits to Iran-*contra*. Yet how did such a dopey president (tolerant of "cronyism" and "sleaze") manage to have so many competent subordinates? And if the president was merely manipulated by his subordinates, how was it that he repeatedly ignored their advice in many areas—the budget deficits being the best example?

The good-luck theory clearly fails to explain Reagan's greatest accomplishment and the pillar of his popularity: the reduction of double-digit inflation. The idea that Volcker ought to receive all the credit, and Reagan none, is preposterous. It's true that Volcker led the attack. But though nominally "independent" of the White House, the Federal Reserve cannot long oppose presidential wishes without facing intense political pressures that no agency of technocrats can easily withstand. William Greider's *Secrets of the Temple*—a chronicle of Volcker's time at the Fed—shows that his policies had Reagan's encouragement and backing. After one 1981 session between the two men,

David Stockman concluded: "Volcker couldn't have come out of that meeting thinking anything but that the White House wanted tightening."

The ensuing 1981-82 recession was more severe than anyone anticipated. Unemployment reached a peak of 10.8 percent in late 1982. But Volcker did not relax the tough, high interest rate policies until inflation was clearly broken—and Reagan didn't force his hand by blasting the Fed in public. That's the important point. It's easy to forget now how much economists agonized in the late 1970s over the difficulty of controlling inflation. Reagan and Volcker showed that government could govern. With nerve and patience, someone could take the unpopular decisions that had huge long-term benefits. . . .

Another anti-Reagan theory is that his success is a mirage. The press was hypnotized by his charm or manipulated by media advisers. This theory is also crazy. First, the press dwelled on Reagan's failures, bad habits, and embarrassments, from the disastrous Lebanon policy to his press conference errors to Nancy's astrologer. Second, the theory makes his popularity a media contrivance separate from public approval of his performance. Opinion polls contradict that. In his first two years Reagan's average approval ratings were below those of every president—except Ford—since Truman. . . . The ratings rose after people found the Reagan presidency more to their liking: that is, after inflation dropped and the 1981-82 recession ended.

Where Reagan's critics hit pay dirt are the budget deficits. There were times (especially after his landslide 1984 re-election) when more energetic leadership might have broken the deadlock. The president held back. Either he wouldn't risk unpopular actions or believed that the deficits would restrain government spending. So the deficits persist. But his failure needs to be kept in perspective. The apocalyptic language often used to describe it has a political purpose: to portray the deficits as such a catastrophe— such an awesome act of irresponsibility—that they cancel any Reagan achievements. This view misrepresents both the politics and economics of deficits.

By 1980 Americans simply wanted more government than they were willing to pay for. They thought taxes were too high and defense spending too low. They opposed cuts in government services, especially entitlements such as Social Security or Medicare. No one wanted budget deficits, [but they] endure because they reflect genuine conflicts in popular demands.

It's true, as charged, that the United States has lived beyond its means. Part of Reagan's prosperity was borrowed from the future. Our excess spending was covered by imports. . . .

These economic consequences are serious, but not calamitous. The economy's main problem is actually the poor growth of productivity—the ability to raise our national wealth. This is the basic cause of the budget deficits. When productivity rose rapidly in the 1950s and '60s, people felt they could afford more government and more private spending. Now the conflict is acute. Economists don't fully understand the productivity slowdown. Nor can government easily cure it. But the Reagan years coincided with an improvement. Since 1979 business productivity has grown 1.4 percent annually. That's twice the 0.6 percent rate between 1973 and 1979, but below the 1947-73 average of three percent. Despite budget deficits and other problems—stubborn poverty and the savings and loan crisis, to mention two—the economy is far healthier today than a decade ago.

A president can't do everything. The presidency is, as political scientist Richard Neustadt has argued, a weak institution. Other centers of power abound, as do opportunities for political failure. The president cannot determine every piece of legislation, which, regardless of his personal views, will be largely shaped by bureaucrats, interest groups, and congressional committees. Foreign relations with most countries have their own drift. A president who tries to do too much risks seeing his reputation sink under the weight of all the visible (and inevitable) setbacks. He must pick and choose what he considers important. Unlike Johnson, Nixon, and Carter, Reagan preserved the authority of his office.

In this, he also resembles Eisenhower. When historians rummaged through Eisenhower's presidency, they discovered that the general was far more crafty and calculated than contemporaries had thought. Perhaps historians will decide the same of Reagan. But perhaps not: the inside of the White House is far more visible today—with tidal waves of media leaks and every janitor writing a memoir—than in Eisenhower's era. Maybe Reagan acted, or didn't, mostly on instinct. But whatever the case, Eisenhower and Reagan shared a common characteristic disparaged by their critics: an ability to stay above events.... Like Eisenhower, Reagan sensed that a president cannot succeed unless he is a unifying figure. And he cannot be that if he becomes too deeply embroiled in too many political firefights.

The truth is that the Reagan presidency falls firmly in the centrist tradition of U.S. politics. A liberal could as easily boast of his major accomplishments: inflation's decline, tax reform, the arms control treaty, welfare reform. Reagan gets blamed for many things that would have happened even if he hadn't become president. Government social spending would have been squeezed anyway, simply because there was less money to pay for old and new programs. Granting this, Reagan's changes to government were modest. He didn't demolish the welfare state or end demands for more government services. Indeed, his success in lowering inflation "had the unintended consequence of ending the revolt against government," as analyst William Schneider has noted.

By the same token, Reagan didn't transform the political landscape. The Great Communicator didn't create a conservative majority. In 1987 only 20 percent of college freshmen considered themselves "conservative," while 25 percent labeled themselves "liberal" and 56 percent "middle of the road." The figures have hardly changed since 1980, when conservatives were 18 percent; liberals, 22 percent; and middle-of-the-roaders, 60 percent. The conservatives are disappointed that Reagan didn't do more. But they misunderstand what happened. "We underestimated the stamina of liberalism," Edwin J. Feulner Jr., head of the Heritage Foundation, recently complained. No, they misjudged Reagan. His presidency has been more cautious than conservative. In the end, it's been a triumph of competence, not ideology.

ALBUQUERQUE JOURNAL
Reagan's World View
[January 14, 1989]

Mr. "Morning in America" Reagan went out in much the same vein as he took office eight years ago, with an upbeat, America's-on-the-move message of almost Pollyanna optimism. And the inescapable reaction is that Reagan's sense of national pride, optimism and good feeling has spread through the land during his term in office.

Never mind the glaring failures of his term—the towering deficit, the Marines dead in Beirut, the Iran-Contra scandal, the numerous investigations and indictments of administration staffers, the cheating scandals on Wall Street and the Black Monday crash of 1987—most Americans want to take the bright view, and with the encouragement of the president, they do.

Further, all those failures notwithstanding, there is indeed much Reagan can point to as justification for his "don't worry, be happy" message. We are still in the longest peacetime economic expansion in the nation's history, with the Federal Reserve tightening credit even now to cool the ardor of a 6-year-old growth cycle. The cancer of inflation has been in remission, and more Americans are working than ever before. The long years of Cold War tension with the Soviet Union seem genuinely to have thawed and there is more reason than at any time since World War II to believe the arms race might be amenable to compromise.

Any meaningful grand analysis of the Reagan presidency must await a longer perspective and more exhaustive analysis than the president's own good-bye speech. But it is undeniably the Reagan legacy and accomplishment that he made us feel good about ourselves as a country and about the office of the presidency. He brought us measurably closer to the ideal of a "shining city upon a hill" by his own powers of persuasion. Perhaps it is in part illusion made reality by the power of positive thinking—but it is reality nonetheless.

America really likes Ronald Reagan.

[Reprinted courtesy the *Albuquerque Journal*.]

Paul Boyer is the Merle Curti Professor of History at the University of Wisconsin and a senior member of the Institute for Research in the Humanities there. Born in Dayton, Ohio, he studied at Harvard University and taught history at the University of Massachusetts, Amherst, before his tenure at Wisconsin. His books include *By the Bomb's Early Light*, a highly regarded study of American thought and culture at the dawn of the nuclear age; *Urban Masses and Moral Order in America, 1820–1920*; and *Purity in Print: Book Censorship in America.*